NEW PROCLAMATION

NEW PROCLAMATION

Year A, Advent through Holy Week

2001–2002

Francis J. Moloney, S.D.B.

Dale C. Allison Jr.

Christine Roy Yoder

Donald Juel

FORTRESS PRESS

Minneapolis

NEW PROCLAMATION
Year A, Advent through Holy Week
2001–2002

Cover and book design: Joseph Bonyata

Illustrations: Tanya Butler, *Icon: Visual Images for Every Sunday,* copyright © 2000 Augsburg Fortress.

Library of Congress Cataloging-in-Publication Data

New proclamation year A, 2001–2002 : Advent through Holy Week / Francis J. Moloney ... [et al.].
     p. cm.
  Includes bibliographical references.
  ISBN 0-8006-4245-7 (alk. paper)
   1. Church year. I. Moloney, Francis J.

 BV30 .N48 2001
 251'.6—dc21

                               2001023746

Manufactured in the U.S.A.   AF 1-4245

05   04   03   02   01   1   2   3   4   5   6   7   8   9   10

CONTENTS

The Season of Epiphany
Dale C. Allison Jr.

The Season of Lent
Christine Roy Yoder

Holy Week
Donald Juel

FOREWORD

Nᴇw *Proclamation* continues the venerable Fortress Press tradition of offering a lectionary preaching resource that provides the best in biblical exegetical aids for a variety of lectionary traditions.

Thoroughly ecumenical and built around the three-year lectionary cycle, *New Proclamation* is focused on the biblical text, based on the conviction that those who are well equipped to understand a pericope in both its historical and liturgical contexts will be stimulated to preach engaging and compelling sermons. For this reason, *New Proclamation*—like its predecessor, *Proclamation*—invites the most capable North American biblical scholars and homileticians to contribute to the series.

New Proclamation retains the best of the hallmarks that made *Proclamation* so widely used and appreciated while introducing changes that make it more user-friendly.

- *New Proclamation* is published in two volumes per year, designed for convenience. The volume you are holding covers the lections for approximately the first half of the church year, Advent through Holy Week, which culminates in the Great Vigil of Easter.

- This two-volume format offers a larger, workbook-style page with a lay-flat binding and space for making notes.

- Each season of the church year is prefaced by an introduction that offers insight into the background and spiritual significance of the period.

- There is greater emphasis on how the preacher can apply biblical texts to contemporary situations and to the actual setting of Christian worship. Exegetical work ("Interpreting the Text") is itself oriented toward proclamation (for the day of Epiphany, for example, learn how the "star of the east" could identify for the magi the place where the infant Jesus lay). Specific suggestions on how the text addresses contemporary persons and issues ("Responding to the Texts") have a prominent place. And read how your worship planning decisions reflect your theology (for example, in the use of the passion narrative in worship during Holy Week).

- Although they are not usually used as preaching texts, comments on each assigned psalm ("Responsive Reading") are included so that the preacher can incorporate reflections also on these readings in the sermon.
- Boxed quotations in the margins help signal important themes in the texts for the day.
- The material for Series A is here dated specifically for 2001–2002, for easier coordination with other dated lectionary materials.
- These materials can be adapted for uses other than for corporate worship on the day indicated. They are well suited for adult discussion groups or personal meditation and reflection.

We are grateful to our contributors, Francis J. Moloney, Dale C. Allison Jr., Christine Roy Yoder, and Donald Juel, for their insights and for their commitment to effective Christian preaching. We hope that you find in this volume ideas, stimulation, and encouragement in your ministry of proclamation.

Marshall D. Johnson

THE SEASON OF ADVENT

FRANCIS J. MOLONEY, S.D.B.

THE CHRISTIAN LITURGICAL YEAR is made up of cycles of seasons, holy days, and the celebrations of saints that combine and sometimes overlap, but it was from "the Lord's day" that a liturgical year developed. Although the celebration of the first day of the week marked a new creation, the earliest church recognized its links with Israel's tradition and also called this day "the eighth day," out of respect for the Sabbath (the seventh day). Every Sunday recalled Easter, and it was not until the first years of the second Christian century that a separate annual Feast of Easter was instituted. Still closely linked with the Jewish celebrations, it became a feast of a "week of weeks" (St. Hilary [315–367])—fifty days between Easter and Pentecost. Easter to Pentecost celebrated the end of Jesus' life, the beginning of his presence as risen Lord, and his gift of the Spirit from his place at the right hand of the Father. Already in the fourth century there is the suggestion of two feasts, the Nativity of the Lord and the Epiphany, that marked the beginning of Jesus' life-story. These two celebrations have always been linked: the birth of Jesus of Nazareth (Christmas) and the manifestation of God that takes place in and through Jesus (Epiphany). A preparation for Christmas and the Epiphany paralleling the Lenten preparation for Easter was soon to follow.

The history of the liturgical cycle works back from the celebration of the end of Jesus' life to its beginning. But the church's year tells a narrative of the saving work of God in and through Jesus by working chronologically through his life-story and beyond. The mystery of Christ is unfolded from the Incarnation and the Epiphany to his Passing Over in death and resurrection, Ascension, and Pentecost. From that point on, the "Ordinary" weeks of the year begin their rhythmic numbering as the liturgical year circles back again to Advent, the celebration of the expectation of the coming of the Lord.

Some History

There is evidence from the fourth century of a number of different ways of celebrating a preparation for Christmas and Epiphany. One element united these early forms of what eventually came to be called Advent; they were not to be identified with Lent. Advent was not a time of penance for Christians accompanying those to be new members through Baptism at Easter. The "birth" of new life within the Christian community, so much a part of the celebration of the new creation that took place in the death and resurrection of Jesus, was not the feature of Christmas and the Epiphany. Looking back across the human story, especially as it is recorded in the Bible, the early church saw that humankind had waited long for the coming of the Savior. The celebration of Advent was to be associated with the experience of waiting. Advent played a more psychological role in the life of the Christian community, waiting in eager expectation for the coming of the Lord.

This understanding of Advent as a period different from Lent determined the eventual establishment of the season in the Roman church. It was Pope Gregory the Great (591–604) who established the four Sundays in Advent, a move deliberately calculated to indicate the difference between this season of preparation for Christmas and the six Sundays of Lent that prepare for Easter. Closely linked with this establishment of Advent as a distinct period of the Christian year was the development of a celebration of Christmas as a feast with a character of its own, distinguished from the celebration of Epiphany. The emergence of the season of Advent, directed specifically toward the preparation of the faithful for the celebration of the coming of the Lord at Christmas enabled the gradual development of an Advent liturgy.

The Twofold Message of Advent

Advent, in many ways, catches a fundamental element of Christian life. It is a season that waits as Christians prepare for the celebration of the remembering of Christ's *first coming*. It does so, however, by focusing the attention of the believer on the need to direct the mind and the heart to await Christ's *second coming* at the end of time. The liturgy of Advent, perhaps more than any other liturgical season, reminds the believing individual and community that they are living in an in-between-time: the time between Jesus' first coming and Jesus' final return. Advent celebrates the tension between the now and the not yet, the givenness of all that God has done for us in and through the life and teaching, death and resurrection of Jesus (the first coming), and the fullness of life, yet to come (the second coming). The Christ-event extends across these two "comings." One has already taken place: "I am bringing you good news of great joy for all the people: to you is born this day in the city of David a Savior, who is the Messiah, the Lord" (Luke 2:10-11). Another lies at some time in the future: "Then they will see 'the Son of Man coming in clouds' with great power and glory. Then he will send out the angels and gather his elect from the four winds, from the ends of the earth to the ends of heaven. . . . But about that day or hour no one knows, neither the angels in heaven nor the Son, but only the Father" (Mark 13:26–27, 32).

The Christian word "advent" is of pagan origin (Latin: *adventus*), used in the pagan world to describe a feast celebrating the manifestation of a divinity that came to dwell in its temple at a certain time of the year. On these days the temple, which was normally closed, would be opened and the statue of the divinity would be moved to a position where it could be publicly viewed. Thus *adventus* celebrated the anniversary of the return of the divinity. In the imperial world of Rome, the *adventus* celebrated the anniversary of the coming of the emperor. Translated into the Christian world, inspired by the Gospel stories and the earliest reflections upon what God had done in and through Jesus Christ, the *adventus* had two points of reference. It described the coming of the Son of God in the flesh, his visit. But it also celebrated, in anticipation, his return.

But the incarnate Son of God does not come again and again, as did the pagan gods. The Christian *adventus* prepares for the one and only coming of Christ, the day of his birth (*dies natalis*). The *adventus* and the *dies natalis* of Christ supplanted the *adventus* and the *dies natalis* of the unvanquished sun of the winter solstice. Christianity gradually became the imperial religion, as Emperor Constantine strove to give freedom to all the religions in the Edict of Milan (313). In an increasing Christian dominance of culture, the adoption of pagan feasts led to the gradual dominance of the Christian significance of certain periods of the year. The pagan associations were forgotten. There was an obvious difference between the Christian understanding of the coming of Jesus Christ and the yearly *adventus* of the pagan gods, but Jesus Christ did not have a yearly *adventus*. He came in the Incarnation, and he will come at the end of time. The unique coming of Christ on the day of his birth was his *adventus* in the Christian tradition. Thus, within the Christian practice of the *adventus,* there was no place for an annual gazing upon the public presence of a divinity in his temple. But there was the promise that he would return: "Men of Galilee, why do you stand looking into heaven? This Jesus, who was taken up from you into heaven, will come in the same way as you saw him go into heaven" (Acts 1:11). Advent is a period that recalls the long wait for the coming of the Messiah and Savior, as it is told in the biblical story. It thus eagerly looks forward to Christmas. But it is also the liturgical

period when the Christian church urges its members to look forward and be prepared for the second coming at the end of time: "Therefore keep awake—for you
do not know when the master of the house will come, in the evening, or at mid-
night, or at cock crow, or at dawn, or else he may find you asleep when he comes
suddenly. And what I say to you I say to all: Keep awake" (Mark 13:35-37).

The Prayers and the Readings of Advent

The readings and prayers of Advent develop a focus upon the *two comings of Christ*,
the coming of Jesus of Nazareth, the Christ, in the event of the Incarnation, and
the return of Jesus Christ at the end of time as final Judge and Savior. The opening prayers on the first two Sundays of Advent in the Roman tradition set the
theme: "Increase our strength of will for doing good that Christ may find an
eager welcome at his coming and call us to his side in the kingdom of heaven"
(First Sunday of Advent). "Remove the things that hinder us from receiving
Christ with joy, so that we may share his wisdom and become one with him when
he comes in glory" (Second Sunday of Advent).[1] The Third Sunday turns specifically to the oncoming celebration of Christmas: "May we, your people, who
look forward to the birthday of Christ experience the joy of salvation and celebrate that feast with love and thanksgiving" (Third Sunday of Advent).[2] But, as
the season closes, the tradition of the two comings returns vigorously: "As you
revealed to us by an angel the coming of your Son as man, so lead us through his
suffering and death to the glory of his resurrection" (Fourth Sunday of Advent).[3]

The lectionary is equally clear on the theme of the two comings. The readings of the first Sunday focus almost exclusively upon the theme of the final
appearance of the Messiah and Savior. Isaiah 2:1-5 speaks of the ideal time in the
future when all hostilities will cease and all the nations will stream to the Temple
of the Lord. Romans 13:11-14 is written to a Christian community already living in the in-between-time, warning its members that they must pay attention to
the quality of their lives. The final *adventus* of the Lord may be nearer now, with
the passing of time, than it was at the time of their conversion to Christianity. In
the Gospel passage, Matt. 24:37-44, the same theme dominates: the need for
Christians to live good lives, to be awake and ready for the unexpected coming
of the Son of Man. There is little of Christmas joy and cheer in these passages!

From that point on, the readings allow the theme of the first coming of the
Christ to develop. The Advent season, however, begins with an uncompromis-
ing commitment to the truth and urgency of the second coming, and that theme
is never absent. The prophet Isaiah dominates the Old Testament readings across
all four Sundays.[4] The selections move steadily through messianic prophecies read
within a Christian community as pointing to the coming of Jesus Christ. They
also retain their original meaning, addressing the final coming of God to restore

his original design for a sinful and fragmented world. The root of Jesse will come forth and introduce the new creation when all will be drawn to that root, a signal to all the peoples (Second Sunday). The coming of the Lord will restore the beauty and freedom of God's original creation (Third Sunday). Both readings point the Christian community toward the first *and* the second coming of Christ. The first coming is heralded by the themes of joy, peace, restoration, and beauty, while the decisive nature of the God entry into the human story, where all will be definitively restored to its original design and purpose, points to the second coming.

The readings from the letters (Rom. 15:4-13; James 5:7-10; Rom. 1:1-7) retain an unrelenting focus upon the final coming of the Christ. On the final Sunday the only hint of the importance of the first coming is provided by Rom. 1:3: "The gospel concerning his Son, who was descended from David according to the flesh." Only on the fourth Sunday does the prophet Isaiah speak to the theme of Christmas, promising the birth of a Son, whose name "Emmanuel" means "God-is-with-us" (Isa. 7:10-14). The Gospel lections of the Second and Third Sundays offer a steady preparation of the community for the celebration of the first coming at Christmas, leading toward a climax in Matt. 1:18-25, a Christian re-reading of Isa. 7:10-14. On the Second Sunday, the preaching of John the Baptist prepares for the coming of the more powerful one (Matt. 3:1-12). On the Third, in a well-chosen reversal, Jesus gives witness to the Baptist, the greatest of all who have been born of a woman. But Jesus' coming and subsequent establishment of the kingdom of heaven has created a new relationship with God where even the least in that kingdom is greater than the Baptist (Matt. 11:2-11). Finally, on the Fourth Sunday, as Joseph receives the annunciation of the birth of Emmanuel, the celebration of Christmas is upon us (Matt. 1:18-25).

The double message of Advent, the product of the history and reflection of two thousand years of Christian life and the celebration of the "coming" of Jesus Christ, Lord and Savior, has been magnificently captured by the prayers and readings selected for the season. Caught between the gift of God in Jesus Christ at Christmas, and the future fullness of the gift of God at the end of time, "we ourselves, who have the first fruits of the Spirit, groan inwardly while we await adoption, the redemption of our bodies. For in hope we were saved. Now hope that is seen is not hope. For who hopes for what is seen? But if we hope for what we do not see, we wait for it with patience" (Rom. 8:23-25).

FIRST SUNDAY IN ADVENT

DECEMBER 2, 2001

REVISED COMMON	EPISCOPAL (BCP)	ROMAN CATHOLIC
Isa. 2:1–5	Isa. 2:1–5	Isa. 2:1–5
Psalm 122	Ps. 122	Ps. 122:1-2, 3-4, 4-5, 6-7, 8-9
Rom. 13:11–14	Rom. 13:8–14	Rom. 13:11–14
Matt. 24:36–44	Matt. 24:37–44	Matt. 24:37–44

A S THE ARRIVAL OF THE FIRST SUNDAY OF ADVENT arouses holiday and Christ- mas sentiments and we turn our minds to that celebration and its accompa- nying experiences, we find that the liturgy and the lections for this Sunday look elsewhere. During Advent, Christians celebrate two "comings" of Jesus as Lord and Savior. He first came in the Incarnation, remembered at Christmas, and he will come again at the end of time. It is the theme of the final coming of Jesus that dominates the biblical texts chosen for this Sunday.

FIRST READING

ISAIAH 2:1-5

Interpreting the Text

Isaiah 2:1-5 tells of a vision of the prophet's in the troubled times that preceded the collapse of the Northern Kingdom, Israel, in the last half of the sixth century B.C.E. During that period, Judah, the Southern Kingdom with its capital and Temple in Jerusalem, was lured into alliances with foreign powers attempting to overthrow the expanding Assyrian Empire. Such alliances, for Isa- iah, were a betrayal of Israel's unique God, YHWH. Isaiah has a vision of an ideal mountain, an ideal Temple, and a dream of what will come to pass. The Temple is no longer the structure erected by King Solomon, nor is the mountain the well- known Temple Mount. The mountain rises to unimagined heights above all the hills, and the Temple becomes the place toward which all the nations stream (v. 2). As Judah prepares for war against Assyria with unwise alliances, Isaiah calls them to a peace that the Law of God will establish, and reminds them that it is God, not armies, who "shall judge between the nations" (v. 3). The Law that will go out from Zion, the oracle of the Lord from Jerusalem, is a message of peace (vv. 3-4). The imagery used to describe the law of peace retains its power: "They shall beat their swords into plowshares and their spears into pruning hooks" (v. 4). The instruments of war, swords and spears, become the instruments of activities that till the land and reap the harvest—plowshares and pruning hooks. The house of Jacob is invited to lead the way in this acceptance of the universal Lordship of the God of Israel. God is still worshiped in the Temple at Jerusalem, but the significance of this worship must be better understood. The House of Jacob is summoned to be the oracle of the Lord of peace. They will walk in the light of the Lord rather than in the darkness of the anger and violence generated by human conflict (v. 5).

Responding to the Text

The theme of peace, so central to the oracle of Isa. 2:1-5, is an important Christmas theme: a time of "Glory to God in the highest heaven, and on earth peace among those whom he favors" (Luke 2:14). However, in its original setting, as Isaiah spoke and his followers wrote it, the oracle pointed to an unknown moment in the future when God will be the Lord of all people and the world will live in the light and goodness of God. The ambiguity and violence of the contemporary world make today's reading from Isaiah a dream yet to be realized. The future orientation of the oracle still holds. Christianity may have created a "culture," especially in the Western world, with its art, music, poetry, philosophy, theology, and ever-deepening understanding and appreciation of the wonders of the creation, but it cannot be said that we are "walking in the light of the Lord."

The great powers continue to manufacture swords and spears—or their modern, more deadly equivalents. Armaments arouse more interest, budgetary considerations, and scientific research than the implements that will till the soil and feed the hungry with the fruit of the earth. The Law of the Lord continues to fall upon deaf ears. We must recognize that our "now" of anger, violence, division, hatred, starvation, and dramatic distinctions between those who have

WE MUST RECOGNIZE THAT OUR "NOW" OF ANGER, VIOLENCE, DIVISION, HATRED, STARVATION, AND DRAMATIC DISTINCTIONS BETWEEN THOSE WHO HAVE AND THOSE WHO DO NOT HAVE IS CHALLENGED AS WE PREPARE FOR THE COMING OF THE LORD.

and those who do not have is challenged as we prepare for the coming of the Lord. Advent is a time when we are summoned to look carefully at the ambiguities of our "now." It is now that we prepare for the second coming when the Lord will "judge between the nations and arbitrate for many peoples" (v. 4).

Responsive Reading

PSALM 122

The exhortation, "Let us go up to the house of the Lord!" (Ps. 122:1) promises that the prophet's vision (above) may become a reality. At the house of the Lord the tribes of Israel gather to give thanks to the Lord, and receive right judgment (vv. 3-5). The psalm closes with a prayer for peace: "Pray for the peace of Jerusalem (v. 6). Peace and the prosperity of those who love Zion are not guaranteed. The peace of the people within the city, and its walls and bulwarks that defend them (vv. 6-7), call for the steady prayer of the people. Thus the psalmist's prayer is that peace may be within Jerusalem, "for the sake of the house of the Lord" (v. 9). The themes of judgment and peace are found in both Isa. 2:1-5 and Psalm 122. The prophet points to a future time when God will draw all the nations to the Temple. There they will be judged, and the word of the Lord will go forth, a word of peace for all the nations (Isa. 2:3-4). For the psalmist, this experience of judgment and peace is already a possibility. However, it calls for the recognition of God's dwelling place and steady prayer and commitment to peace for the prosperity of all who are committed to the presence of the Lord (Ps. 122:6).

Second Reading

ROMANS 13:11–14 (RCL/RC); 13:8-14 (BCP)

Interpreting the Text

Two different, although related issues, are dealt with in Rom.13:8-14. In vv. 8-10 Paul exhorts the Romans to mutual love. Touching a fundamental characteristic of the early church's self-understanding, he points to love as the fulfillment of the Law (v. 8). Paul cites four commandments that retain their significance in a world that increasingly disregards the divine: the prohibition of adultery, murder, theft, and coveting (see Exod. 20:13-17; Deut. 5:17-21). Where genuine love is in place, these terrible scourges have no place! He cites the Law to point to the single commandment that sums up all laws: "Love your neighbor as yourself" (v. 9; see Lev. 19:18). We hear echoes of Jesus' teaching in Paul's interpretation of a law, which sums up all laws (see Matt. 5:43; 19:18-19), an echo that resounds across other parts of the New Testament (see Gal. 5:14; James 2:8; and especially John 13:34-35; 15:12, 17). To commit oneself to genuine love means to place "the other" before oneself. It thus follows logically that those who love cannot possibly harm their neighbor, and thus—without worrying about the detailed legislation of a legal tradition—they live the Law perfectly (v. 10).

Paul also wishes to face another question (see v. 11), that of the end of time (see also 1 Thess. 4:13—5:11; 1 Cor. 15:12-58). God has set a time for the end of the world as we know it, and the passing of each day means that we are approaching the final moment of God's saving intervention into the human story: "Salvation is nearer to us now than when we became believers" (v. 11). Both chronologically and in the increasing awareness of being God's eschatological people, the sense of the nearness of the final coming intensifies. At some point there will no longer be time. The end of the world is further reason for Paul to exhort the Romans to lay aside all forms of life that do not recognize what God has done for them in Jesus Christ. Christians live between the two *advents* of Jesus. Living in an "overlap time," between the saving action of God in and through Jesus Christ (see Rom. 3:21-26) and the end of time (13:11), they are to lay aside all that smacks of darkness: reveling, drunkenness, debauchery, licentiousness, quarreling, and jealousy (v. 13). They are to be bearers of light (v. 12).

The coming of the end of the world leaves no space for overindulgence in the good things it has to offer the flesh and its desires (v. 14). The Romans are to "put on Christ" (v. 14a). This important Pauline image summons up the idea of making entirely one's own the values of Jesus Christ, but it has a deeper meaning. It also means that the Christian enters into relationship with others who have been baptized into Christ, in a new situation where division, hatred, and the pettiness that this world accepts as important, have no place (see especially Gal. 3:27-28; Eph. 4:24; Col. 3:10-11).

Responding to the Text

Human history as we know it, measure it, and discuss it, is not the only history that is crucial for Christian life. We have received an abundance of gifts through God's action in and through the life and teaching, death and resurrection of Jesus. But that is not the end of the story. We look back to Jesus for the model of a quality of love that is unconditional. Jesus' loving is, in its own turn, the revelation of the unconditional love of God for creation: "For God so loved the world that he gave his only Son, so that everyone who believes in him may not perish but may have eternal life" (John 3:16).

Adultery, murder, theft, destructive yearning for the possessions, talents, or achievements of others, the abuse of drink and drugs, quarreling and jealousy that lead to murder—all are deeply embedded in our society. We need something beyond ourselves to summon us into the light, away from the darkness and pain that evil brings. Not only does Paul's list of evils still make sense but so also his suggestions for living in the light: love your neighbor as yourself. Recognize that there is another story, the story of God's saving presence, that transcends the achievements of our human story. Let us put on Christ, joining all those who are "in Christ Jesus" where there is no longer Jew or Greek, male or female, slave or free, but where all are one, waiting for the salvation "which is nearer to us now than when we became believers" (Rom. 13:11).

The Gospel
MATTHEW 24:36-44 (RCL);
24:37-44 (BCP, RC)

Interpreting the Text

The Advent focus on the second coming of Jesus as Lord continues in this lection, from Matthew's version of Jesus' discourse on the end of the world. Jesus insists that only God knows *when* "that day" will come (v. 36), but *that* it will come is certain. In the days of Noah the ordinary things in life went on. No attention was devoted to the threatening presence of God's looming intervention, which would judge the way ordinary, everyday activities were being performed. Not knowing of the flood, the people of Noah's time were careless about the things that pertained to God, and they paid the price (see Gen. 6:11-13). So it will be in the day of the final coming of the Son of Man. The ordinary things in life will go on. People will be given and taken in marriage, they will continue to work in the fields or at the grindstone (v. 38). Yet, at the final coming the Son of Man will make judgment upon these events: one will be saved and another lost (v. 41).

What determines the salvation of one and the loss of the other? The Gospel message as a whole informs us that on this side of "that day" believers are called to go on doing what they are best able to do in this world. It is the way they do these things that matters. The Gospel message about the inevitable end of time should be one of the elements that determine the way things are done. Belief in "the day of the Lord" marks the quality of the everyday performance of the believer who does not live as if there will be no tomorrow but believes that God is the Lord and final judge of all history.

Not only does the threat of what is yet to come determine the Christian life. Jesus' command to "watch" does not ask that the Christian keep one eye on the day-to-day tasks that must go on and the other on the possible appearance of the Son of Man on the clouds. The command summons Christians to be worthy of the one who will come at an unknown and unexpected hour (vv. 42, 44). House-holders know how to care for their house and possessions against surprise attacks.

So also must believers, waiting for the final return of the Son of Man, stay awake and live as disciples should live, resisting all surprising invasion from those who would disturb God's established order (v. 43). Indeed, the house must be ready for the unknown day of the Lord.

Responding to the Text

As Christians we have learned from the life, teaching, death, and resurrection of Jesus that there is a quality of life asked of us that transforms the ordinary into the extraordinary. One day we will be judged according to our response to that lesson. When that day will be is beyond our knowledge, a mystery beyond all human understanding (see Matt. 24:36). Yet, as we look forward during Advent to

> THERE IS A QUALITY OF LIFE ASKED OF US THAT TRANS-
> FORMS THE ORDINARY INTO THE EXTRAORDINARY.

the celebration of the first coming of the Son of Man, our Gospel reading joins the readings from Isaiah and Paul. It summons us to recall the quality of life required from us in expectation of the second and final coming of Jesus. We live in a world where many attempting to live Christian values in an open-minded and courageous fashion are regarded as quaint or outmoded by a secularized society and disloyal by those who see no need for a Christian commitment to a highly fragmented and rapidly changing world. This can be difficult. Thus, as we begin Advent, Jesus calls to us, "Stay awake!" To heed this call is to live the time given to us between the two comings of Jesus in a way that reflects the love of God already made known to us in the person of Jesus and to allow God to draw us more deeply into the mysterious future known only to God.

SECOND SUNDAY IN ADVENT

DECEMBER 9, 2001

REVISED COMMON	EPISCOPAL (BCP)	ROMAN CATHOLIC
Isa. 11:1–10	Isa. 11:1–10	Isa. 11:1–10
Ps. 72:1-7, 18–19	Ps. 72 or 72:1–8	Ps. 72:1-2, 7-8, 12-13, 17
Rom. 15:4–13	Rom. 15:4–13	Rom. 15:4–9
Matt. 3:1–12	Matt. 3:1–12	Matt. 3:1–12

Today's reading of the oracle of the root that shall rise from Jesse is applied within the Christian tradition to the coming of Jesus, but that was not its original meaning. Psalm 72 asks that the king be a true king to the people of God, rendering praise and honor to God alone. In Romans 15 Paul instructs a divided community on the need for oneness, to give honor and praise to the one true God. The suggestion of the first coming returns, however, with the introduction of the figure of John the Baptist, crying out his warnings. The one who is more powerful than John is coming, and the people must repent and prepare themselves for the advent of the one who will baptize with the Holy Spirit and with fire. The liturgy moves gradually from last week's intense focus upon the second coming of Jesus to this week's blending of teaching concerning the time between the first and second comings of Jesus.

FIRST READING

ISAIAH 11:1-10

Interpreting the Text

Spoken late in Isaiah's career, this oracle looks forward to an ideal Davidic king. Immediately prior to Isa. 11:1-10 the prophet had used the image of trees and bushes to tell of God's destruction of wicked rulers (Isa. 10:33-34). But from Jesse, the father of David, will come a shoot, roots, and the branches of an ideal king (11:1). A king from the line of David replaces the condemned kings. Israel is to go back to its true origins and be rid of those who have unworthily usurped royal authority over God's people. Isaiah expresses a hope that a king will arise who is directed by the Spirit of God (v. 2). YHWH's spirit was a divine force given to individuals to enable them to fulfill tasks otherwise beyond them (see Num. 11:17: Moses; Judg. 3:10; 6:34; 11:29: the Judges; 1 Sam. 16:13: David). The action of God sustains the true king.[5]

The gifts of the Spirit indicate that the ideal king will be a charismatic figure. Wisdom, understanding, and counsel will make him independent of foolish advisers (see 1 Sam. 5:21; 9:5; 29:14). The gift of might means that he will not only be able to make wise and God-directed decisions but also will have the authority to ensure that such decisions are effective. Driving the exercise of all the charismatic gifts is "the fear of the Lord." The person who fears the Lord looks to the Lord for direction in all things and delights in doing so (v. 3a; see Prov. 1:7). It is not superficial judgment by externals that direct the governing of God's people but the design of God (v. 3b). The description of the king in vv. 4-5 encapsulates Israel's hope for perfect justice: the poor and the meek will be cared for with righteousness, while the arrogant and the wicked will be smitten by the proper exercise of the authority of a divinely appointed king.

The disorder that exists in creation from the days of the chaos created by disobedience in Eden (see Gen. 2:18-20; 3:14-19) is reversed. Hyperbole heightens the ideal nature of the oracle: wolf and lamb, leopard and kid, lion and fatling, cow and bear, lion and ox, infant and asp are at peace. No harm is done, as all anger, division, and violence come to an end in the reign of a Spirit-filled Son of David. All the earth will come to recognize and know the greatness and goodness of the God of Israel (vv. 6-9). Knowledge of the Lord, the fruit of fear of the Lord, is the key to right order. The root of Jesse will proclaim to all peoples the greatness and glory of the one true God, and Israel and its king will become a rallying point for all who are seeking justice (see vv. 4-5) and peace (see vv. 6-9) (v. 10).

Responding to the Text

The original setting and the close association of the oracle with the Davidic line make the oracle a dream about the best of all possible kings in Israel, after a series of unwise and unfaithful rulers. The oracle retains its idealism when read within the Christian assembly. As long as one is looking for the perfect society, marked by a Spirit-directed and God-oriented leadership, just rule, and subsequent idyllic peace, the future orientation of the oracle must be retained. In this sense, the oracle reminds us that we live in a period of ambiguity. The original order of God's creation, evoked in vv. 6-9, has yet to be reestablished. We still suffer from the profound disorder introduced by selfishness and sin.

THE ORIGINAL ORDER OF GOD'S CREATION, EVOKED IN VV. 6-9, HAS YET TO BE REESTABLISHED. WE STILL SUFFER FROM THE PROFOUND DISORDER INTRODUCED BY SELFISHNESS AND SIN.

Yet in one person this prophecy has been fulfilled. As Mark brings his prologue to a close, he reports that Jesus, in the desert, was "tempted by Satan; and he was with the wild beasts; and the angels waited on him"(Mark 1:13). This is a deliberate affirmation on the part of the evangelist that in the coming of Jesus the disorder established in Eden has been eliminated. Satan is rejected, the enmity between the animal kingdom and human beings, as well as their savagery, has been overcome and, like Adam and Eve (in some Jewish traditions), he is nourished by the angels of God. This understanding of the coming of Jesus Christ enables us to recognize Isa. 11:1-10 as fulfilled in the first coming of Jesus, celebrated at Christmas.

Responsive Reading

PSALM 72:1-7, 18-19 (RCL); 72 or 72:1-8 (BCP); 72:1-2, 7-8, 12-13, 17 (RC)

Psalm 72 is a "royal psalm," a prayer directed to God, asking that the royal dynasty be what God has raised it up to be. In vv. 1-4 the psalmist asks that the king exercise justice and righteousness toward the poor, the underprivileged, and the oppressed. Prosperity, the sign of God's blessing, will be with the people. In vv. 5-8 the psalmist prays for the king's long life and for fertility. Such gifts were essential for the stability of the dynasty and thus the nation. As with Isa. 11:1-10, these prayers expressed something of a dream-wish, but also express a belief that God would give the nation such a king. He would be blessed with a long-lasting and far-reaching reign (v. 8), marked by peace and justice (vv. 1-7). The RCL includes vv. 18-19, which indicate that the prayer of the psalmist, expressing the hopes of the people, was based in confident address to the God of Israel who alone is capable of doing such wondrous things. These final verses bless and render glory to a God who can raise up human beings who correspond to the design of God and thus respond fittingly to human needs.

Second Reading

ROMANS 15:4-13 (RCL, BCP); 15:4-9 (RC)

Interpreting the Text

Throughout the letter to the Romans, Paul is motivated by his desire to show that being Jew or Gentile brings no privilege in the eyes of God. All have sinned, but the action of God in and through the death and resurrection of Jesus

Christ has opened up the possibility that all might be saved (see 3:21-26). Paul turns to more practical matters over the latter part of the document. He utters what might be the inspiring issue of the letter. Israel has been the recipient of its long biblical tradition, and all, both Jew and Greek, are to look upon those Scriptures for instruction, leading to steadfastness and hope (15:4). But the dream of Paul is that both Jew and Greek will be open to the grace of God to live in profound harmony with one another. Obvious tensions were present in the Roman community between those who were the bearers of the biblical tradition and those who were not (see, for example, 3:1-9). This had to be overcome, "so that together you may with one voice glorify the God and Father of our Lord Jesus Christ" (15:6). What God had done in and through Jesus Christ has had universal significance, and the lives of believers had to reflect this truth. There can be no division when all look to the one God and Father of Jesus Christ as Lord.

Practical consequences follow for the community, already foretold in the Scriptures, the source of instruction, steadfastness, encouragement, and hope (vv. 7-13; see v. 4). The barriers of hostility must be broken down, and the different members of the community must welcome one another. As always with Paul, this welcome is not something cosmetic but reflects the unconditional commitment of Jesus to everyone, welcoming all in his self-gift unto death (v. 7). Even the action of Christ can be seen as part of the instruction that comes from the Scriptures. Christ's self-gift for all served and perfected the promises made to Israel. To prove this Paul moves through a series of citations from the Scriptures that highlight the inclusion of the Gentiles (v. 9: Ps. 18:49; v. 10: Deut. 32:43; v. 11: Ps. 117:1; v. 12: Isa. 11:10). The final citation looks back to the first reading. Isaiah dreamed of a king who would "stand as a signal to all the peoples" (Isa. 11:10), and Jesus, Son of God and Son of David (see Rom. 1:3-4), has made this promise possible.

Responding to the Text

Paul's deep sensitivity to the Jewish tradition leads him to present Jesus as the universal savior who brings to perfection the long-standing instructions of God, available in the Jewish Scriptures. The dangers facing the Roman Christians, divided between those who had their roots within Judaism and others who came from a Gentile world, had to be overcome. Paul is calling them all to a recognition of the one true God, under whom there could be no division. It is the universal saving purpose of God that lies behind the saving action of Jesus Christ. One God, one Lord and Savior, Jesus Christ, one people of God.

As we approach Christmas, a time for the celebration of peace and unity, this reading from the closing pages of Romans touches a raw nerve in contemporary Christianity. Beyond the more obvious divisions between the churches, still unresolved after five centuries, there are within our own communions (as was the case with the Roman Christians) the privileged and the less so. The lines of division are not always economic, even though, shamefully, they often are. Increasingly, within one Christian community people from different nations, representing different national cultures, are often marginalized or marginalize themselves into ghetto communities. The fusion of the themes of the two *advents,* Jesus Christ at Christmas, and the expectation of his second final coming, demands that we listen to Paul's urgent words to contemporary Christianity. "May the God of steadfastness and encouragement grant you to live in harmony with one another, in accordance with Christ Jesus, so that together you may with one voice glorify the God and Father of our Lord Jesus Christ" (Rom. 15:5-6).

THE GOSPEL
MATTHEW 3:1-12

Interpreting the Text

John the Baptist, bursting into the Gospel story without introduction (v. 1), proclaims the coming of the kingdom (v. 2) to the masses that went to him from all the regions of Israel (v. 5). His preaching opens with the same words that Jesus will use as he begins his ministry: "Repent, for the kingdom of heaven has come near" (see 4:17). This prophet, dressed like Elijah, the first of the prophets (v. 4), calls for repentance, a response to God's action by a change of heart and mind and a consequent change in life-style. The Baptist does not appear on the scene proclaiming repentance upon his own authority. The Word of God drives him. Isaiah had spoken of his voice "crying in the wilderness" (v. 3; see Isa. 40:3). Fulfilling God's design, as indicated by the prophecy of Isaiah, the Baptist attacks traditional ways to God, those represented by the major religious institutions of Israel: the Pharisees and the Sadducees (v. 7).

Like the prophets before him, John the Baptist attacks any pretence to be religious. He uses expressions that reflect the fierce righteousness of God's prophet and the insidious wickedness that false religious practice produces: "You brood of vipers" (v. 8). The institutions of Israel are attacked because they are not producing the fruit that should come from a true relationship with God. They make the mistake of acting on the belief of their special place in God's hierarchy because of their link with Abraham (vv. 8-9). But blood ties are not the basis of oneness with God. As the Gospel of Matthew will show, the inexhaustible creative power of God can turn stones into children and

THE INEXHAUSTIBLE CREATIVE POWER OF GOD CAN TURN STONES INTO CHILDREN AND GENTILES INTO DISCIPLES.

Gentiles into disciples. One of Matthew's major concerns is that the Christian church bring the good news to all the nations (see 28:16-20).

Despite his exalted role as the fulfiller of the prophecy of Isaiah and the precursor of the Messiah, John the Baptist concludes his witness by subordinating his work and purpose to Jesus. There is a plan of God in which one event follows another, one great prophet leads to another. The baptism of John is only a material rite leading to repentance, while Jesus will bring another experience: a baptism that plunges the believer into the fiery experience of God's Holy Spirit (vv. 11-12). The one who follows John is the stronger one. Normally the master leads and the "one who follows" learns. Here the roles are reversed (v. 11). The one who is to come is the Master, whose sandals the slave is not even worthy to carry. He is unworthy of even the most menial of tasks—so great is the one who is to come.

Responding to the Text

The use of the figure of John the Baptist over the season of Advent is an invitation to join with this figure in a period of "preparation." The preaching of the Baptist does not introduce the coming of Jesus into the world but the beginning of his ministry. The incarnation of God in the person of Jesus at Christmas is not the focus of the Baptist's preaching. Without the event we celebrate at Christmas, however, his description of Jesus as the more powerful one, baptizing with power, and worthy of all praise and respect, would make no sense. The Advent tension between the now and the not yet continues into today's Gospel reading.

The kingdom of heaven is at hand, and the one who is able to separate the wheat from the chaff is coming. We rejoice in the coming event of Christmas that will mark the first coming of the greater one, whose sandals we are not worthy to carry. Yet we are challenged by the preaching of John the Baptist to live in the in-between-time. We know and experience that we have already been gifted by the presence of God among us. The very existence of our worshiping Christian community is tangible evidence of that presence. But does the presence of the greater one influence our lives in any significant and effective fashion? Like John the Baptist we recognize that the Lord is among us because of Christmas (see v. 3). But, also like the Baptist, we are waiting for the Christ who is still to come, to gather the wheat into the granary.

THIRD SUNDAY IN ADVENT

REVISED COMMON	EPISCOPAL (BCP)	ROMAN CATHOLIC
Isa. 35:1-10	Isa. 35:1-10	Isa. 35:1-6a, 10
Ps. 146:5-10	Ps. 146 or 146:4-9	Ps. 146:6-7, 8-9, 9-10
or Luke 1:47-55		
James 5:7-10	James 5:7-10	James 5:7-10
Matt. 11:2-11	Matt. 11:2-11	Matt. 11:2-11

A FURTHER ORACLE FROM ISAIAH (Isa. 35:1-10) looks beyond the royal expectations of earlier weeks and announces the coming of the Lord and the wonders that will accompany it. A sense of Christmas expectation is generated, heightened by the jubilant praising of the Lord in Psalm 146, or the parallel praise of the *Magnificat* (Luke 1:47-55). But a reading from James returns energetically to exhortation for a community, waiting patiently for the final coming of the Lord. The Gospel, Matt. 11:2-11, strikes a balance. The final appearance of John the Baptist enables Jesus to praise him and speak of his greatness. In the light of the greatness of John, Jesus informs believers that because of the incarnation, they are blessed with a greatness that even surpasses that of the Baptist.

FIRST READING

ISAIAH 35:1-10 (RCL, BCP);
35:1-6a, 10 (RC)

Interpreting the Text

Today's oracle from Isaiah describes the transformation that will take place when all the redeemed will be led back to Zion (see 35:10). The fertility of Lebanon, Carmel, and Sharon, rich territories in the north of Israel, will be found in the most arid places of the land: the wilderness and the dry land of the south. The deserts will be transformed by the abundant blossoming of plant life (vv. 1-2). The suffering people as well as the arid land will be transformed. The physically weak and the frightened will be given strength and courage as a powerful God brings vengeance upon all who harmed them (vv. 3-4). The prophet tells of abundant life in a desert now transformed with flowing streams accompanied by sight for the blind, hearing for the deaf, mobility for the lame, and speech for the dumb (vv. 5-7). The coming of God will be welcomed by the transformation of everything that is less than perfect! Within that new world, a way for the righteous will open up, enabling them to travel safely to Zion. Nothing will threaten them—neither beast nor unclean person. No one will lose the way on this journey back to Zion (vv. 8-9). Once there, all sorrow will disappear, and everlasting joy and gladness will be theirs (v. 10).

Although found within the so-called First Isaiah, this passage echoes Second Isaiah (Isaiah 40–55), composed by disciples of Isaiah as the possibility emerged of a return of the exiles in Babylon. It is a fragment placed here as the whole book was assembled but was originally written to encourage the exiles. In its original setting, this is not a messianic text. God's saving action transforms Israel and ensures the lasting happiness of the redeemed. No messianic figure is involved.

Responding to the Text

The theme of the coming of God and the transformation of the world points to Christmas. For us, Christmas makes this text messianic—it points to the coming of our Messiah. Already in the New Testament Jesus' activity was recognized as the fulfillment of this oracle: "He even makes the deaf to hear and the mute to speak" (Mark 7:37; see also Matt. 11:4-6; Luke 7:22). As Advent draws closer to the Christmas period, this passage reminds us that sinfulness, frailty, sickness, powerlessness, and the many problems that dog the human being and our ambiguous world are always with us. Yet the hope of the coming of God and the manifestation of his glory promises transformation. Advent reminds us of these promises and tells us that it is not Christian to "give up on the world." Today's oracle from Isaiah, coming from a period in the history of the people when they felt most abandoned, exiled in Babylon, addresses our own sense of exile.

As Isaiah pointed forward with confidence to the flowering of the land, the restoration of the frail, and the return home of all the abandoned, so do we. As he placed his hope and expressed his confidence in the coming intervention of God, so do we. However, we do so in the knowledge that our God has already come and transformed the human situation. We are about to celebrate that coming of God at Christmas. The incarnation of God has the potential to transform creation. The Word having become flesh and dwelt among us has the power to transform all creation (see John 1:14). We wait for the revelation of God's glory, when joy and gladness will be with us, and sorrow and sighing flee away. The glory of God will be revealed in the birth of a child.

RESPONSIVE READING

PSALM 146:5-10 (RCL);
146 or 146:4-9 (BCP); 146:6-10 (RC);
LUKE 1:47-55 (RCL, alt.)

Psalm 146 is a full-throated song of praise: "I will sing praises to my God all my life long" (v. 2). The psalmist exalts God above all others who might appear to exercise power: princes who are mere mortals and whose plans, like their lives, come and vanish (vv. 3-4). True happiness and peace come from an unconditional trust in God who made heaven and earth and holds them in existence (vv. 5-6). God executes right judgment; gives food to the poor; sets the prisoners free; gives sight to the blind lifts up those bowed down by worry or illness; and cares for the stranger, the widow, and the orphan (vv. 7-9). Fundamental beliefs of Israel are encapsulated in this hymn of praise. What other nation has a God like this, who has called us from nothingness, and in whom we place all our trust.

The *Magnificat* (Luke 1:47-55) comes from the same tradition but begins in a more personal mode. After the greeting received from her cousin Elizabeth, that she is the most blessed of all women (see 1:45), Mary of Nazareth points away from herself to give praise where it is due. Mary's blessings are the gift of God. Her achievements reflect the greatness of God. God has regarded her lowliness and raised her up so that all generations might call her blessed. Holy is the name of God above all else (vv. 47-49). From that point on, the attributes of God praised in Psalm 146 return. Those who look to God with reverence, from generation to generation, will be cared for. The story of Israel tells it: God has put down those who pretend greatness and has raised up the lowly, feeding the hungry and reducing the rich to nothing (vv. 50-53). From the time of Abraham, Israel has received the promise that God would care for the lowly in this way (vv. 54-55). Mary and her praise of God come at the end of a long history of loving, serving, and praising a God who saves.

SECOND READING

JAMES 5:7-10

Interpreting the Text

This reading follows hard on the heels of a severe warning to the wealthy (James 5:1-6). It is not inappropriate that he turns to his fellow believers, encouraging them to patience as they await the second coming of the Lord (vv. 7-10). They may not have a great deal of this world's possessions, but they wait for the coming of the Lord. James does not commit himself to the question of *when* the second coming will take place, but he joins the rest of early Christianity in his unshakable confidence *that* it will take place. He uses a practical and effective image to make his point. Farmers know that once they have sown the seed they must wait for the richness of the earth and the life-giving early and late rains to bring forth "the precious crop" (v. 7). No anxiety or attempt to change the growth process can change the rhythm of nature. Christians also must be patient, confident, and strong as they await God's time (v. 8). But this waiting must be done *together*. As a Christian community waits patiently for the coming of the Lord, it strengthens the hearts of the gathered members (v. 8). James gives urgency to his exhortation that fellow Christians must not offend one another with harsh words. He points to the imminent coming of the Judge: "The Judge is standing at the doors!" (v. 9).

Almost without fail, the great prophetic figures of Israel, especially Isaiah and Jeremiah, were rejected by the religious and political leaders of their times. Early Christians rightly applied the figure of the Suffering Servant to Jesus, but in its original setting (see Isa. 42:1-4; 49:1-6; 50:4-9; 52:13—53:12), it may have reflected the sufferings of the prophet himself, bearing all suffering and insult for the vindication of God's word. Jeremiah's confessions tell his confusion and suffering, but also his unflagging commitment to the demands of the word of God that was like a burning fire shut up in his bones (Jer. 20:9). These figures are to serve as models for the Christians who also have much to suffer (see James 5:1-6) but wait confidently for a future that belongs entirely to God.

Responding to the Text

The Advent theme of the second coming has been reintroduced. Christians are exhorted to wait patiently in the midst of perplexing ambiguities and sufferings. Such experiences are a necessary part of life in the in-between time. Patient waiting reflects belief in the Lordship of a compassionate and merciful God, as the verse that follows this lection states: "You have seen the purpose of the Lord, how the Lord is compassionate and merciful" (v. 11).

As Christmas draws near, James' demand deserves our attention: cease judging one another and grumbling about our lot. The first coming of the Lord and Savior established a Christian community marked by the quality of its mutual love (see John 13:34-35; 15:12, 17). Such love reflects the compassionate and merciful God who so

ADVENT PREPARES US FOR CHRISTMAS BY STRESSING THE CHRISTIAN VOCATION TO LOVE.

loved the world that he sent his Son to save us (see John 3:16). Much of the suffering we endure comes from a lack of such love among us. James teaches the members of Christian communities to live through their troubles with minds and hearts firmly fixed upon the future coming of the compassionate and merciful

Lord. The feature of his teaching is his insistence that they do it *together* (see vv. 8–9). Advent prepares us for Christmas by stressing the Christian vocation to love, so much a part of our annual celebration of the first coming of Jesus in the Incarnation. The liturgy of Advent, however, continues to point us beyond the coming of Christ at Christmas to the final coming of the Lord at the end of time, asking that we celebrate Christmas as a part of the longer journey toward the end time.

The Gospel

MATTHEW 11:2-11

Interpreting the Text

The figure of John the Baptist, used to hail the coming of the Lord in the Gospel for the Second Sunday of Advent, returns in today's reading. In his last appearance in Matthew's story, he wonders if the man whose words and deeds are being reported to him is the one who is to come. Is this the "mightier one" (see Matt. 3:11)? If so, then he can joyfully resign himself to whatever destiny may be ahead of him (11:2-3). Jesus' response sums up his ministry to this point in the Gospel, and he uses the oracle of Isa. 35:5-6, a part of today's first reading. The blind see, the lame walk, the deaf hear, the dead are raised to life, and the good news is proclaimed to the poor. What has been foretold of the messianic era by the prophet Isaiah has been fulfilled superabundantly. There can be no doubt. Jesus is the "one who is to come." The first part of today's passage answers the question posed by the Baptist. But, as the messengers depart, Jesus turns his attention away from a description of his own ministry as the fulfillment of the prophecy of Isaiah. He speaks first of the virtue and courage of his forerunner and then of the dignity and grandeur of all called to a privileged participation in the riches of God's kingdom.

The Baptist is not only a prophet. He fulfills messianic prophecies, as Jesus points out by citing Mal. 3:1: "See I am sending my messenger ahead of you, who will prepare your way before you" (v. 10). Jesus adds further information on the greatness of John the Baptist in God's overall design. Until the time of Jesus, John was the greatest of all human beings (v. 11). This is remarkable praise. As we look back over the great heroes of the story of Israel—the patriarchs, the judges, the kings, the wise men and women, the prophets—we are told that they pale into insignificance before the figure of John the Baptist. They have all displayed great virtue and are rightly regarded as great figures in the story of God's people, but the Baptist emerges as a person unconditionally committed to his call. He was no reed swaying in the breeze or prince dressed in fine clothing. He is God's prophet, prepared to accept his prophetic responsibilities, cost what it may (vv. 7-10).

In this light, Jesus' closing words are all the more surprising. Despite the greatness of the figure of the Baptist, the disciple associated with Jesus in proclaiming the kingdom is superior! The Baptist fulfilled the prophecies of Isaiah and Malachi concerning the one who would usher in the messianic time. The "least in the kingdom of heaven" (v. 11) is associated with Jesus in the greater mission of bringing hearing and sight, of giving power back to the legs of the lame, of preaching the good news to the poor. Above all, the Christian disciple gives witness to the resurrection of the dead. Christians are not *preparing* the messianic time—*they belong to it.*

Responding to the Text

As the liturgy joins Jesus in speaking of the Baptist, we too can praise God for calling and gracing the great people from our sacred history. We look back with love and gratitude to the great people from our past. They too remained firm in their response to the call of God and made straight the paths of the Lord for us (see Matt. 3:3). We can all recall those special people of God in our own lives. Today's Gospel explains the advantage they have had over John the Baptist. They have been part of the messianic era and part of a messianic people of God. Because of them and their loyalty, cost what it may, the Christian tradition has been passed on, and we too have the privilege of being among "the least in the kingdom" (see Matt. 11:11).

Christmas is a time to recall the blessings we have received from those who went before us, those who "made straight" so many of the paths we now tread. Advent, however, asks that we gaze beyond the warm and grateful recognition of our forerunners and ask questions of ourselves. The best way to prepare for Christmas is to ask: How are we responding to the dignity of our call to join the least in the kingdom? Even the least of us is called to a greatness that surpasses that of Jesus' precursor. These words of Jesus are both encouragement and challenge. We bring sight to the blind, healing to the sick, comfort to the poor, and by the quality and joy of our lives show that the dead shall rise into life. This is the "good news" that we are privileged to live and proclaim. Advent reminds us that Christmas is a moment to pause, to thank God for the good that has brought us to this moment in our lives, and to recommit ourselves to our unique place in the Lord's messianic time.

FOURTH SUNDAY IN ADVENT

DECEMBER 23, 2001

REVISED COMMON	EPISCOPAL (BCP)	ROMAN CATHOLIC
Isa. 7:10–16	Isa. 7:10–17	Isa. 7:10–14
Ps. 80:1–7, 17–19	Ps. 24 or 24:1–7	Ps. 24:1–2, 3–4, 5–6
Rom. 1:1–7	Rom. 1:1–7	Rom. 1:1–7
Matt. 1:18–25	Matt. 1:18–25	Matt. 1:18–24

THE THEME OF THE SECOND COMING recedes as the celebration of the first coming approaches. An oracle from Isaiah, although firmly situated in the story of the prophet and an encounter with King Ahaz, climaxes in the promise of the Immanuel: "God is with us" (Isa. 7:10–17). The opening of Paul's letter to the Romans is an initial proclamation of Jesus, Son of David, Son of God, whose coming brings grace and peace (Rom. 1:1–7). The Gospel reading prepares for the birth of Jesus by telling the Matthean account of the annunciation of that birth to Joseph (Matt. 1:18–25). "The virgin shall conceive and bear a son, and they shall name him Emmanuel, which means 'God is with us'" (Matt. 1:23).

FIRST READING
ISAIAH 7:10–16 (RCL); 7:10–17 (BCP); 7:10–14 (RC)

Interpreting the Text

Isaiah exercised his prophetic ministry during a period when the Assyrian Empire was expanding and many of the surrounding nations were attempting to form alliances to bring it to an end. King Ahaz of Judah, faced with an attack from Syria (Aram) and Israel (the Northern Kingdom), who wanted Judah to join their alliance against Assyria, turned away from them and formed an alliance with Assyria, for protection against Syria and Israel. The Lord is prepared to give Ahaz a sign to show that the nation needs no alliances, as it has a powerful God (v. 10). But Ahaz has already made up his mind that he will seek help from Assyria. The king has abandoned his trust in God, and so he sanctimoniously replies that he will not put God to the test (vv. 11–12). Ironically, that is exactly what he is doing.

Into that situation steps the prophet Isaiah with his oracle. Whether or not Ahaz wants a sign from God, he will be given one. There will be hope and future life in the midst of desolation and destruction (vv. 14–17). "The house of David," with Ahaz as its anointed king, must listen to the voice of the Lord, who tires of the deceits of his chosen people and their leaders (v. 13). The first sign will be the birth of a son to a young woman. The Hebrew word (*'almâ*) means a young woman who is of childbearing age and most likely refers to the wife of Ahaz. The birth of a child is a sign of life, a promise of a future for the Davidic dynasty (v. 14). The name of this child, "Immanuel," is an indication of God's ongoing protection: "God is with us." Yet, the child will have to pass through deprivation before he comes to maturity, able to discern between good and evil. The child's food, curds and honey, are basic products available during a time of siege and devastation (v. 15). This child, however, will choose the good and reject evil, and this makes him the antithesis of Ahaz, who has chosen evil. Assyria will descend upon the kings of Aram and Israel, and the land will be devastated (v. 16), and the king of Assyria will reduce Ahaz and his house to a vassal state (v. 17).

Responding to the Text

The Roman Catholic tradition allows the reinterpretation of this passage in the Gospel of Matthew (Matt. 1:23) to determine the liturgical sense of the passage from Isaiah. Eliminating the references to future destruction (Isa. 7:16–17), the Roman lectionary sees the woman who will bear the Immanuel as the Mother of Jesus—not just a young woman capable of bearing a child (Hebrew: *'almâ*) but a "virgin" (Hebrew: *bethulâ*), as she is described in the story of the annunciation to Joseph (Matt. 1:23; Greek: *hē parthenos*). In this reading, the oracle of Isaiah looks forward to the promise of the presence of God that has its beginnings in the birth of Jesus at Christmas and will never be absent from the Christian community. The history of the people of Israel and the promise that God would be with them always have been fulfilled in the flesh and blood of the child born of the virgin at Christmas.

The RCL and BCP read the broader context. This places the promise of a son to the king within the context of the imminent disaster and destruction that will fall upon the nation because of his lack of trust in Israel's one true God (Isa. 7:16–17). This reading also speaks to the ambiguity of the Christian community as it approaches Christmas. The promise made to Ahaz, and through him to the whole of the house of David, holds. God will always be with his people. However, people always wax and wane in response to a God who so loved the world that he gave his only Son (John 3:16). There is no stinting God's superabundant gift to his world. Our

ISAIAH ASSURES US THAT THE PROMISES OF GOD WILL NOT BE THWARTED.

response, however, as we rightly anticipate our joy-filled celebration of Christmas, all too often does not correspond to the love that is lavished upon us. Isaiah assures us that the promises of God will not be thwarted. We have been given a sign, the gift of the Immanuel at Christmas. Our fragile response to this gift can never destroy God's faithful presence to us. Indeed, it is cause for even greater rejoicing at Christmas. We are unfailingly loved by our God despite our many failures.

RESPONSIVE READING

PSALM 80:1-7, 17-19 (RCL); 24 or 24:1-7 (BCP); 24:1-6 (RC)

The theme of Israel's failure to respond to God's election and covenant with them dominates Psalm 80, a "communal lament." The people recognize their need of restoration and salvation (v. 3), that God has rejected their prayers and reduced them to ridicule before their enemies (vv. 4-6). From this situation, an appeal rises to the one "enthroned upon the cherubim." This expression recalls the time when YHWH moved among the people in the Ark of the Covenant, a covenant the people know they have forsaken. They look back to the foundation of that covenant: God's leading of the vine of Israel out of the slavery of Egypt and giving the people a dwelling place where they could flourish. As the psalm closes, there is a focus upon an individual, someone who will rise up from the midst of the people: "Let your hand be upon the one at your right hand, the one [Hebrew: 'the son of man'] whom you made strong for yourself" (v. 17). In its original setting this asks God's support and strength for a leader, possibly a king, who will see to it that the restoring action of God, reestablishing a covenant with a sinful people, will not be neglected. Read within the context of our immediate preparation for Christmas, the first coming of Jesus, Lord and Savior, promises that the face of God will shine upon the people, and we will be saved (v. 19).[6]

Psalm 24 has a very different character. It is a hymn of praise to YHWH, recognizing the greatness of God, the creator of the earth and all that is in it (vv. 1-2). Before such greatness, who is worthy to approach his Temple ("the hill of the LORD")? Only those who have clean hands and pure hearts, who are not false and do not swear deceitfully (vv. 3-4). The separation between the creator and the created, and the possibility that the latter may approach the former is cause for wonder. The psalmist cries out this wonder as he contemplates the approach of the Lord. Confident that God comes to dwell among the faithful, he appeals to the very building of the Temple, the gates and the doors, to prepare themselves for the coming of God. The most wonderful God, the King of glory and the Lord of hosts, is about to visit us.

ROMANS 1:1-7

Interpreting the Text

Through no virtue of his own, Paul has been called to be a servant, a slave of Jesus Christ. This happened to him; he did not make it happen. Out of his total dependence upon the one who called him flows another role. He is an apostle, a sent one of Jesus Christ, announcing the good news of what God has done for us in and through his Son, something long promised in the Sacred Scriptures of Israel (vv. 1-2). The Romans who are to receive this letter are similarly privileged. Because of the gift of Paul's apostolic commitment to the preaching of the good news of Jesus Christ, the possibility of a new relationship with God emerges for the Gentile world, including the Roman Christians (vv. 5-6).

The new relationship is one of obedience. Paul introduces a theme that will emerge as crucial to his more detailed presentation of God's offer to humankind in and through Jesus. Sin has entered the world through Adam, and from that time on the human situation is caught in a situation of sinfulness. No human invention can ever free humankind from that slavery. However, an abundance of grace has come into our story because of the gift of Jesus Christ whose obedience opened up a new way to God. His unconditional yes to God led to death and resurrection. Where sin once abounded, the obedience of Jesus has generated the possibility of a superabundance of grace (see Rom. 5:12-21).

The Roman Christians receive the superabundance of God's gracious gifts of love and freedom. Because of the obedience of faith, they can be called "saints," people made holy by what God has done for them in calling them to belong to Jesus Christ. Grace and peace were expressions often used in ancient letters as a salutation. When Paul uses them to greet his fellow Christians, however, they take on a deeper meaning. The grace they receive is the result of the death and resurrection of Jesus Christ. The peace they have reflects the biblical notion of *shalôm*, a sense of wholeness and holiness that comes from being at one with their creating and saving God and among one another (vv. 6-7).

The other side of the Christian mystery is succinctly summed up in vv. 3-4. In a remarkable statement, Paul tells the Romans of the content of his gospel. It is the good news concerning the Son of God. The Son of God is presented as having taken on the human condition according to the line of David. His coming into the world, however, already places him in a unique situation. As one "descended from David according to the flesh" (v. 3), Jesus is the Christ. He is born into the messianic dynasty and brings that line to its perfection. The man Jesus of Nazareth was Jesus the Christ! But he is more. From the Father, he has returned to the Father, to receive all glory and honor (see Phil. 2:5-11), by means of his death and resurrection. There is a close link between Jesus as the Christ, according to the flesh and Jesus "declared Son of God with power according to the spirit of holiness by his resurrection from the dead" (v. 4).

Paul's understanding of the new relationship between God and humankind made possible by Jesus Christ depends entirely upon Jesus' human experience of life, death, and resurrection as unconditionally determined by God. It is Jesus— the Christ who suffered, died, and rose from the dead—who is Lord. We now have one who has gone before us, the firstborn of many from among the dead (see 1 Cor. 15:20-23). One who experienced the human condition in all its ambiguity leads the way: Jesus Christ is our Lord (v. 4).

Responding to the Text

The incarnation, celebrated annually at Christmas, is a central moment in Paul's understanding of Jesus and what he has done for the human situation. Writing only some twenty years after Jesus' death, Paul understands Jesus as having had a prior existence with God (see Phil. 2:5-11).[7] A response to the Pauline reading rejoices in the light that has come into the darkness because of Jesus Christ's coming as Son of David. Paul saw evidence that the dark reality of sin was everywhere, and human beings were unable to escape the pain and disorder that this reality imposed. Both Jew and Gentile suffered in the same fashion (see Rom. 1:18-3:20). What we celebrate at Christmas is the beginning of a life-story that changed the darkness into light. Jesus comes into the human story as the Christ, the Son of David, and fulfills the Jewish messianic expectation, albeit in a most unexpected way. Jesus begins a journey that will not be completed until, via his death and resurrection, he returns to the Father. There he is our Christ and Lord. Like the Romans, we are the privileged recipients of this gospel. We are saints, blessed with grace and peace because of Christmas: God's action in the incarnation of his Son.

THE GOSPEL

MATTHEW 1:18-25 (RCL, BCP); 1:18-24 (RC)

Interpreting the Text

Like many of the women from Israel's sacred history (Tamar, Rahab, Ruth, and Bathsheba), Mary has been invaded by the mysterious power of God (Matt. 1:19; see 1:1-17). The Lord calls a puzzled Joseph to an act of faith and obedience. Joseph is told of the origin of Mary's pregnancy through the message of the angel, coming to him in a dream. "The child conceived in her is from the Holy Spirit" (v. 20). What is more important, however, as Matthew begins his Gospel, is the proclamation of the future destiny of the son to be born: his name must be "Jesus, for he will save his people from their sins" (v. 21).

Isaiah had asked that Ahaz trust more deeply in the power and caring presence of YHWH to his people rather than enter into an alliance with Assyria. Ahaz disobeyed and was destroyed (vv. 16-17). Joseph, by contrast, in a wordless response to the word of God communicated by an angel, rose and "took her as his wife" (v. 24). A total and unquestioning acceptance of the word of God is Joseph's first action in Matthew's story of Jesus' birth and infancy. Matthew does not only report the fulfillment of the prophecy of Isaiah. He adds an explanatory note to the word "Emmanuel" of Isa. 7:14. A Greek readership needs to be told that the Hebrew "Emmanuel" means "God is with us" (v. 23).[8] As a first example of what the never-failing presence of God means, Joseph is reported as responding to both commands from the angel. He takes Mary to his home as his wife (v. 24), and he calls the son of Mary "Jesus" (v. 25). But Matthew wants to tell all his readers that God is with them. As the Gospel of Matthew comes to its close, Jesus returns to the theme of "Emmanuel." The risen Jesus says to his first disciples, and through them to disciples of all time: "I am with you always, to the end of the age" (Matt. 28:20).

Responding to the Text

God is among us. By means of his messenger, a child to be born of the Holy Spirit has been announced. The word of God, originally proclaimed by a prophet of the Lord, is now fulfilled. God is at the center of all that happens in this story, and Joseph instructs us on our response to the intervention of God. God's presence to us may not be as spectacular as the one described for Joseph in today's Gospel, but we are all aware that the divine seeps into our life in many different ways, sometimes simply and sometimes in a more complex fashion. Joseph leads the way by responding without words, argument, or question. He does what is asked of him.

GOD'S PRESENCE TO US MAY NOT BE AS SPECTACULAR AS THE ONE DESCRIBED FOR JOSEPH IN TODAY'S GOSPEL, BUT WE ARE ALL AWARE THAT THE DIVINE SEEPS INTO OUR LIFE IN MANY DIFFERENT WAYS.

Christmas brings us our Emmanuel. The celebration of Christmas reminds us that in the Incarnation, the Divine has become part of the human story. Christmas also asks us to examine the quality of our response to the presence of the Divine among us. Again, Joseph leads the way and shows the quality of trust and commitment, so different to that of Ahaz, that the coming of God should engender. Our Gospel also reminds us that this "coming of God" is not a yearly event. God will be with us until the end of the age. As each Christmas comes and goes, the church continues to proclaim that in Jesus, God is with us, and that Jesus will be with us until the end of time. May our joy and celebration be highlighted by a deep trust in a God who so loved us that he gave us his only Son (see John 3:16; Rom. 1:3-4).

THE SEASON OF CHRISTMAS– EPIPHANY

FRANCIS J. MOLONEY, S.D.B.

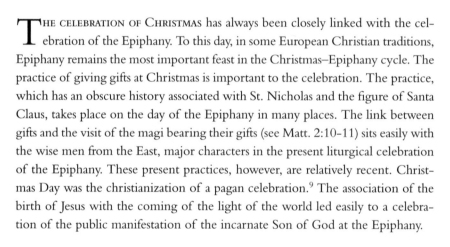

THE CELEBRATION OF CHRISTMAS has always been closely linked with the celebration of the Epiphany. To this day, in some European Christian traditions, Epiphany remains the most important feast in the Christmas–Epiphany cycle. The practice of giving gifts at Christmas is important to the celebration. The practice, which has an obscure history associated with St. Nicholas and the figure of Santa Claus, takes place on the day of the Epiphany in many places. The link between gifts and the visit of the magi bearing their gifts (see Matt. 2:10-11) sits easily with the wise men from the East, major characters in the present liturgical celebration of the Epiphany. These present practices, however, are relatively recent. Christmas Day was the christianization of a pagan celebration.[9] The association of the birth of Jesus with the coming of the light of the world led easily to a celebration of the public manifestation of the incarnate Son of God at the Epiphany.

The Origins of the Christmas–Epiphany Cycle

The birth of Jesus, probably celebrated in different ways, times, and places in an earlier period, is mentioned in a calendar for the first time in the fourth century.[10] The development of the Christian celebration was deliberately (and polemically) associated with the pagan feast of the *sol invictus*, "the invincible sun." The pagan feast had been introduced by Emperor Aurelius (270–275 C.E.), to be celebrated in Rome on December 25. The background of the pagan feast was the gradual waning of the sun from the end of June until the winter solstice, the shortest day of the year. The waning and then the steady waxing of the sun and the lengthening of the daylight hours indicated that the sun could not be conquered.

It would increase in strength as the days became longer and hotter until the summer solstice, its brightest and most glorious moment. The celebration of the *sol invictus* recognized this immutable rhythm of nature and gave it divine status.

The conversion of many to Christianity who had celebrated the feast of *sol invictus* facilitated the substitution of the pagan feast with a Christian feast. The early Christian church searched the Scriptures for guidance as its theological and liturgical thought and practice developed. The prophet Malachi said that one day "the sun of justice" (Mal. 3:20) would arise, and Jesus called himself "the light of the world" (John 8:12; 9:5). The Johannine tradition makes much of Jesus' being the light that breaks into darkness, overcoming sin and evil (John 1:5; 3:19-21; 9:1-39; 12:35-36, 46). The link between Jesus, the light of the world, with the sun that vanquishes darkness was there to be made. Jesus was the light who had triumphed over sin and death (John 1:5, 9). Once the Peace of Constantine (313) was established and Christianity gradually took its place as the imperial religion, the celebration of the Nativity of the Lord steadily supplanted the pagan celebration of *sol invictus* until it became established as the feast to be celebrated on December 25.[11] The Gospel of John, so important in the great theological and christological debates of the early centuries, also played an important role in the recognition of the need to celebrate the coming of the true light into the world at the incarnation of the Son of God.

At about the same time as the Roman pagan feast became the Christian celebration of Christmas, Egyptian and Arabian Christians developed a celebration of the winter solstice that focused on January 6. Largely ignoring the development of Christmas in the West, the feast of the Epiphany came into being. The Greek word *epiphaneia* means "showing forth," "manifestation," or even "revelation." Probably to refute pagan myths, the earliest tradition associated this "manifestation" with the baptism of Jesus, his mission, and the miracle of Cana, where Jesus first manifested his glory (John 2:1-11). Thus, in the East the celebration of the Epiphany and the fact that Christ's coming was the revelation of God developed independent of the Western replacement of the pagan celebration of the *sol invictus*. The feast of the Epiphany, however, was rapidly assumed and celebrated throughout the West. As early as 361 it is mentioned as a great feast in Gaul. A similar adoption of Christmas took place in the East. The universal celebration of a cycle that focused upon the incarnation of the Son of God, and the consequent revelation of God in the Son, was in place in both the East and the West between the end of the fourth and the first half of the fifth Christian centuries.

The Development of the Celebrations

The earliest celebration of Christmas in Rome was a papal Mass at the basilica of St. Peter. This Mass was the forerunner of the present Roman Catholic Mass of

Christmas Day, still reflected in the readings for the Revised Common and the Episcopal lectionaries. The proclamation of the prologue of the Gospel of John (John 1:1-18) was an essential part of the Mass and was one of Rome's many ways of affirming its rejection of the Arian heresy. Arianism, although condemned at the Council of Nicea (325) and finally at the Council of Constantinople (381), remained powerfully present in Christianity for many centuries. According to St. Jerome (c. 347–420), the Christian world had become Arian. Fundamental to Arianism was the teaching that Jesus of Nazareth was not the human manifestation of the eternal God. The papal Mass at Dawn in Rome, beginning in the fourth century, proclaimed John 1:1-18 and developed a liturgy that insisted that the preexistent word of God who was one with God (vv. 1-2) became flesh and dwelt among us (v. 14). This earliest celebration, therefore, was focused upon the person of Christ as the incarnation of the eternal Word. Other episodes from the birth and infancy stories of Jesus were quickly associated with the Christmas Day Mass. By 360 the celebration also commemorated the adoration of the magi and the slaying of the Innocents through the inclusion of readings from the Gospel of Matthew (Matt. 2:1-18). The celebration of Christmas was not only about the doctrine of the incarnation but also an important part of the Christian "story."

A night Mass was celebrated every year in the cave of the nativity at Bethlehem for the Epiphany. From the fifth century, a night Mass was adopted in Rome. Instead of the Epiphany, however, the Roman tradition celebrated the Mass at Christmas. The night Mass in Rome took on a special significance because of its association with the Church of St. Mary Major, built after the Council of Ephesus (431). The pope celebrated this Mass in a chapel of the basilica, and within that chapel was placed wood from a crèche, to recall the event of the birth of Jesus, especially as it is recorded in the Gospel of Luke (see Luke 2:1-21). The Mass eventually took on the name of the *Missa ad praesepe*, which means, "the Mass at the crib." Our present pageantry and the long iconographic tradition associated with the crib at Christmas have their beginnings in 1223. St. Francis of Assisi set up a crib, with a child and animals (on the basis of the "sign" of the manger in Luke 2:12, read in the light of Isa.1:2-3) in a cave in the Italian village of Greccio.[12] Yet the presence of a crib at Christmas celebrations reaches back to the earliest liturgical celebrations of a night Mass. As with the day Mass, the need to affirm traditional doctrine associated Christmas liturgy with the narrative of the Gospel reporting of the events that marked the incarnation of the Son of God. The association of the events of Bethlehem linked the liturgy of Christmas with the Gospel narratives of the birth of Jesus. The Gospel reading for the night Mass was Luke 2:1-14. This tradition remains in all contemporary lectionaries.

A third Christmas Mass developed around the Greek colony in Rome. Its members also recalled the birth of Jesus on December 25 at their church,

St. Anastasia (Holy Resurrection). To honor this tradition, the pope went to the Church of St. Anastasia and celebrated a Mass before the Mass at St. Peter's. This third Christmas Mass announced the nativity by reading the Gospel of the good news announced to the shepherds and their visit to find the Christ child (Luke 2:15-20). This completed the development of a threefold Christmas liturgy in Rome. Each of these moments had its own history: the night Mass celebrated at St. Mary Major (*Missa ad praesepe*), a Mass at early dawn, originally at St. Anastasia, and the Mass during the day at St. Peter's.

Today's Celebration of Christmas and the Epiphany

The development of the liturgical cycle of Christmas to Epiphany described above is still present in contemporary lectionaries. The RCL, the Episcopal lectionary, and the Roman lectionary have a selection of readings for an evening or a night celebration of Christmas highlighted by the Lukan account of the birth of Jesus (Luke 1:1-14). All three lectionaries also have a Christmas Day celebration with a focus on the Johannine prologue (John 1:1-18). The earliest traditions of Christmas celebrations have thus been preserved. We continue the tradition of a night celebration looking back upon the Gospel narratives' events that report the birth of a child, traditionally the Roman Mass at St. Mary Majors "at the crib" (Luke 2:1-14). This is coupled with a day celebration that affirms that in Jesus Christ the eternal Word had become flesh and dwelt among us. Both of these themes were already part of Christmas celebrations in the fourth Christian century.

One might expect an "octave," a week of liturgical celebration that looks back to Christmas Day. But, because of the intimate link between Christmas and the Epiphany and the fact that the new calendar year begins on January 1, an octave would lessen the significance of these important moments in the Christian year. Thus, there are several Sunday celebrations scattered across the weeks between Christmas and the Epiphany associated with the central theme of the incarnation of the Son of God and its consequences for the human condition. For many centuries, January 1 was variously dedicated to the commemoration of the circumcision of Jesus or the motherhood of Mary. Despite the biblical background for the former celebration (see Luke 2:21), this aspect of Jesus' infancy fell out of favor in Roman Catholic tradition, as circumcision is not part of Christian practice and meant little to the faithful. In 1969 the reformation of the Roman Liturgy called for by Vatican II (1962–1965) favored the dedication of January 1 to the Solemnity of Mary, Mother of God, an important Christian tradition that had its original doctrinal formulation at the Council of Ephesus in 431. Other Christian traditions retain the memory of the circumcision but recognize that the celebration is not so much a recalling of the Jewish practice of circumcision but the "naming" of a child (see Luke 2:21) and thus have developed a celebration of the Holy Name of Jesus. All three lectionaries read the Gospel of the shepherds' journey to discover the newborn child in a manger, climaxing in the circumcision and the naming of the child "Jesus" (Luke 2:15-21).

Instituted for the Roman tradition by Pope Benedict XV in 1921, the Sunday between Christmas and January 1 is a celebration of the Holy Family. If there is no Sunday between December 25 and January 1, this feast is celebrated on December 30. All three lectionaries have readings for the celebration of the Holy Family. Traditionally, the celebration of the Epiphany was a fixed feast, always celebrated on January 6. In many European and Latin countries this tradition is still in place. But in the United States, in order to maintain the foundational association between celebrations of Christmas and Epiphany, it is celebrated on the Sunday that falls between January 2 and January 8. In this way, both Christmas Day and the Epiphany are publicly celebrated "holy days." On the Sunday following the Epiphany, the Christian church moves away from the infancy of Jesus and opens the door to his public ministry with the celebration of the Baptism of the Lord. This celebration closes the season of Christmas–Epiphany.[13]

The celebration of the death and resurrection of Jesus stands at the heart of the liturgical year. Yet, as this brief history of the development of the Christmas–Epiphany cycle demonstrates, the early church quickly recognized that, despite the fundamental importance of the way the story of Jesus Christ came to an end, it was important to celebrate the beginnings of his life. Within the threatening context of the

"GOD, OUR FATHER, OUR HUMAN NATURE IS THE WONDERFUL WORK OF YOUR HANDS, MADE STILL MORE WONDERFUL BY THE WORK OF YOUR REDEMPTION. YOUR SON TOOK TO HIMSELF OUR HUMAN CONDITION; GRANT US A SHARE IN THE GODHEAD OF JESUS."

Arian heresy, the earliest celebrations wished to proclaim Jesus of Nazareth as the eternal Word of God become flesh. It was not enough, however, to celebrate this doctrinal truth. The birth of Jesus was also the beginning of a life-story, and Gospel narratives that told of that beginning were available to the church. From early times Christmas recalled the newborn child, a crib, wonder and openness to what God had done in this child (the Shepherds), and rejection and violence from others (Herod and the slaying of the Innocents). It is this marriage of the doctrine of the incarnation and the significance of the enfleshment of the divine for the human condition that makes Christmas–Epiphany a period that has brought such joy to centuries of Christian celebration.

> God, our Father, our human nature is the wonderful work of your hands, made still more wonderful by the work of your redemption. Your Son took to himself our human condition; grant us a share in the godhead of Jesus.[14]

THE NATIVITY OF OUR LORD I (CHRISTMAS EVE)

DECEMBER 24, 2001

REVISED COMMON	EPISCOPAL (BCP)	ROMAN CATHOLIC
Isa. 9:2-7	Isa. 9:2-4, 6-7	Isa. 9:1-6
Ps. 96	Ps. 96 or 96:1-4, 11-12	Ps. 96:1-2, 2-3, 11-12, 13
Titus 2:11-14	Titus 2:11-14	Titus 2:11-14
Luke 2:1-14 (15-20)	Luke 2:1-14 (15-20)	Luke 2:1-14

THE ADVENT PRACTICE OF READINGS from Isaiah continues. The prophet promises the appearance of the light that will accompany the birth of a child who will free the nation from its burdens. The letter to Titus boldly proclaims the universal salvation made possible through the appearance of God's grace among us in the person of Jesus Christ. Jesus is born of Mary in Bethlehem, and angels announce to shepherds a message of "peace on earth" among those whom God favors (Luke 2:14). The coming of the saving light of God into a sinful world begins with the birth of Jesus of Nazareth.

FIRST READING

ISAIAH 9:2-7 (RCL); 9:2-4, 6-7 (BCP); 9:1-6 (RC)

Interpreting the Text

This oracle is to be dated shortly after Isaiah's encounter with Ahaz, on the occasion of the king's refusal to ask God for a sign and Isaiah's giving him the sign of Immanuel (Isa. 7:10-17).[15] The Davidic dynasty would survive the devastation (see 7:14-15). Today's passage opens with a hope-filled oracle concerning the northern parts of Israel subjected to Assyria (9:1). They had been enslaved and walked in darkness. This situation will be reversed by the action of God. A great light will come among them, and their sufferings will be turned into light (v. 2), their families will multiply and prosper, the harvests will be great (v. 3). The yoke of the Assyrian lordship will be broken, and all the signs of war: the boots of tramping warriors and garments rolled in blood, will be destroyed by fire (vv. 4-5). Such a reversal of the fortunes of the northern lands will not be the result of any mighty human action but the fulfillment of the promise of Immanuel: "For a child has been born for us, a son given to us" (v. 6a). Royal authority has passed to him, and he is named "Wonderful Counselor, Mighty God, Everlasting Father, Prince of Peace" (v. 6b). The first of these titles claims that the new king will have no need for the type of advisers who led Ahaz into a false alliance. The remaining titles do not claim divinity for the king but insist that his rule will manifest extraordinary authority, last forever, and bring an undisturbed peace. The son of Ahaz, promised in 7:14-15, will be very different from his father.

As the passage closes, the association with the Davidic dynasty is made clear. The never-ending authority, peace, justice, and righteousness that will be established is "for the throne of David and his kingdom." The crucial point in the oracle about the role of the son of Ahaz, however, is that his success comes from God: "The zeal of the LORD of hosts will do this" (v. 7d). The alliance that led to the destruction of the northern regions and turned them into vassal states dependent upon Assyria was the fruit of *human design* (see 7:16-17; 9:1). Isaiah insists that the lasting peace and just rule to be established by the son of Ahaz will be the result of *the action of God*.

Responding to the Text

Darkness, the oppressive yoke upon the shoulders of so many, the incessant tramping of the boots of soldiers, and garments rolled in blood are still dramatically present in all four corners of the globe. As we celebrate Christmas, the prophet calls out that a Son has been given to us, and we immediately identify that Son with Jesus of Nazareth, Son of God. A message of hope rings out in the darkness of our evening celebration: the darkness will be dispelled, the oppression will be eliminated, peace and justice will be established. As we all know so well, such a reversal seems impossible for any human individual or organization to achieve.

> A MESSAGE OF HOPE RINGS OUT IN THE DARKNESS OF OUR EVENING CELEBRATION: THE DARKNESS WILL BE DISPELLED, THE OPPRESSION WILL BE ELIMINATED, PEACE AND JUSTICE WILL BE ESTABLISHED.

Two world wars and other major conflicts, such as the wars in Korea and Vietnam, highlighted the century we have just left. No place on the face of the earth was without war, from Europe to Africa, Asia, and the Americas. As the new millennium opens, there is no sign of an easing of the sound of "the boots of the tramping warriors" or destruction of "the garments rolled in blood," now spreading into the peace of Oceania. The League of Nations, followed by the United Nations has struggled in vain to impose a new world order. We stand in the darkness of Christmas night with hearts afire as we hear of a Son, a Mighty God, a

FRANCIS J.
MOLONEY, S.D.B.

Prince of Peace, who has been given to us at Christmas. There is joy and hope as we confess our belief that, despite the good efforts and many failures of human beings to resolve the many sins of violence and oppression, "the zeal of the Lord of hosts will do this" (v. 7d).

RESPONSIVE READING

PSALM 96 (RCL, BCP); 96:1-3, 11-13 (RC); 96:1-4, 11-12 (BCP, alt.)

Probably written for the enthronement of a king, this psalm is unique in its "missionary" character. Unlike much of the Hebrew Bible, it exhorts all the earth to sing to the Lord (v. 1) and the people to declare the glory of God among the nations (vv. 3, 10). The hymn is unrestrained in its recognition of the greatness, glory, justice, and righteousness of God, and prays a threefold prayer. The psalmist first addresses God's people and asks that they make known to the nations the glory of God by means of a new and joyful song. All the gods of the other nations are idols, and only one God deserves reverence. Beauty and strength are found in his sanctuary (vv. 1-6). He then turns to the nations, asking all the "families of the people" (v. 7) to recognize the glory and strength of the one true God. In this recognition they will make their way to his sanctuary, bringing their offerings and rendering him due worship (vv. 7-9). This movement of addressees from the people of God to the families of all the nations, however, reaches further. The final section of the psalm addresses creation: the world (v. 10), the heavens and the sea, the fields, the trees, and the forests (vv. 11-12). The beauty of the sky, the roar of the sea, and the majesty of the fields and the forests call out in praise of the God who made them.

Due recognition of the goodness, strength, and beauty of God are called for, because God is coming to judge everyone and everything in the earth. He will judge the creation with righteousness (v. 13a), and all the people of the world he will judge in the light of his truth (v. 13b). At Christmas we recognize the first stage in this coming of God. In Jesus of Nazareth the light has come into the world to bring life and judgment to all who accept or refuse the revelation of the truth that takes place in him (see John 3:11-21). Christmas celebrates the first step in a process that will come to an end when the same Jesus returns as the Son of Man to judge with righteousness.

TITUS 2:11-14

Interpreting the Text

The two epistles to Timothy and the epistle to Titus called, since the eighteenth century, "pastoral" epistles, are concerned with the everyday life of Christian communities. They were written by followers of Paul who used the name of their inspiration "Paul" to give their directions authority.[16] Immediately prior to the lection for Christmas Eve, the author exhorts various groups in the Christian community in Crete: teachers, older women, younger men, and slaves (Titus 2:3-10). But it is not enough to exhort. The Christmas reading looks at the uniqueness of the Christian situation: Why is it that a certain quality of life, love, and service is required of the followers of Jesus?

The event celebrated at Christmas provides the answer: "For the grace of God has appeared, bringing salvation to all" (2:11). There is a progression here from the reading from Isaiah that spoke of the gift of a Son, to Psalm 96, which called upon the whole of creation to sing praise to the God who is coming as life-giver and judge. The author points to the event of Jesus Christ as the appearance of the possibility of universal salvation. Writing to Christians in Crete, he includes the Gentile world, but this coming is not the only coming. The central theological theme of the period of Advent returns as Christians are exhorted to right living because they are living in the in-between-time. The grace of God *has appeared* in the incarnation. But believers are to live lives marked by that grace (see v. 12) as they "wait for the blessed hope and the manifestation of the glory of our great God and Savior, Jesus Christ" (v. 13). He has come, and *he will come again* to judge the way Christians have lived the time between the two comings. But Jesus is not only at the beginning and end of the Christian way of life. Jesus is the one who gave himself unconditionally to free all people from their sin, to offer the possibility of a new people of God who live the in-between-time in a way modeled upon his self-gift (Titus 2:14).

Responding to the Text

The reading from Titus arouses at least two sentiments. We recognize the importance of Christmas as the beginning of the revelation of God's gracious self-gift in Jesus Christ (see v. 11). Perhaps more important is the church's insistence, even on Christmas Eve, that we must not lose ourselves in the joy and gratitude that flow from the coming of the Son of God into the world. Christian life is made up of moments of great happiness, delighting in the gifts of God that we already enjoy: love, family, community, the word of God, our shared faith, our celebrations, the ambiguous beauty of the creation. However, it must never be *only* that. Even on Christmas Eve the church asks us to pause, in the midst of our joy and celebration, to recall that we are to live lives marked by the tension demanded by the Christian belief in the wonder of the "now" and the unknown mystery of the "not yet." In all situations we have our model: "He it is who gave himself for us" (v. 14). We are asked, at Christmas, to go on giving ourselves for one another.

THE GOSPEL

LUKE 2:1-14 (15-20) (RCL, BCP); 2:1-14 (RC)

Interpreting the Text

The development of the feast of Christmas was associated with the need to proclaim the Christian belief that in Jesus Christ the eternally preexistent Word of God became flesh. Behind this truth, however, lies the story of the birth of a child. The author of the Gospel of Luke deliberately links even the most sublime moments in God's dealings with the human story to recognizable events from that story. Luke's account of the birth of Jesus, the moment when the Son of God enters the human scene, opens with a series of names and places (Luke 2:1-3). Jesus did not simply come among us; he came into the world at a given place in a given time. The names of the people involved begin with the greatest of human figures: Caesar Augustus, issuing a decree for a census *of the whole world* (v. 1). His delegate, the lesser but still significant Quirinius, sees to the administration of that census *in the area of Syria* (v. 2). Two simple people, unknown by the great people of their time, set out for *Bethlehem,* the city of the family of David in the Jewish tradition, but, for the rest of the world, an insignificant town in the hills to the south of Jerusalem (v. 3).

At Bethlehem they find that the usual resting place for travelers (Greek: *kataluma*) is full (v. 7). The traditional English translation of *kataluma* as "inn," preserved in the NRSV, does not accurately render the original. The word "inn" suggests a snug, softly lit place where people gather in comfort. The *kataluma* was a large area, perhaps covered with a tent, where wandering travelers found a place to lie down for the night. Joseph and Mary had begun a journey from Nazareth, and they have arrived in Bethlehem. This is a long and arduous journey, made more so by Mary's being in an advanced state of pregnancy (v. 6). There is no place for them in the *kataluma,* and thus they must journey further. Jesus is born on a journey, for a journey, and he will later call others to follow him (see especially Luke 24:44-49; Acts 1:6-11).

At birth Jesus was wrapped, as a king, in bands of cloth (see Wis. 7:4-5), laid in a manger (Greek: *phatnē*) so that the prophecy of Isa. 1:2-3 might be reversed: "I reared children and brought them up, but they have rebelled against me. The ox knows its owner, and the donkey its master's crib (Greek: *phatnē*); but Israel does not know, my people do not understand" (Luke 2:7). The children of Israel summoned to the manger are not the high and mighty (v. 8). Shepherds are summoned from their flocks by angels (v. 9), who bring them good news of great joy for all the people: "To you is born this day in the City of David a Savior, who is the Messiah, the Lord" (vv. 10-11). The details used by the narrator to describe the care of the newborn child, the bands of cloth, and the manger (see v. 7), are described by the angels as "a sign" (v. 12). They will find a child cared for as a king should be cared for (see Wis. 7:4-5) and lying in a manger at which Israel might find right nourishment (see Isa. 1:2-3). The shepherds begin their journey to the crib, responding to the word that has come to them from heaven (see v. 15). They are accompanied by a heavenly song of praise, announcing the glory of God and the wonder of his blessings upon all who are open to God's goodness (v. 14).

Responding to the Text

There is more to this story than the birth of a child in a stable. Luke's story of the birth of Jesus tells of a reversal of the value systems of the world. It opens with a list of people whom one might regard as the greatest (Caesar Augustus), to the less important (Quirinius), to the unimportant (Joseph and the pregnant Mary) (vv. 1-3). It closes with an angelic song praising God who has given us a Savior in the newborn son of a humble woman (see Luke 1:46-55) and who calls shepherds, people marginal to society at large, to come from their fields and flocks. They are to be the first to acknowledge their Christ and their Lord, "this thing that has taken place," made known to them by the Lord (v. 15).

> LUKE'S STORY OF THE BIRTH OF JESUS TELLS OF A REVERSAL OF THE VALUE SYSTEMS OF THE WORLD.

Christmastime in our prosperous society can often lead to a search for the gift with the correct label. But, more significantly, it is a time when the liturgy asks us to stop and reassess our values. The readings for Christmas Eve announce that a people who walked in darkness have seen a great light (Isa. 9:2). The readings from Titus and the Gospel of Luke urge us to recognize that the darkness of the night can be filled with the light of *love given* and *love received*. The proclamation of this event from the beginning of the Christian story asks that our contemporary Christian lives reflect the love of a God who has unconditionally entered our story in the birth of his Son, Jesus Christ.

THE NATIVITY OF OUR LORD II (CHRISTMAS DAY)

DECEMBER 25, 2001

Revised Common	Episcopal (BCP)	Roman Catholic
Isa. 52:7-10	Isa. 52:7-10	Isa. 52:7-10
Ps. 98	Ps. 98 or 98:1-6	Ps. 98:1, 2-3, 3-4, 5-6
Heb. 1:1-4 (5-12)	Heb. 1:1-12	Heb. 1:1-6
John 1:1-14	John 1:1-14	John 1:1-18 (1-5, 9-14)

The Christmas Day readings focus on the theological significance of the incarnation. They feature the reading of the prologue to the Gospel of John (John 1:1-18), the great hymn in praise of the incarnation of the eternally pre-existent Word of God (v. 14). Similar sentiments are expressed by the opening verses of the letter to the Hebrews. The author celebrates the culmination of a long history of the various ways in which God has communicated with humankind (Heb. 1:1-12). An oracle from Third Isaiah, read as an introduction to the christological readings of John and Hebrews, announces the coming of God's comfort, redemption, and salvation.

First Reading
ISAIAH 52:7-10

Interpreting the Text

The prophet rejoices in God's saving action, restoring the people to their land, and addresses the difficulties they faced on their return.[17] Having established that Israel's freedom and the return of the nation to the land and the city given to them by God is for the greater glory of the name of God, Third Isaiah announces God's salvation. Excitement rings out as the messenger of God's peace announces the good news that "God reigns" (v. 7). The first to hear this message are those in Zion. They have suffered at the hands of the wicked (vv. 1-2), and there had been times in Babylon when they wondered why God had allowed such tragedy. Now both the fact of their return and the word of the prophet assure them that God reigns. The joyful shout of the messenger who brings the good news to Zion is picked up by the sentinels who are guarding the ruined walls of Jerusalem against the incursions of those who oppose the renewed presence of God's people within the Holy City (vv. 8-9). Within the city, and from the ruined walls of the city, the shout goes up, announcing "the return of the LORD to Zion." The city may be destroyed, but its heart and soul, the people and their God, rejoice in its midst.

The reigning presence of God, the return of the Lord to Zion, however, is not only a message for Israel. Against all odds, the slaves have been freed, the exiles have returned home. This has happened because of the "mighty arm" of the Lord. The power of God had made the impossible possible. The prophet insists that "all the nations shall see the salvation of our God." It is not only Israel who shouts with joy at the freedom a gracious and powerful God has granted them. The action of God reveals a power unheard of among the nations. What God does for Israel reveals the glory of the Lord to all the nations.

Responding to the Text

The Christian liturgy cries out this song of jubilation at Christmas to express the belief that with the coming of God in Jesus Christ the good news of redemption and freedom has been announced. The pressures of life and the distractions of the year gone by may have generated "ruins of Jerusalem" (v. 9) for us, but Christmas proclaims our freedom. God reigns, all the earth sees the salvation of our God, and we are the blessed recipients of the freedom granted by his mighty arm.

There is a sense in which the Christian often shares the experience of Israel in exile in Babylon. There the exiles lived an experience of a foreign cult, strange language and customs, and the birth of a new generation that had never known Israel, Jerusalem, and the dwelling place of God. Increasingly marginalized in our highly fragmented postmodern world, we often wonder about our roots. We wonder if the God who led us into our community of faith and nourished us with word and action still cares. Christmas announces that we are free. This season is not the time for a grim hanging on to principles that have become no more than principles. It is a time for us to welcome the messenger who brings this good news, to stand up in the midst of the many ruins that we have often created for ourselves, aware that "the Lord has comforted his people" (v. 9). A joyful acceptance of God's powerful presence, redeeming us, freeing us, and bringing us home at Christmas can be an evangelizing force. In our joy "all the ends of the earth shall see the salvation of our God" (v. 10).

> IT IS A TIME FOR US TO WELCOME THE MESSENGER WHO BRINGS THIS GOOD NEWS, TO STAND UP IN THE MIDST OF THE MANY RUINS THAT WE HAVE OFTEN CREATED FOR OURSELVES, AWARE THAT "THE LORD HAS COMFORTED HIS PEOPLE."

FRANCIS J.
MOLONEY, S.D.B.

RESPONSIVE READING

PSALM 98 (RCL, BCP); 98:1-6 (RC, RCL, alt.)

Psalm 98 is an enthronement hymn, recognizing in the joyful moment of the enthronement of a king that God is the agent of all that is good and beautiful.[18] To this God all praise is due. The psalmist calls upon God's people to recognize that God has saved Israel in the midst of its failures and difficulties and to praise God with a new song (vv. 1–3). As this summons to God's people comes to a close, they are reminded that God's saving action has taken place before all the nations. This leads the psalmist to call upon all the earth to recognize what God has done for Israel, and to join the people's worship of YHWH as Lord (vv. 4–6). Creation reflects God's grandeur and is summoned to rejoice in the coming of the Lord. The roaring of the seas, the "clapping" of the foam-capped waves, and the majestic praise of the hills join to welcome the coming of God (vv. 7–8).

This chorus of joy and praise from Israel (vv. 1–3), all the nations (vv. 4–6), and the whole of creation announces the coming of the just God to judge creation and all who dwell there. Righteousness and equity are the features of God's coming in judgment (v. 9). There is no need for fear, except for those who are unable to accept that all that is good, joyful, and holy in their lives is the result of a gracious gift of God. Nowhere is that gift more obvious than in God's coming among us at Christmas. Let the whole earth rejoice!

SECOND READING

HEBREWS 1:1-4 (5-12) (RCL); 1:1-12 (BCP); 1:1-6 (RC)

Interpreting the Text

The letter to the Hebrews forcefully argues that, through Christ, faithful Christians have direct access to God. The letter presents Jesus as the unique mediator between God and humankind and exhorts Christians to remain faithful, following Christ's example—loving, hopeful, and patient in the face of persecution. Hebrews 1:1-12 is read in its entirety (Episcopal lectionary) or in part (RCL: 1:1-4 [with the option of also reading vv. 5-12]; Roman Catholic lectionary: 1:1-6). In fact, Hebrews 1:1-14 might be called a "prologue" to the letter to the Hebrews, functioning very much like the prologue to the Gospel of John. The christological issue of Jesus as the unique mediator between God and humankind is established by means of affirmation (vv. 1-4) and a Christian exegesis of the Hebrew Scriptures (vv. 5-14).

Two epochs are described by the author: "long ago" (v. 1) and "in these last days" (v. 2). There is a sense in which God's speaking to our ancestors "in many and various ways" was imperfect. It was incomplete in its variety. Nevertheless, God's prophetic word to Israel, and to all outside Israel who would listen, must be regarded as a communication between God and humankind, however imperfect. "In these last days" is an expression from the Hebrew Scriptures that generally refers to the end of time. The author of the letter to the Hebrews shares with St. Paul the idea that the coming of Christ instituted an eschatological time. Christians have been granted access to God in a once-and-for-all final fashion because of the coming of the Son of God. The communication of the Son, however takes place not only through the word of Jesus Christ but in his being the heir of all things, the redeemer and the model of all creation. These are exalted ideas. Although they happen in reverse order (creation first and redemption later), they act as one to indicate that all that is of God is also of the Son, the heir of all things.

The story of Jesus of Nazareth lies behind vv. 3-4. The author affirms that the presence of the Son in human history is the unique revelation of God in our history: "the reflection of God's glory . . . the exact imprint of God's very being" (v. 3). If one seeks the face of God, one need only look to the Son. Not only is the Son at the beginning (creation) and the end (redemption) of the human story, but he sustains it. Just as Wisdom "reaches mightily from one end of the earth to the other, and she orders all things well" (Wis. 8:1), so does the word of the Son. Not unlike John 1:1-18, the author presents the Son as preexistent, coming into the human sphere to make "purification for sins," to return to "the right hand of the Majesty on high" (v. 3). It is on the basis of this dignity that the author turns to one of the issues that will return regularly through the letter: the superiority of Jesus to the angels (v. 4). In Jewish traditions, angels delivered the Law, the fundamental communication between God and humankind. A levitical priesthood administered the cult of the Mosaic covenant, but this ministry was effective because of the parallel ministry of the angels in a heavenly sanctuary. In some Jewish traditions, the archangel Michael was particularly important in the heavenly model of the Temple cult. Jesus surpasses all angelic mediation and cultic worship.

The Christian reading of the passages from the Hebrew Bible that follow is scriptural proof that the author's claims for the Son in vv. 1-4 are true. Words addressed to the Son (v. 5, citing Ps. 2:7 and 2 Sam. 7:14) have never been addressed to an angel, and God has explicitly charged the angels to worship his firstborn (v. 6, citing Deut. 32:43). The description of the angels as winds and flames of fire (Ps. 104:4) is outstripped by the description of the Son in Ps. 45:6-7 as "anointed with the oil of gladness" beyond all others (vv. 8-9). The lection concludes with a long citation of Ps. 102:25-27. The psalm was originally addressed to God, but the Son becomes "Lord" in this Christian reinterpretation. The Scriptures reaffirm the claims of vv. 1-4: the Son is the everlasting one, the creator and the sustainer of all that exists (vv. 10-12).

Responding to the Text

Against all who might claim to have access to God, we have been privileged to be called to belief in the unique revelation of God to humankind. Incredible claims are made for the Son: preexistent, Savior, and returned to the right hand of a majestic God. As such, the Son lies hidden behind all the beauty of the created world, and he has saved us by his death on a cross.

THE SON LIES HIDDEN BEHIND ALL THE BEAUTY OF THE CREATED WORLD, AND HE HAS SAVED US BY HIS DEATH ON A CROSS.

Traditionally, the liturgy of Christmas Day was dominated by the desire of the early church to affirm the uniqueness of Jesus Christ, the incarnation of the eternally preexistent Word (see vv. 1-4). At the time of the author of the letter to the Hebrews there were some who suggested that angels were the unique mediators of God's graciousness to humankind (see vv. 5-12). As the celebration of Christmas developed, the church found that it needed to affirm its full belief in Jesus as the Christ, the Son of God, the incarnation of the preexistent Word against a powerful heresy that argued that this was not the case. Our world has its own subtle (and not so subtle) attempts to negate what God has done for us in and through Jesus Christ. There is little need to list the many contemporary "mediators" who promise the divine to unwary people forever in search of some ultimate answers to the deepest desires of their hearts. Christian tradition affirms that they are all ephemeral—like the angels and the Arian understanding of Jesus of Nazareth. Reading the letter to the Hebrews on Christmas days summons us to assess our personal and community understanding of the person of Jesus Christ: Who is he, and what has he done for us? Why do we celebrate the day on which we recall his birth?

JOHN 1:1-14 (RCL, BCP); 1:1-18 (1-5, 9-14) (RC)

Interpreting the Text

Stories surrounding Jesus' birth were developed in the preaching of the early church to capture the wonder of God's action in sending his only Son to be our Savior. We have read selections from these narratives, taken from the Gospels of Matthew and Luke, during Advent and on Christmas Eve. In the final liturgy for the celebration of Christmas Day, the prologue of the Gospel of John has been traditionally used by the Christian church to summarize the significance of the events celebrated at Christmas.

John's prologue has always been rightly remembered for its famous words, "And the Word became flesh and lived among us" (John 1:14). But this Gospel reading tells us more about the incarnation than the simple fact of the enfleshment of the Word and his dwelling among us. Several times throughout the hymn the author preaches another message basic to Christianity. The Word exists from all time (v. 1), before the Baptist, the God-sent witness (vv. 6-8, 15), in a union with God so close that what God is, the Word also is (v. 2). But to speak of a "word" means that a message is communicated. God speaks, and the Word who is one with God dwells among us (v. 14). This word provides the only place among us where we can find God. No one has ever seen God, but Jesus Christ, the Word of God, makes God known to us (v. 18).

The Word shines in our darkness (v. 5); the Word comes unto his own (v. 11); the Word is the fullness of a gift that is the Truth (v. 17). How one responds to the gift of the Word is up to the listener. God will not force his truth upon us. He may have come to his own people, but they did not receive him (v. 11). He shines in the darkness, but the darkness still attempts to overcome the Word (v. 5). The Gospel promises that all those who accept the Word spoken by God in the incarnation of his Son, Jesus Christ, become children of God (v. 13). We are born as believing Christians, sons and daughters of the one true God as a result of God's gift of his Son, not by any human means but by the gift of God.

Responding to the Text

This is certainly poetry and, like all great poetry, does it not touch upon our own experience? We did not *earn* the gift of faith through our own good works or our intelligence. Through all sorts of apparent coincidences—birth, friends, religious experience, a word passed on in a time of need—we were *drawn* to the Word who became flesh and dwells among us. At Christmas it is urgent that we recognize the gift we have received and treat it joyfully as the most precious of all possessions.

Unlike many gifts, the gift of the Word will give life and light if we respond to its challenge (see vv. 3-4). The light still shines in our darkness, but we remain free, able to choose between light and darkness in our everyday lives. Our freedom to say yes or no to a never-failing light summoning us to life is remarkable evidence of God's love for us. While freedom is the greatest feature of the human condition, nowhere do we exercise it more crucially than in our acceptance or refusal of the Word who became flesh, and who dwells among us. In our Christian celebration of Christmas as the coming of the Eternal Word, Son of God, Jesus Christ, into our story, we exercise that freedom.

THE LIGHT STILL SHINES IN OUR DARKNESS, BUT WE REMAIN FREE, ABLE TO CHOOSE BETWEEN LIGHT AND DARKNESS IN OUR EVERYDAY LIVES.

FIRST SUNDAY AFTER CHRISTMAS / HOLY FAMILY

DECEMBER 30, 2001

REVISED COMMON	EPISCOPAL (BCP)	ROMAN CATHOLIC
Isa. 63:7-9	Isa. 61:10—62:3	Sir. 3:2-6, 12-14
Ps. 148	Ps. 147 or 147:13-21	Ps. 128:1-2, 3, 4-5
Heb. 2:10-18	Gal. 3:23-25; 4:4-7	Col. 3:12-21
Matt. 2:13-23	John 1:1-18	Matt. 2:13-15, 19-23

THE CHRISTMAS SEASON CREATES AN OPPORTUNITY to recall the family of Jesus and address the importance of the family as such. While this celebration is present in the Roman Catholic lectionary, Christmas themes, the action of God in and through Jesus Christ, continue in the RCL and the Episcopal lectionary. As each lectionary approaches this Sunday differently, there are eleven passages that call for commentary. The presentation of the readings will differ from earlier reflections on the Advent–Christmas cycle.

FIRST READING
ISAIAH 63:7-9 (RCL)

Third Isaiah reflects upon the situation of Israel after its return from exile in Babylon.[19] Isaiah 63:7-9 expresses a strong faith in God's deeds. There is perplexity in this confession of faith. How could Israel ever have abandoned such a powerful God? The facts of the immediate past, however, cannot be denied. Nevertheless, despite that past, the lived present reveals "the gracious deeds of the Lord" (v. 7a). The prophet wants to tell of these deeds, the acts of God, "the great favor to the house of Israel" (v. 7b), because they manifest "his mercy" and "the abundance of his steadfast love" (v. 7c).

The word of God effects the transformation, raising sinful and distressed children from their misery. The Lord disregards the falseness of the people's dealings with him and does not deal with them in like manner. God loves them, pities them, lifts them up, and carries them as he did in the days before their failure (vv. 8-9). Placed within its literary and historical context, this passage speaks eloquently to the Christian condition of all times. We are challenged by the action of the God who has saved us, despite our falseness, to do likewise with those who, despite their failures, look to us in hope.

ISAIAH 61:10—62:3 (BCP)

The Episcopal lectionary also looks to Third Isaiah, choosing a passage that belongs to a series of songs that open this final part of the book of Isaiah (60:1—62:12). The passage focuses on the prophet's desire to proclaim his joy in the saving activity of the Lord (61:10), who has restored Israel to righteousness. Images are used to speak of Israel's righteousness: the rich preparation of bride and bridegroom, the fertility of the land, sending forth its shoots showing new life. Such shall be the restored righteousness of Israel (v. 11). But what God has done for Israel is never an end in itself. It makes God known to the nations: "her vindication shines out like the dawn" (62:1). The kings of the world recognize what God has done. God's action generates something new that does not simply restore what had existed earlier. The prophet announces, "You shall be called by a new name that the mouth of the Lord will give" (v. 2). The gift of a new name begins something new in the relationship between the one named and the one giving the name. With great confidence, the prophet foretells a different and blessed future for the once sinful Israel: a crown of beauty and a royal diadem "in the hand of your God" (v. 3). This passage, taken from a similar literary context, urges the same sentiments as Isa. 63:7-9. It issues a challenge to recognize and live what God has done for us.

SIRACH 3:2-6, 12-14 (RC)

The Roman Catholic lectionary focuses on the theme of the family, looking to instructions from one of the great Jewish manuals of Wisdom. The passage works systematically through the responsibilities children have toward their parents. Reflecting a patriarchal tradition, the father is given priority of honor, but the mother is also included. The mother is also to be honored, because the father confirms her rights over his children (v. 2). The passage, however, is remarkable in its association of the children's honor, respect, and prayer for both father and mother as the source for the atonement of their sins and the laying up of treasure, a long life, and the blessings of the Lord (vv. 3-6). The reading closes with reference to the aged father, even addressing the possibility of the failing mind, as well as the failing body, of an old man. He is to be loved and honored "as long as he lives." Faced with the fragmentation of many structures that sustained our traditional social fabric, we may find these words of advice from Israel's Wisdom traditions outmoded. However, they ring true. It is not false to suggest that honor, love, and respect for those who have given you life and supported you, even in their frailty, is to "obey the Lord" (see v. 6).

RESPONSIVE READING
PSALM 148 (RCL)

This psalm continues the theme of praise for the Lord. After an opening shout of praise, the hymn invites all those that one might call "on high" to join in the praise (vv. 1-2). The creation is summoned to join the praise, starting with everything in and behind the heavens, created by God: sun, moon, stars, and the waters behind the heaven (vv. 3-6). The psalmist then moves to the earth, insisting that both inanimate and animate creation join the praise: sea monsters, the elements of the weather, mountains, hills, trees, animals, and all creeping and flying things (vv. 7-10). Following the order of Genesis 1, the psalmist finally comes to the sphere of human beings. Kings and princes, young and old men and women are all to praise the name of the Lord. Finally, the uniqueness of the chosen people emerges. The creator God of all that exists has called some to be "close to him." The chosen people must recognize their dignity and "Praise the Lord!" (v. 14). Gazing at all that surrounds us, animate and inanimate, recognizing the beauty of all that we enjoy and celebrate, and accepting the dignity to which we have been called provides reason for joy and praise.

PSALM 147 or 147:13-21 (BCP)

This lection repeats the sentiments of Psalm 147. The psalmist tells of the time of its writing, after the return from Babylon: "The LORD builds up Jerusalem; he gathers the outcasts of Israel" (v. 2). It is on the basis of what God has done for the return of a chosen people to their holy land and city (see vv. 1-6), that this psalm can turn to sing praise to the creator God in a fashion that parallels Psalm 148. The creation is listed from the heavens to the animals (vv. 7-10), but singles out for special attention "those who fear him and those who hope in his steadfast love" (v. 11).

It is to Israel, therefore, enjoying the fruits of the Lord's steadfast love, that the psalmist directs his summons. The freed city of Jerusalem must raise its voice in praise of the wonderful God of creation (vv. 12-18), who has singled out Jacob and Israel for his special love and concern. No other nation has ever been dealt with in this way. Typical of the spirituality of the postexilic period, Israel is reminded that its way to God is in the observance of the Law. It is only Israel who knows God's ordinances. The call to recognize God in creation and in all that God has done for us in Psalm 148 (RCL), as with Psalm 147 (BCP), calls us to sing praise joyfully to our creator God.

PSALM 128:1–5 (RC)

The Roman Catholic lectionary continues its focus on the family with the choice of a so-called "Wisdom Psalm." Blessed is the one who exercises the wisdom virtue of "fear of the LORD," further clarified as walking in the ways of the Lord (v. 1). The fruits of such wisdom are not, in the first instance, great spiritual blessings. The psalmist speaks generally of having enough to eat and enjoying a good life (v. 2). These fundamental and practical experiences, the result of "fear of the LORD," are then further spelled out. The association with the celebration of the feast of the Holy Family becomes obvious. The person who walks in the way of the Lord will have a fruitful wife and healthy children (vv. 3-4). The psalm closes with a prayer that this might be the experience of all in Israel: the prosperity of Jerusalem, and generations who will see their children and their children's children. Such is the measure of true peace (v. 6).

SECOND LESSON
HEBREWS 2:10–18 (RCL)

The RCL continues its reflection on the wonder of the incarnation with this selection from the letter to the Hebrews, following the use of the same epistle at the celebration of the Nativity of the Lord. Themes continue from Heb. 1:1-4. God, as the Lord and sustainer of creation (v. 10a), has established the restoration of many to the glory that has been lost by allowing the one who would lead them to glory to pass through suffering (v. 10b). Jesus is brother to all to whom he has been sent. There is but one Father, and thus Jesus calls all his brothers and sisters (v. 11). A Christian use of the Old Testament (Ps. 22:22; Isa. 8:17-18) allows the author to place certain sentiments on the lips of Jesus. On the one hand, he proclaims the names of his brothers and sisters before God, "in the midst of the congregation" (v. 12). On the other, he places his unconditional trust in the one God and Father of all (v. 13).

Jesus' experience of the human condition, a theme important to Hebrews, is developed in vv. 14-18. He has taken on the human condition without reserve. He is flesh and blood, accepting suffering and death so that the one who is regarded as determining the power of death will be vanquished. Death is no longer the inexplicable experience of a Satan-dominated humankind (vv. 14-15). It is now the way to God, opened up by Jesus, "the pioneer" of salvation (see v. 10). Humankind was to be blessed in Abraham and in all his children (see Gen. 12:3), and Jesus brings salvation to the descendents of Abraham. He does this by his unconditional acceptance of what pertains to being a child of Abraham, on the one hand, and the high priest in the service of God, on the other. The bridge that joins heaven and earth has been opened in the flesh and blood of Jesus Christ. As we are tested, so he was tested, but he has won through this testing "to make a sacrifice of atonement for the sins of the people" (vv. 17-18). The unique claims that we make for Christmas and the incarnation have again been stated powerfully. One who is from God and of God has taken on the human condition and in this way made it possible for human beings to regain the glory lost by sin. A sinless one has taken on our condition, our trials, and our sufferings. He has won through in his death and become our pioneer, our "trailblazer" in the journey back to the God and Father of us all.

GALATIANS 3:23-25; 4:4-7 (BCP)

The selection from Paul's letter to the Galatians continues the Christmas theme of the incarnation. Paul sets up two different times in the history of salvation. In an initial period the people of God lived under the Law. This time *before faith* must not be understood in an entirely negative fashion. The Law came from God, and it was to maintain the people's focus on God, to live in a protected and guarded way, and thus not to wander away from God's design (v. 23). The Law was a "disciplinarian" to look after us (v. 24). The expression in Greek (*paidagōgos*) was used of the slave (generally) who took charge of the child to see to his or her every need: discipline, health, learning, dressing, proper behavior, and all such matters. The "disciplinarian" was to ensure right behavior. This situation has now been transformed in the period *after faith*. The coming of faith, the possibility of justification and standing in right relationship in and through faith in Jesus Christ, makes us free (v. 25). Now we live in the "fullness of time," initiated by the birth of a Jewish boy from a Jewish mother. His Jewishness meant that he was born under the Law (4:4). But his situation under the Law was transformed by his relationship, not with his human mother, but with his Father. It was God who sent his Son! This Son, by means of his unconditional obedience to his Father, culminating in his death and resurrection, has freed all who believe in him from their slavery to the Law. They are now filled with the gift of the Spirit and have the privilege to join the Son of God in calling out to the God and Father of Jesus as our God and Father. All who believe in what God has done for us in and through his Son, sent at Christmas and obedient unto death at Easter, have become sons and daughters in the Son. It is for that reason that we can cry out to our God, with him, "Abba, Father!"

COLOSSIANS 3:12-21 (RC)

The Roman Catholic lectionary continues its focus on the question of the family, here using a so-called "house-table" from Paul's letter to the Colossians. These tables were widespread in the ancient world and were used to determine the behavior of various groups in society: slaves, freed people, children, wives, husbands, and other persons who formed a "house." There are similarities and differences between the use of these tables in Hellenistic society and in the Pauline literature. The similarities come from the desire to see that correct order is maintained within the community of the family. Wives, husbands, and children are to relate to one another in the correct and accepted fashion (vv. 18-21). Customs and relationships can change over the centuries, and we are not asked by this reading to repeat exactly what Paul asked of the Christian families in Colossae. Much remains true, however, in Paul's word of advice to fathers: "Fathers, do not provoke your children, or they may lose heart" (v. 21).

The important difference, however, which deserves our attention, is the motivation for good behavior, provided in vv. 12-17. Nowadays we understand family relationships in ways impossible in the ancient world. Yet what God has done for us in Jesus should determine our relationships. We have been chosen by God and thus should match God's compassion, kindness, humility, meekness, and patience (v. 12). The saving love of God, made manifest in the self-gift of his Son, forgiving us our sins and restoring peace to a situation where once there was enmity, must also live on in the behavior of those who have been called into this peace: "Let the peace of Christ rule in your hearts" (v. 13; see vv. 13-15). Finally, we respond to the word of God alive, preached, and lived among us. As it touches us, we respond with joy, recognizing what God has done for us (v. 16). Relationships are the "stuff" of human existence. We cannot live without them, and the way we conduct them determines our state of heart and mind. We have every right to look upon what God has done for us and shown us in and through his Son. We have every right to "do everything in the name of the Lord Jesus, giving thanks to God the Father through him" (v. 17).

MATTHEW 2:13–23 (RCL);
2:13–15, 19–23 (RC)

Interpreting the Text

In the early chapters of the Gospel of Matthew the angels of the Lord repeatedly lead Joseph, the husband of Mary, into strange behavior. He is asked to take to himself a young bride who is already with child by the Holy Spirit—whatever that might have meant to him (Matt. 1:18-25). He is further asked to flee his homeland and set out for Egypt (2:13-15). Looking at a map, one might think that the journey from Bethlehem to Egypt was not a great ordeal. Maps "tell lies." Even today such a journey is extremely arduous but, for the first-century Jew, a journey to Egypt would have been a traumatic experience. Joseph responds to all the commands of the Lord without word or hesitation. "Then Joseph got up, took the child and his mother by night, and went into Egypt" (v. 14). The ways of God must have seemed strange to this "righteous man" (see 1:19), but through his obedience the Christ, a Son of David, has been born into the world (see 1:18-25).

The RCL includes the response of Herod to the disobedience of the wise men from the East (vv. 16–18), excluded in the Roman Catholic lectionary.[20] They had been told to inform him of the birthplace of the new king (see 2:8), but warned in a dream, they returned home by another way (v. 12). Enraged, Herod slays all the young males from Bethlehem, and Jeremiah's prophecy is fulfilled as the lamenting of Rachel, weeping for her children in Ramah is heard (vv. 16-18; see Jer. 31:15). The Roman Catholic lectionary rejoins the story at this point, and another prophecy is fulfilled. As Moses had come from Egypt, so Jesus, the man who surpassed all that Moses had been and done, comes out of Egypt. The journeys to and from Egypt took place because of the rejection and violence of Herod. The words of Hosea, originally recalling the experience of the Exodus, now apply to Jesus: "Out of Egypt I have called my son" (v. 15).

Joseph responds obediently to a further divine intervention into his life and leads his family back to its own land. Again he is "warned in a dream" (v. 22): there can be no returning to his home in Bethlehem. Along with Joseph and Mary, Jesus is to be a wanderer, unwanted and persecuted by the powers in the land, responding trustingly and unfailingly to the ways of God. These passages from the early sections of the Gospel of Matthew are written with one eye on the past and another on the future. Jesus' birth, like that of Moses, is accompanied by the slaying of innocent children. He, like Moses, will come out of Egypt. The lamenting of Rachel is heard in Ramah. These stories also echo the experiences of the adult Christ, unwanted, persecuted, and finally slain by the powers in the land. As was the case with the flight into Egypt, his further flight into Nazareth may have been difficult, but it fulfilled the promises of God made through the prophets: "He will be called a Nazorean" (v. 23). The stage is set for the life-story of Jesus of Nazareth.

Responding to the Text

Throughout the infancy stories of Jesus, understandably present at this time of the liturgical year, there have been repeated references to the fulfillment of the sayings of the prophets. In the Gospel of Matthew the reader is reminded of this explicitly. In the Gospel of Luke the fulfillment is more allusive but real nevertheless. The final saying in today's Gospel: "He will be called a Nazorean" (Matt. 2:23), cannot be traced back to any individual prophet. But the author claims that it fulfills all that "the prophets" (plural) had said. There is a long line of prophets, indeed the ongoing prophetic presence of the word of God in the human story, behind this final word on Jesus, the man from Nazareth. Jesus fulfills the hopes of Israel and reaches beyond these origins. He will be with us until the end of the age (see Matt. 28:16-20).

Throughout his life he will be known as Jesus of Nazareth. At his death, the final act of obedience, a sign will be nailed upon his cross: "Jesus of Nazareth, the King of the Jews" (Matt. 27:37). The words spoken through the prophets are fulfilled. To be family, Joseph, Mary, and Jesus had to accept so much that was difficult, from scandal to flight to crucifixion. It is this all-too-common aspect of suffering that is part of our humanness, and therefore family experience that must be read in a different key, if we are to make sense of it. The courageous acceptance of all that challenged the original family of Jesus, cost what it may, led to the public ministry of Jesus of Nazareth. The enigma of suffering that can lead to light and life must always be seen as part of the following of Jesus. This is not to say that all suffering is to be understood in this way. We are not asked to condone the slaying of the innocents at Bethlehem, just as we are not to condone the many parallel atrocities taking place on every side, despite (and sometimes because of) the increasing sophistication of modern life. Yet we must always be open to the possibility that suffering may be part of God's design, a cross that leads to resurrection.

WE MUST ALWAYS BE OPEN TO THE POSSIBILITY THAT SUFFERING MAY BE PART OF GOD'S DESIGN, A CROSS THAT LEADS TO RESURRECTION.

JOHN 1:1-18 (BCP)

See the comments on the Gospel for the Nativity of Our Lord II (Christmas Day).

THE NAME OF JESUS / HOLY NAME / MARY, MOTHER OF GOD

JANUARY 1, 2002

REVISED COMMON	EPISCOPAL (BCP)	ROMAN CATHOLIC
Num. 6:22-27	Exod. 34:1-8	Num. 6:22-27
Ps. 8	Ps. 8	Ps. 67:1-2, 4, 5, 7
		(Heb. Bible 67:2-3,
		5, 6, 8)
Gal. 4:4-7	Rom. 1:1-7	Gal. 4:4-7
or Phil. 2:5-11	or Phil. 2:9-13	
Luke 2:15-21	Luke 2:15-21	Luke 2:16-21

DIFFERENT CHRISTIAN TRADITIONS HIGHLIGHT different themes in the celebration of January 1. The traditional celebration of Jesus' naming and circumcision (see Luke 2:21) has been maintained in the Revised Common and the Episcopal lectionaries. Since 1969 the Catholic tradition has taken this opportunity to celebrate the doctrine first articulated at the Council of Ephesus (431): Mary as the Mother of God. As with the First Sunday after Christmas, the different traditions generate a selection of readings.

FIRST READING
NUMBERS 6:22-27 (RCL/RC)

This lection uses the occasion of the celebration of a new calendar year to proclaim a blessing. The Lord, through Moses, grants to the sons of Aaron, the privilege of blessing the people of Israel. The blessing, now found in Lev. 5:1—6:21, forms a conclusion to a long series of instructions from the Lord on how the Israelites were to show their unconditional, voluntary commitment to God. The observance of purity in the place where the Israelites dwell (5:1-4), among the members of the community itself (6:1-21), and the purity of their relationships (5:5-31), was to be met with a blessing (6:22-27). The sons of Aaron are given the right to invoke God's name over the people. The regular repetition of "the LORD" in vv. 24, 25, and 26 stresses the power of the name of the Lord. The

sacredness of the four letters YHWH that formed the name of God in Israel cannot be overestimated. Never pronounced, because of its sacredness, "the name of
the LORD" is not so much a description of who God is, but what God has done,
is doing, and will always do for a chosen people (see Exod. 3:1-22). YHWH blesses
and keeps, is gracious and grants peace.

The unique God of Israel, YHWH, in response to the people's preparedness to
adopt a unique lifestyle in the midst of many conflicting voices and cultures, communicates his blessing. God assures them his care, the shining of his face upon
them as he turns his countenance steadily toward them. There are two sides to a
covenant with the Lord: a God who will never fail in faithfulness to a people and
a people called to live in a way that manifests to the nations their unconditional
commitment to that God. When both agents in the covenant actively correspond
to their commitment, blessings flow freely.

EXODUS 34:1-8 (BCP)

The original covenant between God and Israel was established at Mount
Sinai in Exodus 19. However, since that time the people have fallen away. Immediately prior to this passage, Moses has come down from the mountain only to
discover the people worshiping the golden calf (see Exod. 33:1-35). Moses
returns to the mountain to receive the covenant once again. The Lord commands
Moses to take two tablets that the Lord might inscribe "the words" that were on
the former tablets destroyed by Moses in his disgust and rage in the face of the
sins of Israel (34:1; see 32:19). Repeating many of the rituals that marked the first
gift of the Law, Moses cuts the two new stones and returns to meet the Lord. He
is not disappointed. As in the blessing of Lev. 6:22-27, the holy name of "the
LORD" dominates the encounter: "The LORD descended in the cloud and stood
with him there and proclaimed the name, 'the LORD' (YHWH)."

The renewal of the covenant is made with a promise that cannot fail. It opens
with a double use of the name YHWH, describes that God, and then makes a series
of promises: "The LORD, the LORD, a God
merciful and gracious, slow to anger, and
abounding in steadfast love and faithfulness" (see 20:5-6). As with the overall context of the priestly blessing in Leviticus,
however, there are two sides to the covenant. The Lord will never fail in his powerful, gracious, and forgiving presence to the people. But they must play their
part. No easy remission of guilt will pass on to the third and fourth generation.
The event of Jesus Christ has developed further God's saving intervention into
the sinfulness of the human condition. Yet the point made at the renewal of the

THE LORD WILL NEVER FAIL IN HIS POWERFUL, GRA-
CIOUS, AND FORGIVING PRESENCE TO THE PEOPLE.
BUT THEY MUST PLAY THEIR PART.

covenant remains true: sin against God is no light matter. The steadfast love and forgiveness of God, now more evident in the death and resurrection of Jesus Christ, must not be taken for granted.

RESPONSIVE READING
PSALM 8 (RCL, BCP)

The year begins with a fitting proclamation of God as creator, recognizing that all on earth reflects the majesty of "the name," glorious in the heavens, yet confessed by even the most simple, to the confusion of all who would oppose this majesty (vv. 1-2). Gazing into the night sky, the poet sees the beauty of the heavens, the moon and the stars, marveling that God would deign to make human beings even more beautiful, little less than a God. The words of the creation, as God creates man and woman in his own image (see Gen. 1:26), lie behind the psalmist's song. But God has done more: the whole of creation—animals, birds, and the fish of the sea—are given over to the care of the human being. Little wonder that the psalmist cries out again, as he comes to the end of his song, in the words he used at its beginning. We join the poet in praising the creator God: "O Lord, our Sovereign, how majestic is your name in all the earth." We also recognize the grandeur of what God has done for us and accept our responsibilities as God has given us dominion over all the works of his hands (see v. 6).

PSALM 67:1-2, 4, 5, 7 (RC)

The Roman Catholic lectionary continues the sentiments of the blessing from Numbers 6 into the reading of Psalm 67. The poem renders thanks to God, asking for continued blessing, asking again that he "make his face shine upon us" (v. 1; see Num. 6:25). The blessing, however, is not only that the people might prosper and live long. As so often across the Christmas period, the liturgical use of biblical texts asks that the blessings of God make the ways of God known upon the earth (v. 2). The justice and fairness of God are reasons for all the nations to be glad and to sing with joy. The psalm, therefore, extends the sentiments of the blessing of the priests in Numbers 6. Not only does God bless a faithful people, but the blessings showered upon that people reflect the wonder of God to the nations. The God of Israel whose face shines upon his chosen people is the God of all the nations. We pray that this may become better known, that all the people might praise God (v. 3). In our ambiguous response to the blessings of God, we begin the new year with a song which is also a petition: "May God continue to bless us; let all the ends of the earth revere him" (v. 7).

SECOND LESSON

GALATIANS 4:4–7 (RCL/RC)

Comments on this lection are found under First Sunday after Christmas / Holy Family, above.

ROMANS 1:1–7 (BCP)

Comments on this lection are found under Fourth Sunday in Advent, above.

PHILIPPIANS 2:5–11 (RCL, alt.); 2:9–13 (BCP, alt.)

Interpreting the Text

In order to unite the new Christians in Philippi, Paul instructs them to have in the same mind that was in Christ Jesus (v. 5). At this point Paul inserts a hymn to Christ, probably well known to the Philippians. Paul's appeal to them to be more Christ-like is based on something they already confessed about Jesus.

The hymn passes through the various stages of Christ's existence. His origins are in God, and he has the very form of God. He is equal to God, but he does not grab hold of this honor in a jealous and selfish fashion (v. 6). On the contrary, he adopts a life-style of measureless self-emptying. He takes on the human condition, but a human condition so humble that he gives himself unto death. This death, however, was not the normal process that comes at the end of life: he was crucified (vv. 7–8). The hymn is based on the life of Jesus, interpreted as a remarkable gesture of total self-abandon in love. God enters the drama of the experience of Jesus. As the result of the unconditional self-gift, God raises him on high and even gives him "the name" that leads all in heaven and on earth to bow their knee (vv. 9–10). Jesus is raised up, returning to the divine status that was his, but which he never used for selfish purposes. The hymn comes to a climax by announcing the universal recognition of Jesus, as all confess "the name" given by God to Jesus: "Jesus Christ is Lord!" The Lordship of Jesus, attained by his unconditional obedience to God, shown in his death and subsequent resurrection, renders glory to the God and Father of Jesus (v. 11).

The divisions in the community are to be resolved by their continued obedience to Paul, the one who has given them this hymn to Jesus as their point of reference. He is no longer among them, as he has journeyed south toward Athens and Corinth. However, the power of the risen Lord is among them. They must have in themselves the mind that was in Christ Jesus (see v. 5), working out their salvation guided and empowered by the presence of their Lord and God among them (vv. 12-13).

Responding to the Text

The primary meaning of the Pauline passage in its original context must not be lost in our response to this remarkable hymn from the earliest years of the Christian expression of its faith. To a community marked by division, as are all our communities made up of fragile human beings, Paul tells the story of Jesus Christ. There is to be no selfish arrogance on the basis of one's achievements of gift-edness. Nothing that a human has or achieves can ever match the wonder of Jesus' being in the form of God, equal to

> TO A COMMUNITY MARKED BY DIVISION, AS ARE ALL OUR COMMUNITIES MADE UP OF FRAGILE HUMAN BEINGS, PAUL TELLS THE STORY OF JESUS CHRIST.

God. Yet we do cling selfishly to honor and achievement, lord it over others, and create pain and division in doing so. This is not the way of Jesus Christ, and it must not be the way of the Christian. The paradox is that Jesus' self-gift, humbling himself even unto an ignominious death, leads him to the lordship and the glory many of us seek. Paul reminds the Christian community at Philippi of the person they are following by recalling a familiar hymn. What he asks of the Philippians, and what the reading of this passage asks of any Christian community that uses it in the liturgy, is that we put our lives where our words are. Our lives should be public evidence of the faith we have in Jesus, Christ and Lord.

The hymn ends with a remarkable claim (vv. 9-11). God has given the crucified and risen Jesus Christ "the name." We have seen in our earlier readings the importance of "the name" (YHWH). This is the name that is given to Jesus. He is given the divine name, that all might worship him and sing his praise. The celebration of the first day of the year as the "name" of Jesus, places the year under his lordship. As with the Old Testament readings, we go into this year rejoicing in the covenant blessings we have because of God's action for us in and through Jesus, Lord. However, there are two sides to the covenant. God's action is irreversible and steadfast. We are challenged to bend the knee and to confess by word and deed that "Jesus Christ is Lord, to the glory of God the Father" (v. 11).

THE GOSPEL

LUKE 2:15-21 (RCL, BCP); 2:16-21 (RC)

Interpreting the Text

The two directions taken by the Christian liturgical traditions are well represented in this reading. On the one hand, the bulk of the passage is devoted to the response of the shepherds to the revelation of the angel, the discovery of the newborn child, and his being named "Jesus." On the other, Jesus' mother's response to the birth of Jesus and the visit of the shepherds continues her important presence in the Lukan account of Jesus' infancy.

The angel who appeared to the shepherds did not command them to find the child. He announced joyful news, the birth of the Savior Messiah in the city of David and gave them signs of his significance: the bands of cloth and his lying in a manger (2:10-12). The shepherds respond to this initial revelation. The action of God begins in them as they decide, "Let us go now to Bethlehem and see this thing that has taken place, which the Lord has made known to us" (v. 15). The shepherds accept that the revelation of the angel was something made known to them by God, and they set out for Bethlehem to look for the child whose dignity will be revealed by the sign of the manger. Looking for a Savior Messiah born in the royal city of Bethlehem, paradoxically they find "Mary and Joseph and the child lying in the manger" (v. 16). The sign indicated by the angel is present, and the lament of Isaiah is overcome, that Israel does not know its Lord, as the ox knows its master and the donkey its master's crib (see Isa. 1:3). Marginal people, shepherds, come from the fields, recognize the Savior Messiah, and begin to proclaim what the angel had told them and how this had been fulfilled in the child they found with Mary and Joseph (v. 17).

There are three possible responses to the proclamation of what God has done in this birth. As the shepherds make known the good news, "all who heard" are astonished at what the shepherds had to say (v. 18). But there is no indication that their hearing leads to faith. Nor do those who hear the good news attempt to "see" the newly born child, as did the shepherds (see v. 15). The response of those who heard is one of wonder. They were "amazed at what the shepherds had told them" (v. 18). The shepherds themselves, having found the newborn king wrapped in bands of cloth (see Wis. 7:4-5) and laid in a manger, the source of nourishment for all who would look to him as Lord (see Isa. 1:2-3), return to the fields (v. 20). They are never heard of again. No shepherds stand by as Jesus begins his public ministry. There are no witnesses to the wonder of his birth during his preaching, ministry, and journey to Jerusalem for the cross, the resurrection, and the return to his Father. They fall silent.

However, set between "all who heard" (v. 18) and the shepherds who disappear from the story (v. 20) is a woman who is present during the ministry of Jesus (see 18:19-21; 11:27-28) and still present in the life of the earliest Christian community (see Acts 1:14). Mary, the mother of Jesus, "treasured all these things and pondered them in her heart" (v. 19). Often throughout the Bible, women and men receive revelations from God that are beyond their ken. The person of faith, unable to understand the mysterious nature of God's designs, treasures and dwells upon them with ultimate trust in God, waiting to be led where God wills. So it is with Mary. Though unable to understand fully what has happened to her, she has said yes (see 1:38) and from that point on is open to all that the Almighty might do for his lowly servant (see 1:46-48). The closing verse of today's Gospel continues this theme. Obedient to the command of the angel at the annunciation (see 1:31: "You will name him Jesus"), when the time of circumcision and naming arrived, the Law fulfilled, "and he was called Jesus, the name given to him by the angel before he was conceived in the womb" (v. 21). Luke does not explicitly tell the reader what the name means. It is understood by all who have read thus far: "You are to name him Jesus, for he will save his people from their sins" (Matt. 1:21).

> THE PERSON OF FAITH, UNABLE TO UNDERSTAND THE MYSTERIOUS NATURE OF GOD'S DESIGNS, TREASURES AND DWELLS UPON THEM WITH ULTIMATE TRUST IN GOD, WAITING TO BE LED WHERE GOD WILLS. SO IT IS WITH MARY.

Responding to the Text

Across all the traditions celebrating the beginning of a new Christian year, the theme of the name of Jesus, Lord and Savior, dominates. The focus of the Gospel reading lies with the shepherds and Mary, but they are characters used to lead the reader to an acceptance of what God has done in and through Jesus. The sign of the linen cloths and the manger support the message of a Savior Messiah born in Bethlehem. The Christian reader responds to the proclamation of the coming of Jesus by accepting what God has done in the man named "Jesus," the one who has saved us from our sins.

Mary is subordinated to the figure of the child she has born, but she models the Christian response. She is presented in the Gospel of Luke as the mother of Jesus, the one who bears the Son of God. Her place within the Christian tradition, however, originating in the Gospel of Luke, relies not so much in the physical bearing of the child. As Jesus replies to the woman from the crowd who cries out in praise of his mother's physical blessedness: "Blessed rather are those who hear the word of God and obey it" (Luke 11:27-28). Her faithful acceptance of God's will shows her as a person who bears Jesus in her heart and soul. Thus, Mary is not the only one who "bears the Son of God." As Christian believers, and as the Christian Church, we learn to wait *patiently and trustingly* in the midst of misunderstanding that we too may bring Jesus Christ into our world.

For Further Reading

The Advent–Christmas lectionaries make selections from many biblical books. First Isaiah dominates the Old Testament readings, and the Psalms are always present. As throughout Year A in the three-year cycle, Matthew regularly provides the Gospel reading.

1. For a thorough investigation of the history, theology, and liturgy of Advent, Christmas, and Epiphany, as well as a commentary on the readings for every day (not only the Sundays and holy days) of the Roman lectionary, see: R. Gantoy and R. Swaeles, eds., *Days of the Lord: The Liturgical Year,* 7 vols., trans. G. LaNave and D. Molloy (Collegeville, Minn.: Liturgical Press, 1991–94). Volume 1: *Season of Advent: Season of Christmas/Epiphany.*

2. For up-to-date and informed commentary on all the biblical texts, see the following collections:

R. E. Brown, J. A. Fitzmyer, and R. E. Murphy, eds., *The New Jerome Biblical Commentary* (Englewood Cliffs, N.J.: Prentice-Hall, 1989).

W. R. Farmer et al., eds., *The International Bible Commentary: A Catholic and Ecumenical Commentary for the Twenty-First Century* (Collegeville, Miinn.: Liturgical Press, 1998).

L. E. Keck et al., *The New Interpreter's Bible,* 12 vols. (projected) (Nashville: Abingdon, 1994–). This is an outstanding resource. Each commentary offers up-to-date scholarship and also applications for contemporary Christianity.

3. For more detailed commentaries on First Isaiah, the Psalms, and the Gospel of Matthew, consult one or several of the following:

First Isaiah

B. S. Childs, *Isaiah* (Old Testament Library; Louisville: Westminster John Knox, 2000).

C. R. Seitz, *Isaiah 1–39* (Interpretation; Louisville: Westminster John Knox, 1993).

G. M. Tucker, "Isaiah 1–39," in *The New Interpreter's Bible,* vol. 6 (Nashville: Abingdon, 1994–).

J. D.W. Watts, *Isaiah 1–33* (Word Biblical Commentary; Waco: Word Books, 1985).

The Psalms

H. J. Kraus, *Theology of the Psalms,* trans. K. Crim (Continental Commentaries; Minneapolis: Augsburg, 1986).

———, *The Psalms,* 2 vols., trans. H. C. Oswald (Minneapolis: Augsburg, 1988).

J. Limburg, *Psalms* (Westminster Bible Companion; Louisville: Westminster John Knox, 2000).

J. L. Mays, *Psalms* (Interpretation; Louisville: Westminster John Knox, 1994).

J. C. McCann Jr., "The Book of Psalms," in *The New Interpreter's Bible* (Nashville: Abingdon, 1994–) 4:641–1280.

M. Eugene Boring, "The Gospel of Matthew," in *The New Interpreter's Bible* (Nashville: Abingdon, 1994–), 8:89–505.

J. P. Meier, *Matthew* (New Testament Message 3; Wilmington: Michael Glazier, 1980).

4. Two significant large-scale scholarly commentaries on the Gospel of Matthew have appeared recently:

W. L. Davies and D. C. Allison, *A Critical and Exegetical Commentary on the Gospel according to Saint Matthew*, 3 vols. (International Critical Commentary; Edinburgh: T. & T. Clark, 1988–98).

U. Luz, *Matthew 1–7: A Commentary* (Continental Commentaries; Minneapolis: Fortress Press, 1999); *Matthew 8–20* (Hermeneia; Minneapolis: Fortress Press, 2001).

THE SEASON OF CHRISTMAS– EPIPHANY

FRANCIS J. MOLONEY, S.D.B.

Notes

1. International Commission on English in the Liturgy, *The Sacramentary: Book for Use at the Chair on Sundays, Solemnities and Certain Feasts* (Huntington, Ind.: Our Sunday Visitor, 1976), 2, 4.

2. *The Sacramentary*, 6.

3. *The Sacramentary*, 8.

4. The interpretation of prophecies from Isaiah is complicated by the fact that our present book of Isaiah has three parts, reflecting different periods in the history of Israel. Oracles and events from the time of Isaiah form First Isaiah (Isaiah 1–39), reflecting a period before 701 B.C.E., when Sennacherib besieged Jerusalem. His followers continued his tradition into Second Isaiah (Isaiah 40–55), written in the latter years of the exile in Babylon (540s). A later continuation of this tradition, Third Isaiah (Isaiah 56–66), reflects the time after the return from Babylon (536 B.C.E.). The Advent–Christmas season is dominated by readings from First Isaiah (First, Second, and Third Sundays in Advent, Christmas Eve), but passages from Second Isaiah (Fourth Sunday in Advent and Christmas Day) and Third Isaiah (First Sunday after Christmas) also appear. See W. A. Meeks, gen. ed., *The HarperCollins Study Bible: New Revised Standard Version* (New York: HarperCollins, 1993), 1011–13.

5. The presentation of the ideal Davidic King in Isa. 11:1-5 can be regarded as an example of the messianic thought of the Old Testament period. This and other passages within the context of weak and sinful kings develop the idea of an ideal sacred kingship. See J. Becker, *Messianic Expectation in the Old Testament*, trans. D. E. Green (Philadelphia: Fortress Press, 1980), 37–47.

6. It appears that the son of man in Psalm 80 (and in Psalm 8) was reinter-

preted in a messianic direction in the Aramaic Targums. In that version, v. 17 asks God to lay his hand upon the "the King Messiah," rather than "the Son of Man." On this, see F. J. Moloney, "The Reinterpretation of Psalm VIII and the Son of Man Debate," *New Testament Studies* 27 (1981): 656-72, especially pp. 664–65.

7. For this understanding of Phil. 2:5-11, a detailed examination of various scholarly perspectives, and some important theological reflections on the Pauline notion of the preexistence of Jesus Christ, see B. Byrne, "Christ's Pre-Existence in Pauline Soteriology," *Theological Studies* 58 (1997): 308–30.

8. The NRSV uses the English "Immanuel" in its translation/transliteration of the Hebrew of Isa. 7:14. In Matt. 1:23 one finds "Emmanuel," a translation/transliteration of Matthew's Greek. The two forms (Hebrew and Greek) of the same name have been respected in the commentary.

9. See above, "The Season of Advent."

10. See A.-G. Martimort, *The Church at Prayer,* 4 vols. (Collegeville, Mn.: Liturgical Press, 1986), 4:77–96.

11. The shift from a predominantly pagan to a Christian culture after 313 was not as simple and immediate as is sometimes thought. For social, political, and religious reasons, Constantine sought to give due respect to both pagan and Christian traditions. See the important study of R. L. Fox, *Pagans and Christians in the Mediterranean World from the Second Century A.D. to the Conversion of Constantine* (Harmondsworth: Viking, 1986), 609–62. On the process of "Christianizing" pagan practices and traditions, see also pp. 663–81.

12. The Franciscan monastery in Greccio, dating to the time of St. Bonaventure (c. 1260), preserves a cave, decorated by Giotto, where Francis set up the crib in 1223. The present monastery houses a remarkable collection of Christmas cribs from all over the world. Many of them are outstanding works of art.

13. The Eastern churches do not have a separate celebration of the Epiphany and the Baptism of the Lord. The Epiphany, the Investiture, and the Manifestation of the Lord are all celebrated on January 6. However, in the West, at the end of the eighth century, an octave of the Epiphany was established. In this calendar, the pericope of the baptism of Jesus was read on January 13. It is this tradition that generated a feast of the baptism of the Lord. It became part of the Roman calendar in 1960 and was ratified in the post-Vatican II renewal of the Liturgy in 1969. It is widely followed by the other Western Christian traditions.

14. Concluding Prayer for Evening Prayer I and II of Christmas Day in *The Divine Office: The Liturgy of the Hours according to the Roman Rite,* 3 vols. (London: Collins, 1974) 1:186, 202. Slightly adapted to more inclusive language.

15. See the commentary on the Fourth Sunday in Advent, above.

16. This practice, which we may regard as dishonest, was widespread in the ancient world, and is present in a number of biblical documents. See F. J.

Moloney, *From James to Jude* (The People's Bible Commentary; Oxford: Bible Reading Fellowship, 1999), 76–77.

17. See above, n. 4.

18. There are many similarities between Psalm 98 and Psalm 96. See the commentary on "Christmas Eve," above, for reflections on the latter psalm.

19. See above, n. 4.

20. The Roman Catholic Lectionary uses Matt. 28:13-18 for the Feast of the Holy Innocents on December 28.

THE SEASON OF EPIPHANY

DALE C. ALLISON JR.

EPIPHANY IS A GREEK WORD meaning "appearance" or "coming into light." Greeks used it of the dawning of a new day and especially to refer to the visible manifestation of a usually invisible deity. Christians early on applied it both to Jesus' first coming (2 Tim. 1:10) and to his second coming (2 Thess. 2:8; 1 Tim. 6:14; Titus 2:13). But in some circles in the second century, *epiphany* came to be the name for the commemoration of Christ's baptism in the Jordan as well as (maybe a little later) of his birth in Bethlehem. The feast was celebrated on January 6, which had nothing to do with the Egyptian winter solstice, although one often reads otherwise. Some Eastern Christians still celebrate the feast of the Nativity, which they call "Theophany," that is, "Manifestation of God," on January 6. In the West, however, calendrical reforms in Rome eventually moved the celebration of Christ's birth to December 25. Epiphany then came to center on the visit of the magi, the baptism of Jesus, and the wedding at Cana. (The antiphons for the Benedictus [Lauds] and Magnificat [Vespers] in the Roman liturgy still speak of these three together.) With time, however, the wedding at Cana fell into the background and the baptism of Jesus came to be celebrated the week after the Epiphany. So January 6 has become the feast of the magi, which celebrates the coming of light to the Gentiles.

The entire season of Epiphany, which spans the time between Advent and Lent, is one of light. It begins with the star of the magi and ends with Jesus' transfiguration into light, and on the way we hear prophetic texts about the divine light dawning (Isa. 60:1-6 on Epiphany, Isa. 42:1-9 on the First Sunday after Epiphany, and Isa. 9:1-4 on the Third Sunday after Epiphany). Now this light

DALE C.
ALLISON JR.

shines in the darkness (cf. Isa. 9:2; 60:2), and why such darkness should exist at all in God's good world is a mystery Epiphany does not attempt to solve. But the light we see suffices to bring us the great joy of the magi (Matt. 2:10) and to guide us in the way we must go.

Epiphany tells us that, into the uncertainties of this life, God has spoken to us, that we are the recipients of revelation. While much remains hidden, much has been revealed. Further, our season locates God's self-disclosure above all in the Christ event. The magi's heavenly light leads us to Jesus, and the divine voice at the baptism and transfiguration identifies Jesus as the Son of God. Him we should heed (Matt. 17:5).

> EPIPHANY TELLS US THAT, INTO THE UNCERTAINTIES OF THIS LIFE, GOD HAS SPOKEN TO US, THAT WE ARE THE RECIPIENTS OF REVELATION.

That God's revelation to us in Christ is associated with a word once used for the rising of the sun is particularly apt. For just as the sun, upon which all life depends, rises without any help from us, so too the divine Word, upon whom our life depends, comes to us apart from our deeds or merits. Epiphany arrives not because we have earned it, but because we are loved. Epiphany is pure grace.

Once this grace overtakes us, however, God calls us to account. The Word does not just save us; it also commands us. So our season includes Mic. 6:1-8, which demands that we who celebrate the advent of the light of the world walk in newness of life. Our celebration issues in a challenge to be faithful to our baptism. We must emulate the one who, after himself being baptized, did justice, acted kindly, and walked humbly with his God.

THE EPIPHANY
OF OUR LORD

JANUARY 6, 2002

Revised Common	Episcopal (BCP)	Roman Catholic
Isa. 60:1-6	Isa. 60:1-6, 9	Isa. 60:1-6
Ps. 72:1-7, 10-14	Ps. 72 or 72:1-2, 10-17	Ps. 72:1-2, 7-8, 10-11
Eph. 3:1-12	Eph. 3:1-12	Eph. 3:2-3a, 5-6
Matt. 2:1-12	Matt. 2:1-12	Matt. 2:1-12

TODAY IS THE DAY OF LIGHT FOR THE GENTILES. The first reading begins with, "Arise, shine; for your light has come," and it goes on to speak of the nations coming to that light. The Gospel features a heavenly luminary guiding Gentiles to the Jewish king, in anticipation of the church's mission to the whole world. So we celebrate this Sunday the divine revelation expanding beyond the few toward the many. We celebrate the universality of God's rule, both present and coming.

FIRST READING
ISAIAH 60:1-6 (RCL/RC);
60:1-6, 9 (BCP)

Interpreting the Text

This poetic depiction of the eschatological transformation of Zion (cf. Isa. 59:20-21) was probably composed shortly after the return of exiles from the Babylonian captivity in the sixth century B.C.E. Many of those exiles no doubt came to Jerusalem with the dramatic expectations of Second Isaiah (chaps. 40–55 of Isaiah) before them. But as yet the promises were unfulfilled, indeed dramatically unfulfilled. The entirety of Isaiah 60–62 appears to be addressed to such exiles as well as to those who initially hoped their return to Jerusalem would be the beginning of a glorious new day. Such people were already, as Isaiah 59 implies, beginning to suffer doubts and discouragement. Their enthusiasm had waned, for reality had left hope unsatisfied. What then were people to make of the promise of a new exodus and of God's help, of the vision of pools of water flowing in the wilderness (Isa. 41:18) and of all people seeing the glory of God (40:5)? Had the prophecies been illusions? We know from the prophet Haggai that even after—and maybe especially after—the building of the Second Temple there was a sort of national inferiority complex. The present suffered by comparison both with Isaiah's prophecies of the future and with the memories of the preexilic past. So the beginning of Isaiah 60 is an attempt to sustain or rekindle hope among people whose faith is weakening, among a group that has discovered it has not gone home again.

Our oracle opens with a declaration that the light has already come (v. 1), a declaration that recalls both Isa. 9:2 ("The people who walked in darkness have seen a great light"—quoted in Matt. 4:12-17) and 42:16 ("I will turn the darkness before them into light"). The emphasis is on the nearness of salvation; it is so near that it can be spoken of as already here. Darkness may yet cover the earth, but the Lord will soon arise, and God's glory will dispel the darkness. Indeed, Zion will become a beacon, to which the world, both Gentiles and dispersed Jews, will be drawn (vv. 2-4). Everything will soon change.

Responding to the Text

What do we make of Isaiah's promises, which in no literal way came to fulfillment? This is the problem of much biblical prophecy in general, from the Tanakh's promise that the line of David would never die out to the avowal of Revelation's Jesus that he will "come quickly" (Rev. 22:20)—a statement made fully nineteen hundred years ago. One interpretive move urges that, once upon a time, everybody knew that the fantastic prophetic depictions of the future were metaphorical, so that it is only our modern literalness, our lack of a poetic sense, that makes us misread the prophets and so become disturbed. Another option is to give a functional interpretation to the prophetic language. One could, for instance, hold that, notwithstanding the failure of the prophecies, Isaiah's words were the right words because they brought hope to a people who otherwise would have given up their faith and dreams. Further, an eschatological or utopian vision need not be realized in order to perform the service of measuring the shortcomings of the transient against the transcendent and so give us much-needed perspective on the contingencies that we too often misinterpret as necessities.

The first move is the least satisfying, because it probably underestimates the supernatural expectations of ancient Jews and Christians. Beyond that, we should not give up on God's utopia and banish it to the realm of mythology and imagination. Surely the Creator must win in the end—even if one does not know how to think concretely about such a hope. Someday, somewhere, somehow there must be a divine victory that produces meaning and justice for all, the dead no less than the living. If, on the contrary, nothing ever happens in this world or in the world to come that measures up to the scriptural dreams, that is, if there remain lives empty of meaning, if the weak and needy are never rescued once and for all from the hand of the wicked, then how could the biblical God be God? We may not be able to share Isaiah's expectations about time and place, but does not our faith still move us to share his hope for a future or a place in which wrongs are made right and our wounds are healed?

The reading of Isa. 60:1-9 alongside today's Gospel is appropriate for several reasons. For one thing, Christians have traditionally thought of this prophetic text as actually foreseeing the coming of the magi and their giving of gold, frankincense, and myrrh to the new-born king, Jesus (see below). In fact, our passage, which says that "nations shall come to your light, and kings to the brightness of your dawn" (v. 3), is one of the sources of our tradition that the magi were kings. (Although Matthew's text does not call them such, we all sing every Christmas, "We three kings of Orient are . . .").

> WE MAY NOT BE ABLE TO SHARE ISAIAH'S EXPECTATIONS ABOUT TIME AND PLACE, BUT DOES NOT OUR FAITH STILL MOVE US TO SHARE HIS HOPE FOR A FUTURE OR A PLACE IN WHICH WRONGS ARE MADE RIGHT AND OUR WOUNDS ARE HEALED?

Another reason that Isaiah 60 is so appropriate for Epiphany is its opening words about light. The term itself, *epiphaneia,* means in Greek "manifestation" or "appearance," and originally the feast of Epiphany celebrated the baptism of Jesus, which in the early tradition was thought of as being, like the transfiguration, a luminous divine manifestation. Already in the second century, Justin Martyr says that a fire was kindled in the Jordan when Jesus was baptized, and just such a light appears in some of the Old Latin manuscripts at Matt. 3:15 and in Tatian's *Diatessaron,* among other places. Although in the West Epiphany is no longer directly associated with Jesus' baptism, it is now connected with yet a second story in which a light plays a leading role: the magi are guided by the light of the star.

A third way in which Isaiah 60 links up with the Gospel takes us back to eschatology. Everything in both Jewish and human history has fallen short of Isaiah's expectations. Christians, however, believe that the life, death, and resurrection of Jesus have somehow made real in our experience at least some of the hopes and dreams of the Jewish prophets. In the present case, who can deny that, soon after Jesus' death and resurrection, unprecedented numbers of Gentiles came to know and worship the God of Israel's Scriptures?

RESPONSIVE READING

PSALM 72:1-7, 10-14 (RCL); 72 or 72:1-2, 10-17 (BCP); 72:1-2, 7-8, 10-11 (RC)

Whatever its origin, Psalm 72, like Psalm 2, came to be used at the coronation of Davidic kings. Moreover, when it was recited after the failure of the monarchy, it must have been read messianically, that is, as a psalm of hope for the restoration of Israel's kingship. This is in any case how Christians, from at least Justin Martyr on, have read it when they have seen it as a prophecy fulfilled by the magi bringing gifts and gold to Jesus. From the Jewish side, the Targum on the Psalms, the Aramaic paraphrase for Jewish liturgical reading (of uncertain date), similarly understands the psalm to be a prophecy of the future Davidic Messiah.

The psalm is notable for its juxtaposition of great glory and prosperity with a keen awareness of the poor: the psalmist does not think of the one without thinking of the other. Indeed, the verses that lead off the psalm focus first on righteousness and justice—"May he [the king] defend the cause of the poor of the people, give deliverance to the needy" (v. 4)—and the theme is taken up again in vv. 12-14. So the great wealth that comes to the king (vv. 10, 15-16) and that brings glory to God (vv. 18-19) comes to a ruler who judges justly on behalf of the whole people and so uses his resources to counter the oppression of the unfortunate.

The justice and righteousness of the king are not grounded in sentimentality but in theology. Verse 1 is a prayer: "Give the king your justice, O God, and your righteousness to a king's son." So the king is to act as God would act, and that means with justice for all, not just some. It is particularly striking that this is all the king does in this psalm. So the logic seems to be that, if the king were to defend the cause of the poor and judge with justice, then peace would abound (v. 7), and even the nations would behave as they ought (vv. 8-15). In fact, vv. 8-14 appear to envisage the royal rule of Israel becoming worldwide—and this not through political maneuvering or military policy but on account of justice. The psalm, then, in giving us a big, utopian picture, sees the king doing the will of God, with the result that the poor, the nations, and even nature (see v. 16) become what they are supposed to be. The eschatological orientation of Psalm 72 unites it with Isaiah 60: both envisage God's lordship becoming universal through the glorification of Israel.

The final verse tells us that "the prayers of David son of Jesse are ended" (v. 20). This originally served to mark the end of a collection of psalms or, as it does today, a division between sections of the Psalter. But Psalm 72 opens with

"Of Solomon" (so NRSV), the Hebrew of which can equally mean, "For Solomon." This raises the intriguing possibility that our psalm was intended by a collector to be a psalm *by David* written *for Solomon*. This would add great poignancy to the text when read in light of the ultimate failure of the Solomonic kingdom. Solomon may have rendered just judgments and received gold from afar, but his kingdom split upon his death. Neither he nor his offspring "live[d] while the sun endured, and as long as the moon, throughout all generations" (v. 5). Such language Christians reserve for Jesus alone.

Second Reading
EPHESIANS 3:1–12 (rcl, bcp); 3:2–3a, 5–6 (rc)

Interpreting the Text

Verses 2–13 are a long autobiographical narrative interrupting the prayer that begins in v. 1 and continues in v. 14. The parenthesis in vv. 2–13 is a statement of the apostle's unique role in bringing the mystery of God's grace to the Gentiles. The apostle's knowledge of this mystery has neither been learned from others nor been figured out through exegesis or reflection but rather given by divine "revelation" (v. 3). This revelation, furthermore, has not come to Paul in vain: he has worked to proclaim it throughout the world. The result is of cosmic consequence. For even "the rulers and authorities in the heavenlies" (v. 10) now know, through the existence of the church of Jew and Gentile, things that were formerly hidden to them (vv. 8–9).

Responding to the Text

Ephesians 3 makes the New Testament's most exalted claims on behalf of Paul. Those who admire the apostle and think of his doctrine of justification by faith as the heart of Christianity may be quite happy with this sort of extravagant praise. But the large number of people—there are now many in the churches—who feel that Paul was somehow far removed from Jesus and did not get everything quite right will be bothered by it.

Although the issue of theological continuity between Paul and Jesus is complex, it does seem that in one particular at least there is significant continuity between the two figures—and precisely regarding the subject common to today's four readings. Both Isaiah 60 and Psalm 72 foresee the day when Gentiles will recognize the reality of the Jewish God, while in Matthew 2 Gentile magi adore the young Jesus, and here in Ephesians 3 the mystery given to Paul is the inclusion of the Gentiles in God's dealings.

Now it cannot be said that the historical Jesus had much to do with Gentiles. Our sources record only a few incidental encounters, and he seemingly had very little to say about non-Jews. Jesus was, however, apparently known for keeping company with certain sorts of disreputable people. His detractors accused him of consorting with "toll collectors and sinners," for instance (see Matt. 11:19 and Mark 2:15). Such people were probably viewed by many as individuals who had disobeyed the law and so lost their birthright; that is, they had left the covenant with Abraham by not obeying Moses. Their religious standing was then very similar to that of the Gentiles: they were outsiders, and their souls were in jeopardy. If then Jesus, as it appears, went to them and offered them salvation on the condition that they throw in with him or adopt his cause, then the step toward Paul is not so large. Both made salvation depend not on birth or covenant or law but on the cause of Jesus. So Paul's mission to the Gentiles, his inclusivity, which Ephesians presents as given by revelation, was not wholly out of the blue, nor did it develop in isolation. It rather stands in continuity with an important part of Jesus' ministry. Those of us who have our problems with Paul may find this one way of appreciating him more.

> PAUL'S MISSION TO THE GENTILES, HIS INCLUSIVITY, WHICH EPHESIANS PRESENTS AS GIVEN BY REVELATION, WAS NOT WHOLLY OUT OF THE BLUE, NOR DID IT DEVELOP IN ISOLATION. IT RATHER STANDS IN CONTINUITY WITH AN IMPORTANT PART OF JESUS' MINISTRY.

THE GOSPEL
MATTHEW 2:1-12

Interpreting the Text

Matthew 2 continues the theme of Davidic kingship already so prominent in chap. 1 (vv. 1, 2-17, 20). Jesus is born in Bethlehem, where David was brought up and anointed (1 Samuel 16); and Mic. 5:1, 3, which is here quoted as fulfilled in Jesus (vv. 5-6), is about a promised Davidic king. But the central theme, and the theme that aligns our passage with the other readings for this day, is the homage of Gentiles. Although their country of origin is unspecified—Persia, Babylon, and Arabia are the usual guesses—the magi clearly represent the Gentile world. And it is they, not the Jewish chief priests and scribes, who seek to honor the newborn king. Our story in fact overturns the traditional motif of the superiority of Jewish hero to foreign wise men (recall Genesis 39, where Joseph but not the magicians of Egypt can interpret Pharaoh's dream, and the similar stories in the first half of Daniel). Matthew 2 foreshadows Matt. 13:57 ("Prophets are not without honor except in their own country and in their own home"), and it shows that, from the beginning, Jesus kept unexpected company. The insiders are outsiders and the outsiders are insiders.

It is quite plausible that the evangelist Matthew and his first Jewish-Christian audience, like most modern commentators, associated Matthew 2 with both Isaiah 60 and Psalm 72. The former (which has certainly influenced Rev. 21:23-26) speaks of the dawning of a light (v. 1), of Gentiles coming to Israel (v. 3), of them bringing wealth with them (v. 5), and indeed of gold and frankincense (v. 6). As for Psalm 72, it speaks of foreign islands rendering tribute to the Jewish king (v. 10), of prostration before him (v. 11), and of gold being given to him (v. 15). So the liturgical readings are texts that can be and have been viewed as promise and fulfillment.

The Septuagint (Greek translation) of Num. 23:7 says that Balaam is "from the east," and commentators throughout the ages have also associated this Old Testament text with Matthew's story of the magi. They have viewed the magi as Balaam's descendants. Jewish tradition made Balaam a *magos* and the father of magi; and, in the Tanakh, when the evil king Balak tries to enlist Balaam in the cause against Israel, the seer instead prophesies the nation's future greatness and the coming of a great ruler. This is close to Matthew, where the cruel Herod, attempting to destroy Israel's king, employs foreign magi who in the event bring only honor to the king's rival. So Matthew's magi are successors to Balaam. Moreover, Justin Martyr and other commentators have found the scriptural key to 2:2 in another text in Numbers, namely, 24:17, where Balaam prophesies that a star will come out of Jacob and a scepter will rise out of Israel. This text was given messianic sense by ancient Jews (as in the targums). Sometimes they identified the star with a messianic figure (as in the Dead Sea Scrolls), other times with a star heralding the Messiah. Matthew, then, recounts the fulfillment of Balaam's prophecy.

> MATTHEW 2 SHOWS THAT, FROM THE BEGINNING, JESUS KEPT UNEXPECTED COMPANY. THE INSIDERS ARE OUTSIDERS AND THE OUTSIDERS ARE INSIDERS.

The "star" goes before the magi and then comes "to rest over the place where the child" is. This is no ordinary star, and the attempts, repeated by the planetariums every Christmas season, to identify it with a planetary conjunction, comet, or supernova, are futile. Such objects do not go ahead of people, nor do they stop over a particular place. And that a light high above could precisely guide people below just does not make sense. The text rather seems to support Chrysostom, who wrote that Bethlehem's star did not "remain on high and point out the place, for it was impossible for the magi so to learn it; instead it came down and performed this office. For you know that a star could not possibly mark out a spot as small as that taken up by the body of a newborn." The *Protevangelium of James,* from the second century, and later Ephrem the Syrian in his commentary on the *Diatessaron,* also assume that the so-called star does not stay on high but moves as a guide and indeed comes to rest very near the infant Jesus; and Chrysologus, Leo the Great, Theophylact, Aquinas, and Nicholas of Lyra further agree in telling the tale of a Tinker Bell–like light flying hither and yon. So what is going on here?

The ancient conception of a star was not our conception of a star. Matthew did not imagine stars to be immense, inanimate, energetic masses billions of light-years away from, and thousands of times larger than, our planet. Matthew lived in antiquity, and in antiquity stars were alive; they were living beings. In Judaism, moreover, stars were often spoken of as angels, and angels were often spoken of as stars. According to Job 38:7, "The morning stars sang together, and all the sons of God shouted for joy." In Rev. 1:20, "The seven stars are the angels of the seven churches." And Rev. 12:4 says of the devil that "his tail swept down a third of the stars of heaven." When we reckon with texts such as these—and there are dozens more—and then recall that in the Bible angels are bright, that they come down from heaven to earth, and that they can serve as guides, as in the story of the exodus (Exod. 23:20, 23; 32:34), then modern astronomical ideas, which are after all modern ideas, become irrelevant. As Origen, Theophylact, and Maldonatus saw, we have here the story of an angel. The old *Arabic Gospel of the Savior* got it right: "Behold, magi came from the east. . . . And there were with them gifts of gold, frankincense, and myrrh. And they adored him [Jesus], and presented the gifts to him. . . . In the same hour there appeared to them an angel in the form of that star that had before guided them on their journey; and they went away, following the guidance of its light. . . ."

Matthew 2:1-12 contains several elements that anticipate the story's end. Here as there the issue is Jesus' status as "king of the Jews" (2:2; 27:11, 29, 37). Here as there the Jewish leaders gather against him (2:3-4; 26:3-4, 57). Here as there plans are laid in secret (2:7; 26:4-5). And here as there Jesus' death is sought (2:13, 16; 26:4). Obviously the end is foreshadowed in the beginning. But there are also artistic contrasts. Here a light in the night sky proclaims the Messiah's advent; there darkness during the day announces his death (2:2; 27:45). Here Jesus is worshiped; there he is mocked (26:67-68; 27:27-31, 39-44). Here it is prophesied that Jesus will shepherd his people Israel; there it is foretold that Jesus the shepherd will be struck and his sheep scattered (26:31). Here there is great rejoicing; there we find mourning and grief (26:75; 27:46).

Responding to the Text

The Gospel for today has a special power to fascinate readers and to stay in the memory because it incorporates ever-popular and perennially pleasing characters and motifs: the mysterious magi from the East, the anomalous star coincident with the birth of a king, the threat to the life of an infant hero, the warning that comes in a dream. Regardless of our verdict on their historicity, these are things to delight and enchant, to entertain and cause wonder.

While many themes run through Matt. 2:1–12, a sermon might focus on the element it shares with today's other readings. Both Isaiah 60 and Psalm 72 look forward to the day when the Gentiles will share in the salvation bestowed by Israel's God, and Ephesians 3 exalts Paul because, through his ministry, the Gentiles now dwell in the church beside Jews. Amid these texts, Matthew 2 stands as the beginning of the fulfillment of an Old Testament hope and as a foreshadowing of the latter, inclusive church known to Paul. Taken together, the four texts move us from the Old Testament's awareness that God's lordship cannot be full unless the Gentiles participate in that lordship through Matthew's narrative, in which Gentiles recognize the Jewish king, and on to Ephesians 3, which recounts the equal standing of Jew and Gentile before God. So the four readings map a movement towards inclusivity. Their collective lesson is that God's lordship is not complete as long as there are people outside of it, as long as there are insiders and outsiders, as long as some are reckoned strangers.

One of the interesting points about the citation of Scripture in v. 6 is that Matthew felt free to change the prophet's wording. Micah 5:2 speaks of Bethlehem as being among the little clans of Judah: its insignificance is emphasized. But Matthew, without any textual authority, quotes the prophet as saying that Bethlehem is "not at all the least among the rulers of Judah." Here the evangelist shows a freedom foreign to the fundamentalist. If Job could gripe, "What are human beings, that you make so much of them, that you set your mind on them?" (7:17), and thereby invert and mock the famous line from the liturgy, "What are human beings that you are mindful of them, mortals that you care for them?" (Ps. 8:4), and if the author of Isa. 45:7 could say, in opposition to Gen. 1:2, that God creates darkness, so Matthew in like manner felt the rhetorical freedom to revise Scripture to speak to his new situation. Isn't their precedent our example?

That Matt. 2:1–12 foreshadows the end of Matthew comes to expression in T. S. Eliot's poem, "Journey of the Magi." In this the visitors from the East see, on their way to Bethlehem, "three trees on the low sky" and "six hands at an open door dicing for pieces for silver." The three trees stand for the three crosses while the men dicing for silver represent the soldiers casting lots for Jesus' garments and Judas' betrayal of his master for thirty pieces of silver. Thus at Jesus' birth his death is already anticipated: the end is in the beginning.

THE STORY OF THE MAGI IS MEANINGFUL ONLY BECAUSE WE KNOW THE FULL IDENTIFY OF JESUS FROM THE END OF THE GOSPEL. WITHOUT THE CRUCIFIXION, THE INFANCY NARRATIVE LOSES ITS MEANING; THIS IS WHY IT LEANS FORWARD, TOWARD THE END.

This is a theological point we should never neglect. Without the crucifixion, the infancy narrative loses its meaning; this is why it leans forward, toward the end.

The story of the magi is meaningful only because we know the full identify of Jesus from the end of the Gospel.

Leonardo da Vinci's *Adoration of the Magi* highlights another aspect of Matthew's text that some exegetes have missed: Matt. 2:1–12 has not only a foreground but also a background. In da Vinci's painting, behind the magi and Jesus and Mary, are buildings in ruin and horsemen at joust. The meaning is manifest. The world into which the Messiah comes is in chaos and decay; things need to be righted. This is an element of Matthew's story. When Jesus is born, Jerusalem, instead of being overjoyed, is troubled at the news. And there is upon Israel's throne a wicked and illegitimate ruler. And innocent blood is about to be shed (cf. 2:1–13). In brief, the world is ill. Is it any wonder that the first word of Jesus' public proclamation is "Repent" (4:17)? And isn't this still God's word to us, who even in the light of Epiphany fail to recognize the hidden God in our midst even as we, like the scribes of Matt. 2:5–6, quote the Bible?

There is an ancient Christian legend that gives Matthew 2 a canonical reading, and retelling the legend creates some memorable intertextual links. The story, told in the apocryphal *Cave of Treasures*, runs as follows. When Adam and Eve, at the beginning of the world, and before the fall, lived in the Garden of Eden, Adam had many beautiful and precious treasures. After the first parents sinned, but before they were forced to leave Eden, Adam pleaded with God that he might be permitted to take some of his treasure with him. God graciously granted his request. Many years later, when Adam's soul flew to heaven, his family buried his wealth in a cave. This cave, like the entrance to Paradise, was guarded by an angel, so that no one might enter and take Adam's property. And there the treasure rested throughout the ages.

But in the fullness of time, a star arose in the East, and three magi, in response, went on a long voyage to follow its light to the newborn king of the Jews. As they were making their way, the star lead them to the ancient, hidden cave of Adam, and the angelic sentry gave up its guard. There, among the riches, the magi found gold, frankincense, and myrrh, and they took some of each that they might with them honor the royal Jewish infant. This then was how the three wise kings came to offer their gifts to Jesus in Bethlehem. In this entertaining legend, Matthew 2 gets tied to the primeval history and Matthew's Jesus becomes the "last Adam" of Pauline Christology (1 Cor. 15:45).

> *"Disguised, O Savior, you were born in a cave; but heaven proclaimed you to all, taking for its mouth a star. And it offered you the magi worshiping you in faith. Wherefore, with them, have mercy upon us."*
>
> FROM THE EASTERN GREAT VESPERS FOR CHRISTMAS EVE

THE BAPTISM OF OUR LORD / FIRST SUNDAY AFTER THE EPIPHANY

JANUARY 13, 2002

REVISED COMMON	EPISCOPAL (BCP)	ROMAN CATHOLIC
Isa. 42:1-9	Isa. 42:1-9	Isa. 42:1-4, 6-7
Ps. 29	Ps. 89:1-29 or 89:20-29	Ps. 29:1-2, 3-4, 9-10 (11b)
Acts 10:34-43	Acts 10:34-38	Acts 10:34-38
Matt. 3:13-17	Matt. 3:13-17	Matt. 3:13-17

TODAY WE REMEMBER THE BAPTISM OF JESUS, which among other things gives us opportunity to reflect upon our own baptisms. For if our baptisms unite us to him (Rom. 6:1-4), his baptism unites him to us: we cannot think of the one without the other. So just as we must celebrate what has been done for us at the Jordan, we must also ask ourselves how our lives measure up to the radical newness pledged in baptism. Today's prophetic reading speaks of "new things" (Isa. 41:9). This is a promise to us. But how has it been fulfilled apart from and after the ritual that has brought us to "newness of life" (Rom. 6:4)?

FIRST READING
ISAIAH 42:1-9

Interpreting the Text

The Babylonians destroyed Jerusalem in 581 or 582 B.C. Soon thereafter their empire crumbled, to be replaced by the Persians. The Persian king Cyrus (who is named in Isa. 44:28 and 45:1) decided that it would be to his advantage to have allies on his southern and western fronts, so in 538 he allowed the Jewish people to return to Judea and rebuild their city and temple. This is the context for Isaiah 41–55, which offers consolation rather than judgment and focuses on God as the creator, the Lord of history, and the redeemer of Israel. The chapters open by announcing deliverance in a new exodus (40:1-31) and follow with a long section on the impending deliverance (Isaiah 41–48, written during Cyrus's rise to power) and then a second long section depicting joy and sorrow in the land (Isaiah 49–54, composed after Cyrus's decree letting Israel return to its land). The conclusion (Isaiah 55) is an invitation to turn to God.

Embedded within all this are the so-called Servant Songs, which perhaps orig-inally belonged to a separate collection. Isaiah 42:1-9 has to do with the call and ministry of the servant, and 49:1-6 further clarifies his ministry, while 50:4-11 and 52:13—53:12 have to do with the servant's suffering. Exactly who this mys-terious, unnamed servant is supposed to be remains unclear (cf. Acts 8:34). Chris-tians, beginning with the New Testament writers, have naturally thought of Isaiah foreseeing Jesus the Messiah. Jewish tradition has often thought of Israel, although some Jewish interpreters have identified the servant with the Messiah. But there are also additional possibilities—the prophet, the Persian rulers, Cyrus in particular, Jeremiah, Zerubbabel, and Zion, for example. The truth seems to be that the servant is a fluid figure whose identity may vary. Sometimes the ser-vant is clearly Israel, but at other times this equation does not work so well because an individual seems to be depicted.

In 42:1-4, God in the first person presents the servant (to the heavenly coun-sel?). Here we learn that the servant is upheld by God, chosen, and possessed of the Spirit (v. 1), but that he is at the same time self-emptying and humble, so humble that he will not lift up his voice (v. 2), break a bruised reed, or quench a dimly burning wick (v. 3; the old Jewish targum on Isaiah clarifies the lack of self-assertion in v. 3 this way: "The poor who are like a bruised reed he will not break, and the needy who are like a dimly burning wick he will not quench"; many modern interpreters, however, think of reed and wick as standing for Gentiles). The servant comes not to be served but to serve, and his service is to bring jus-tice, even to the ends of the earth: the coastlands wait for his Torah, his instruc-tion. Thus the servant, in addition to being a royal guardian of justice (v. 7), is a prophet and a teacher.

In 42:5-7 and maybe also 8-9 (are these clarifying additions?), God speaks directly to the servant, not to the court audience, which now in effect overhears. After establishing God's credentials as the one who created and sustains all (v. 6), we learn that the servant is God's instrument for enlightening the nations, open-ing the eyes of the blind, and bringing prisoners out of dungeons. (Here the interpretation that identifies the servant with Cyrus works well: one can think of Israel in exile being brought back from darkness and freed.) The passage ends with a declaration of newness (cf. 41:15; 42:10; 43:19; 48:6), something akin to res-urrection: the age before the exile is past, and the creator (cf. v. 5) has now deter-mined to bring in an age heretofore unsurpassed.

Responding to the Text

Whatever the original intent and functions of the servant songs, it is inevitable that Christians have always seen Jesus as their incarnation. Not only did Jesus himself directly relate his ministry to prophecies in the last part of Isaiah (note, e.g., the use of Isa. 60:1-2 in Luke 7:18-23), but the New Testament writers clearly do the same. Luke, for instance, thinks it appropriate that Jesus open his ministry by declaring a passage from Isaiah fulfilled in himself (4:16-21), and the divine voice at the baptism and transfiguration borrow from Isa. 42:9 (Mark 1:11; 9:7). Matthew's longest formal quotation from the Old Testament appears in 12:15-21, which is a citation of Isa. 42:1-4. Moreover, the teaching or Torah of Jesus has literally gone to the coastlands (Isa. 49:4); and words about a bearer of the Spirit who does not cry or lift up his voice, who does not break a bruised reed or quench a dimly burning wick, who is a light to the Gentiles and opens the eyes of the blind, cannot but be for Christian readers a transparency through which we see the anointed prophet and teacher of Nazareth who embodied his command to turn the other cheek.

The application to Jesus holds also, and even especially, for 42:9: "See, the former things have come to pass, and new things I now declare." For this is what Jesus is all about. He brought and continues to bring a new creation that allows us to grow beyond our past. Jesus does not just promise to make the future new (Rev. 21:5), but rather, as Paul puts it, he brings a new creation in the here and now, so that the former things have passed away (2 Cor. 5:17). One understands why, when C. H. Dodd looked at the New Testament, he came to speak of "realized eschatology." The New Testament declares that the Messiah has already come, that dead have been raised (Matt. 27:51-53; 1 Cor. 15:3-7), that judgment has fallen (John 5:24), that Satan has already suffered defeat (Luke 10:18; John 13:31), that sin has met its match (Rom. 8:1-4). In short, the kingdom of God has come (Matt. 12:28; Luke 17:20-21).

These are astounding convictions, and they reflect extraordinary experience. The New Testament claims that, in the ministry of Jesus and then in the social and religious lives of the early Christians, people had encountered the kingdom of God, the fullness of God's will. Put otherwise, they had been overtaken by the truly new—things not just new in time but new in quality. Jesus, according to Mark, had brought a "new teaching" (Mark 1:27; cf. 2:21-22). Similarly, the writer of Hebrews could speak of a "new and living way" (10:20), the author of Col. 3:10 of a "new self," and the author of Eph. 2:15 of a "new humanity."

The church remains the steward of this sense of newness, and it is our duty to see that, beyond our sins and the sins of others, there is always the possibility of a new beginning. Perhaps the best way to encourage ourselves in this seemingly unjustifiable optimism is to think of collective and individual cases of renewal that

> THE NEW TESTAMENT CLAIMS THAT, IN THE MINISTRY OF JESUS AND THEN IN THE SOCIAL AND RELIGIOUS LIVES OF THE EARLY CHRISTIANS, PEOPLE HAD ENCOUNTERED THE KINGDOM OF GOD, THE FULLNESS OF GOD'S WILL. IT IS OUR DUTY TO SEE THAT, BEYOND OUR SINS AND THE SINS OF OTHERS, THERE IS ALWAYS THE POSSIBILITY OF A NEW BEGINNING.

we have know firsthand. In my own life an effective antidote to my natural cynicism has been friendship with a man who grew up without father or mother, a man who became, in his twenties, truly reprobate, of whom the most flattering thing one could say about him was that he was addicted to both drink and heroin. Anyone who met him then would have known him to be beyond hopeless—just as anyone who met him today would never dream that this pious, well-spoken, father of four and prosperous owner of a drug and alcoholic rehabilitation center was once in the gutter himself. One night, however, this hopeless man happened to walk into a church service and was magically transformed—he came to "newness of life" (Rom. 6:4). The difference between the old person and the new person is in this case so dramatic that one naturally begins to think about God's working in the world and about the miraculous plasticity and potential of those created in the image of God.

Responsive Reading
PSALM 29 (rcl);
29:1-2, 3-4, 9-10 (11b) (rc)

This is widely reckoned to be a polemical rewriting of an old Canaanite hymn to Baal, the god of storm and fertility. It is perhaps premonarchical and the oldest psalm in the Psalter. It opens with a scene in the divine council (cf. Gen. 1:26), where the "heavenly beings" (the pagan gods or, less likely, the angels) are ordered to ascribe glory to the Lord, the God of Israel. Verses 3-10 then offer a dramatic, theological interpretation of a tremendous thunderstorm—it is not Baal but the Lord God of Israel who is enthroned as king and in control above the waters. It is God, not Baal, who sends forth the mighty voice of thunder and flames of fire, lightning. The land shakes, trees break. The response to the awe-inspiring spectacle is prayer that the Lord will give strength to the faithful and bless them with peace.

Perhaps most of us in the church, even in this day and age when we have all moved permanently inside, happily still know what it is like sometimes to encounter God in the natural world. Our psalm, however, is not about the sort of natural beauty that makes us intuit a good Providence. It is rather about a violent nature that calls forth awe and even terror. The poetic description of a stupendous thunderstorm, with its destructive winds, deafening sounds, and frightful strikes of fire does not, if I may borrow from Blake, make one think about the gentle God who made the little lamb but of the power that made the dreaded Tyger: "What immortal hand or eye dare frame thy fearful symmetry?"

Consider how our feelings about God may be roughly congruent with our feelings about nature and what happens to the one when the other changes. Has not our increasing physical security, our withdrawal from howling storms and from "Nature, red in tooth and claw," altered our feelings about the world and so altered our feelings about God? Surely the modern dismissal of hell stems partly from an increasing lack of direct contact with nature's indifference and darkness. A friendly nature begets a friendly God.

The Christian message—whose sponsors have even sometimes spoken of "election" and "predestination" to underline our utter feebleness—presupposes feelings of helplessness and sin. It presupposes that we cannot save ourselves, that certain matters are out of our hands. What happens, then, as we continue to isolate ourselves from nature, not just from the night sky and other sources of wonder but from the less hospitable side of nature that has in the past left us feeling exposed and helpless?

PSALM 89:1-29 or 89:20-29 (BCP)

Psalm 89, a communal lament on kingship, is attributed to Ethan the Ezrahite, a figure mentioned in 1 Kings 4:31: Solomon "was wiser than anyone else, wiser than Ethan the Ezrahite, and Heman, Calcol, and Darda, children of Mahol. . . ." So Ethan is a famous sage. Interestingly enough, Psalm 88 attributes itself to the Heman of 1 Kings 4:31, so perhaps the two psalms are intended, in their canonical presentation, to be some sort of wisdom instruction, statements from particularly insightful people.

Psalm 89 opens with a declaration of the Lord's steadfast love (vv. 1–2). This is then illustrated by God's promises to David and his line. God has made a covenant with David, the chosen one, "for all generations" (vv. 3–4). The connection between the monarchical promise and the following verses, which describe God's incomparable greatness, power in creation, justice, and protection (vv. 5–18), is not perfectly clear. But vv. 19-37 (in the form of a divine oracle) return to David and stress that, despite the sin of the people (vv. 30–32), God's faithfulness to the king will last forever (v. 21). Indeed, the theme at this point becomes the continuation of David's throne without end (vv. 28–29, 33–37). Seemingly incongruous, then, is the final part of the psalm, which becomes a lament: God has renounced the covenant, the scepter has departed, and the promises have been undone (vv. 38-46). The psalm naturally ends with searching questions. How long will God hide (v. 46)? Where is God's steadfast love (v. 49)? In other words, has God not failed?

So Psalm 89 raises the question of evil and returns no answer. The pious reader is left in the dark; there is no resolution. Psalm 89 nonetheless does not lose faith. For while it asks questions, it addresses those questions to God (v. 49). Indeed, it goes further to call upon God (vv. 50-51) and even to bless God (v. 52; this is the doxology for the third book of the Psalter). The Psalm's last word, then, is that faith in Israel's God can endure despite the confusions and questions thrown up by a seemingly chaotic, unintelligible history.

SECOND READING
ACTS 10:34-43

Interpreting the Text

Peter here speaks to Cornelius, his relatives, and some close friends (10:25). Luke no doubt intends the words to focus on what Gentiles needed most to hear. Two themes are to the fore. First, Peter stresses the universal character of the Gospel. "God shows no partiality" (v. 34). Everywhere those who fear God and do right are acceptable (v. 35). Jesus is "Lord of all" (v. 36). "Everyone who believes" is forgiven (v. 43). Second, the good news takes the form of an outline of Jesus' ministry. The story began in Galilee with the movement around John the Baptist (v. 37). Anointed with the Spirit and power, Jesus did good deeds and healed the oppressed, and after being killed was raised from the dead (vv. 38-41). And he is now ordained to be judge of the living and the dead (v. 42).

Peter's little sermon is densely intertextual. Readers of Luke's first volume are regularly sent back to the Gospel. Verse 37 (John's ministry), for example, recalls Luke 3 (where John's ministry is introduced). Verse 38 (Jesus being anointed with the Holy Spirit and with power) reminds one of the story of Jesus' baptism (Luke 3:21-22; cf. 4:1, 14) as well as of Luke 4:16-21, where Jesus applies Isa. 61:1-2 ("The Spirit of the Lord is upon me, because he has anointed me. . .") to himself. The reference in v. 38 to good deeds and to healing the ill brings to mind many stories throughout Luke, and vv. 39-41, which speak of Jesus' death, resurrection, and his post-Easter appearances and commands, stir up memories of Luke 22–24.

But it is not just to Luke that Acts 10 sends us. Peter's words are also full of the Old Testament. That God shows no partiality (v. 34) is an Old Testament conviction (e.g., Deut. 10:17). "The message he sent . . . preaching (Greek: *euangelizomenos*) peace" adopts the language of Isa. 52:7 ("the messenger [Greek: *euaggelizomenou*] who announces peace, who brings good news [Greek: *euangelizomenos*]"). Being anointed with the Holy Spirit (v. 38) alludes to Isa. 61:1-2 (see above). "They put him to death by hanging him on a tree" (v. 39) uses the language of Deut. 21:21 (a text Jews applied to crucifixion and which Paul uses in Gal. 3:13). And the apostle ends by saying that "all the prophets" testify that forgiveness comes to those who believe in Jesus (v. 43), perhaps an allusion to Isaiah 53; Jer. 31:34; or Dan. 9:24.

One might wish to make Acts 10:34-43 an opportunity to stress the importance of the historical Jesus. While Luke, like the later creeds, here passes over Jesus' teaching, much of Jesus' pre-Easter ministry is outlined. Luke at least would not have been satisfied with Rudolf Bultmann's argument that theology should care only about the "thatness" of Jesus, not his words and character. And the lively, on-going quest for the historical Jesus, conducted mostly by Christians, and the high sales of many recent books on Jesus, show us how many people want to know the real Jesus. This desire is theologically legitimate. For the historical study of Jesus shows us some very important things. It keeps us, for instance, from forgetting that Jesus was a Jew. It also helps us to focus on Jesus' political and social environments and in this way broadens interpretive options and makes him more concrete to us. And it can help us to be critical of Christian experience and theology when they appear to conflict with things we can reasonably know about Jesus.

But Acts 10 also qualifies our enthusiasm for the historical Jesus. For Peter's universalism is not anchored in the Galilean or Judean ministry of Jesus. Peter does not say that Jesus preached good news to the Samaritans or the Gentiles, nor could he say such a thing. On the contrary, the wider narrative of Luke-Acts (here incidentally in harmony with Paul's epistles) reveals that the mission to the Gentiles began not before Easter—there it was at best only foreshadowed or hinted at—but only after Easter, and then with much hesitation and opposition. So Luke's narrative teaches that there are some central tenets of our faith that must be traced to the risen Lord, not to the historical Jesus, and further that divine disclosure is not circumscribed by Jesus' historical life but extends into the life of the church, where new revelations can be given and received.

THE GOSPEL
MATTHEW 3:13-17

Interpreting the Text

Matthew focuses not on the baptism itself but on a prefatory episode—John's protest of Jesus' desire for baptism—and subsequent events. Although Jesus' sinlessness is not taught in Matthew, it is evidently assumed (cf. John 8:46; 2 Cor. 5:21; Heb. 7:26; in Judaism the patriarchs and others were regularly said to have been without sin: *Jubilees* 23:10; *Testament of Abraham* A 10:13-14; Prayer of Manasseh 8; et al.). And because John's baptism involves the confession of sins (3:6), Jesus' submission to it is awkward. But Matthew's Jesus declares that the act fulfills all righteousness. Here fulfillment is probably, as elsewhere, a reference to biblical prophecy. In line with this, 3:17 draws upon both Ps. 2:7 and Isa. 42:1 (see below). So Jesus, knowing the messianic prophecies, obediently fulfills them and thereby fulfills all righteousness. Because prophecy declares God's will, to fulfill prophecy is to fulfill righteousness.

The appearance of the symbolic dove has occasioned much speculation. Ever since Tertullian, it has often been connected with Noah's dove: the former dove announced deliverance from the flood; the latter dove, deliverance from sins (so the commentary of Theophylact; cf. 1 Pet. 3:20-21). It is also possible to associate the dove with the new exodus motif, for in the earliest Jewish commentary on Exodus the Holy Spirit rests upon Israel as they cross the Red Sea, and the people are compared to a dove and granted a vision.

But the best guess relates the text to Gen. 1:2. This last involves the Spirit of God, water, and the imagery of a bird hovering. Further, in the Talmud (in *b.Hag.* 15a) the hovering of the Spirit over the face of the waters is represented more precisely as the hovering of a dove. The meaning is then once again that the last things are as the first: Jesus inaugurates a new creation.

The correctness of this interpretation is seemingly confirmed by a Dead Sea Scroll fragment, 4Q521. In line 6 ("his Spirit will hover over the poor") the language of Gen. 1:2 characterizes the eschatological redemption: just as the Spirit once hovered over the face of the waters, so too, at the end, will the Spirit hover over the saints and strengthen them. This pre-Christian application of Gen. 1:2 to the eschatological future has the Spirit hovering over human beings as opposed to lifeless material. The striking parallel with Matthew evidences a similar creative application of Gen. 1:2.

What exactly does it mean that the baptism of Jesus is like what happened when the world began? Early Christians, drawing upon the eschatological expectations of Judaism, imagined the better world of the future as a return to the beginning: the end would be paradise regained. "The last things [will be] like the first," to quote the second-century *Epistle of Barnabas.* This is why Rev. 22:1-5 depicts the future as a return to Eden. Just as God, in the beginning, created a paradise with a tree of life in it (Gen. 2:9; 3:22, 24), so too will the divinity create a second paradise with another tree of life (Rev. 22:2). And just as God, in the beginning, set a river in Eden (Gen. 2:10), so too will a river be set in the new Jerusalem of a new earth (Rev. 22:1). Furthermore, because early Christians thought of Jesus as bringing the eschatological renewal, they often likened his advent and its consequences to the creation of the world. Consider just three New Testament texts:

> EARLY CHRISTIANS, DRAWING UPON THE ESCHATO-LOGICAL EXPECTATIONS OF JUDAISM, IMAGINED THE BETTER WORLD OF THE FUTURE AS A RETURN TO THE BEGINNING: THE END WOULD BE PARADISE REGAINED.

- "The first man, Adam, became a living being; the last Adam became a life-giving spirit" (1 Cor. 15:45).
- "If anyone is in Christ, there is a new creation; everything old has passed away; see, everything has become new!" (2 Cor. 5:17).
- "He [Jesus] is the image of the invisible God, the firstborn of all creation; for in him all things in heaven and on earth were created. . . . He is the beginning, the firstborn from the dead . . ." (Col. 1:15-21).

In the light of passages such as these, very near to hand is the thought that the descent of the dove at Jesus' baptism, designed to trigger memories of Gen. 1:2, signified to readers steeped in Jewish Scripture and tradition that Jesus was the bringer of a new creation. If at the commencement of things the Spirit of God hovered over the face of the watery chaos, at the Messiah's advent the Spirit fluttered over the waters of the Jordan. In other words, when Jesus came into the world, a new age commenced, and God, through the Holy Spirit, renewed the great work of creation. (It is appropriate that, in Eastern Orthodox tradition, Gen. 1:1-13 is read for the Great Vespers on Epiphany.)

The divine voice of 3:17, which anticipates the voice of the transfiguration in 17:5, conflates two scriptural texts, Ps. 2:7 and Isa. 42:1 (which is formally quoted in 12:8). The result is that Jesus is revealed to the Baptist and perhaps to those standing by (it is not exactly clear who hears the voice) as the Son of God (cf. Ps. 2:7) and the suffering servant of Isaiah (Isa. 42:1; cf. Matt. 8:17; 12:18-21; 20:28; 26:28). Here "Son of God" refers first to Jesus' special relationship to God the Father (cf. 11:25-30). But one cannot give a simple or single definition to the title as it appears in Matthew, for its connotations vary from place to place. In 4:1-11, as in 2:15, it is, for example, associated with an Israel typology; and in 16:13-20 and 26:59-68 it is linked with Jesus' status as Davidic Messiah (cf. 2 Sam. 7:14; perhaps this is so also in 3:17, for Psalm 2 is a royal psalm).

Responding to the Text

Christians have often remembered Jesus' baptism in order to remember and interpret their own baptisms. Calvin wrote that Jesus "undertook baptism with us that the faithful might be more surely persuaded that they are engrafted into his body, buried with him in baptism, that they might rise again to newness of life." In one of Ephrem the Syrian's Hymns for Epiphany, we find the following: "The Spirit came down from on high and hallowed the waters by brooding over them. In the baptism of John, the Spirit passed by the rest and abode on the one (Jesus); but now the Spirit has descended and abides upon all that are born of the water. Out of all that John baptized, on only one did the Spirit dwell, but now the Spirit has flown and come down in order to dwell on the many; and as each one after another comes up from the water, they are loved and abide in God."

In analogous manner, Gregory of Nyssa, in "On the Baptism of Christ: A Sermon for the Day of Lights," speaks of Christian baptism as being in imitation of our Lord and teacher. That Jesus was baptized becomes an imperative for his followers. Gregory then goes on to insist that "there is certainly need of some manifest proof, by which we may recognize that we are new-born, discerning by clear tokens the new from the old." Despite Gregory's glorification of the ritual of baptism, he yet knows that it is empty without deeds of renewal, unless the old person disappears, to be replaced by another dressed in works of righteousness. "You see how Zacchaeus by the change of his life slew the publican, making fourfold restitution to those he had unjustly damaged, and the rest he divided with the poor—the treasure which he had before got by ill means from the poor he oppressed." Similarly, "Paul was a persecutor, but after the grace bestowed on him as an apostle, he bore the weight of fetters for Christ's sake, as an act of amending and repentance. . . ." These stand as examples: "Such ought you to be in your regeneration. So ought you to blot out your habits that tend to sin; so ought the children of God to have their manner of life, for after the grace bestowed we are all God's children, and thus we ought narrowly to examine our Father's characteristics, that by fashioning and framing ourselves to the likeness of our Father, we may appear true children of the one who calls us to the adoption according to grace." As John Climacus put it, "Repentance is the renewal of baptism and a contract for a second life."

The dramatic change baptism was thought to bring is strikingly represented in some of the depictions of Christian baptism in the Roman catacombs, on which the people being baptized are all depicted as children. It is even the case that some of the old icons of Jesus' baptism picture him as a child. The idea is that baptism is truly a new birth, a starting over. One recalls John 3, Jesus' dialogue with Nicodemus, where Jesus declares that one cannot see the kingdom of God without being born again or from above, a declaration Nicodemus naturally enough misunderstands to mean crawling back into the womb. Many early Christians, as we again know from the catacombs and their burials, counted their age from their baptism. There are burials with adult bones that declare the age of the interred to be in the single digits. One would be hard pressed to find better expression of the conviction that one's past is as nothing, knowing Christ everything (cf. Phil. 3:7-11).

The realization that baptism does not in itself save has been one of the reasons Jesus' baptism has been associated with his atoning death, the central saving event. Thus in the old icons the baptized Jesus stands in what appears to be a cave, which represents a grave. One might in this connection observe that, on the literary level of Matthew, Jesus is confessed as God's Son at both his baptism and crucifixion (3:17; 27:54). There is also the striking fact that Mark (in 10:38-39) and Luke (in

12:50) refer to Jesus' death as a baptism and that Paul (in Rom. 6:3) says that baptism into Christ is baptism into his death (cf. Col. 2:12). So a canonical interpretation of Matt. 3:13-17 might well wish to explore the relationship between Jesus' baptism and his death.

If the association between Jesus' baptism and ours has often been made, especially in Eastern churches, for which Epiphany was, next to Easter, the favored time for baptisms, interpreters have also done other things with our text. They have, for example, often set it within the wider context of salvation-history. One way of doing this has been to contrast Jesus' baptism with Adam's fall: the latter closed the heavens and let loose the wiles of the

A CANONICAL INTERPRETATION OF MATT. 3:13-17 MIGHT WELL WISH TO EXPLORE THE RELATIONSHIP BETWEEN JESUS' BAPTISM AND HIS DEATH.

devil; the former opened the heavens and trampled upon Satan. Also very common has been the cataloguing of biblical stories and miracles involving water, all of which are interpreted as foreshadowing Christ's descent into the Jordan. Paul himself, in 1 Cor. 10:1-5, already does this with Israel passing through the Red Sea (Exodus 14). Later interpreters have recalled Noah and his family being saved in the ark (Genesis 6–8; cf. 2 Pet. 3:21), Hagar's thirst for water (Genesis 16), Isaac digging wells in the desert (Gen. 26:18), Jacob meeting Rachel at a well (Genesis 29), Moses being borne in a little ark (Exod. 2:1-10), Joshua crossing the Jordan (Joshua 3), Elisha healing Naaman the Syrian in the Jordan (2 Kings 5), and so on. Many of the older liturgies—which also cite Ezek. 36:25 ("I will sprinkle clean water upon you, and you shall be clean from all your uncleannesses") as a prophecy of Christian baptism—make similar moves, and in our day such intertextual links would at least have the merit of helping our biblically challenged congregations to associate Scripture with Scripture and discourage us from isolating the New Testament from the Old.

Finally, the baptism of Jesus has frequently been understood as a pictorial depiction of the Trinity. Theodore of Mopsuestia said that "the Father was the testifier, the Son the one testified to, and the Holy Spirit the one who pointed out the one testified to." This way of looking at the baptism became a commonplace and thus appears in the old liturgies for Epiphany: "By thy baptism, O Lord, in the river Jordan, worship to the holy Trinity has made its appearance. For the voice of the Lord did come forth to you with the testimony, naming you the beloved Son; and the Spirit in the likeness of a dove, confirmed the truth of the word. Wherefore O Christ, glory to you, who did appear and light the world." A link between the baptism and the Trinity is suggested by Matthew's Gospel, for if near the beginning of the book there is a baptismal story in which the Father, the Son, and the Holy Spirit all appear, the Gospel ends with a triumphal declaration that speaks of baptism in the name of the Father, and of the Son, and of the Holy Spirit (28:16-20).

"Why are your waters troubled, O Jordan, and why do you turn backward, not pro-ceeding forward according to your natural flow? The Jordan answers, saying, 'I cannot bear a consuming fire. Thus do I marvel and tremble at your exceeding condescen-sion; for I am not accustomed to wash the pure. I have not learned to purify the sin-less, but to purify impure vessels'. . . . Let us believers thus cry unto him, saying, O God that has appeared for our salvation, glory to you."

FROM THE EASTERN LITURGY FOR THE FEAST OF THE DIVINE EPIPHANY

SECOND SUNDAY
AFTER THE EPIPHANY

JANUARY 20, 2002
SECOND SUNDAY IN ORDINARY TIME

REVISED COMMON	EPISCOPAL (BCP)	ROMAN CATHOLIC
Isa. 49:1-7	Isa. 49:1-7	Isa. 49:3, 5-6
Ps. 40:1-11	Ps. 40:1-10	Ps. 40:2, 4, 7-8, 8-9, 10
1 Cor. 1:1-9	1 Cor. 1:1-9	1 Cor. 1:1-3
John 1:29-42	John 1:29-41	John 1:29-34

L AST WEEK WE MEDITATED UPON Matthew's account of the baptism. This week we read John's version, which has its own special features. John's account and its context highlight the central role of human testimony in the divine economy. In the Fourth Gospel, Jesus' baptism comes to us solely through the testimony of the Baptist (John 1:32-34). This is then followed by John encouraging two of his own disciples to follow Jesus, after which one of those disciples tells Peter about Jesus. Jesus may be the light of the world (John 8:12; 9:5), but so are we (Matt. 5:14), and if our light is under a bushel, then so is his. His testimony comes through our testimony. The revelation of God in Christ is carried in us, earthen vessels.

FIRST READING
ISAIAH 49:1-7

Interpreting the Text

These verses make up the second of the so-called Servant Songs (see above, the First Reading for January 13). The passage has long confused commentators, because whereas, in chapter 42 the servant appears to be Israel and while in 49:3 the same identification seems to be made, otherwise in chap. 49 the servant sounds very much like an individual. In 49:5, moreover, the servant ministers to Israel and so cannot, it would seem, be identified with the nation. Some have solved the problem by excising "Israel" from 49:3 (without any support from the textual tradition). This, however, posits a consistency that may not be in the text: the servant may be a fluid figure, now Israel, now the prophet, now someone else. Perhaps we might even think of the servant as an office or vocation waiting to be filled.

One can also argue that the attempt to find consistency overlooks the larger narrative flow. In chap. 42 Israel the servant is called to its mission. But the people remain blind (42:19), obstinate, and unfaithful (chap. 48), so the mission has not been completed. It is in this context, then, that we find the next Servant Song, and it may be that, with Israel's failure, the role of servant is taken up by or opened up for an individual or a remnant within Israel, that is, by a representative. Maybe v. 3 even marks the moment in which the servant has become the embodiment of true Israel.

The new depiction of the servant's mission takes the form of a first-person call narrative reminiscent of Jeremiah's call (cf. v. 5 with Jer. 1:5), and there are additional parallels between Jeremiah and the servant (cf. 50:6-7 with Jer. 20:11; 53:7-8 with Jer. 11:19). No less striking are the parallels between the second Servant Song and the first and last songs, for example:

49:1: "Listen to me, O coastlands"
42:4: "the coastlands wait for his teaching"

49:6: "I will give you as a light to the nations"
42:6: "I have given you as a covenant to the people, a light to the nations"

49:7: "deeply despised, abhorred by the nations . . . kings shall stand up and see"
52:15 and 53:3: "kings shall shut their mouths . . . despised and rejected by others . . . he was despised, and we held him of no account"

The mission in chap. 49 remains the same as in 42, but the servant has become despised (49:4, 7; 53:3), and so the promise in 42:3 ("He will not grow faint or be crushed") has seemingly been undone. The future, however, will undo the present; the lowly servant will become exalted.

Responding to the Text

The metaphor of the servant's mouth as a "sharp sword" in v. 3 is memorable and was picked up by the author of the Apocalypse (1:16, "from his mouth came a sharp, two-edged sword"; 2:16, "make war against them with the sword of my mouth"; 19:15, "from his mouth comes a sharp, two-edged sword with which to strike down the nations"; 19:21, "killed . . . by the sword that came from his mouth"). The image, like that of speech as a polished arrow (see the end of v. 3), effectively communicates how powerful words can be, whether for ill or (as in the present case) for good. Hebrews 4:12 makes the point with reference to God's word this way: it is "living and active, sharper than any two-edged sword, piercing until it divides soul from spirit, joint from marrow; it is able to judge the thoughts and intentions of the heart." It is no wonder that John's Gospel exalts Jesus by calling him "the Word" (1:1). But because the forceful divine speech that comes through the prophet and can change things often stirs up opposition, the servant here takes solace in another metaphor: "In his quiver he hid me away." Those who speak the prophetic word encounter opposition, but they will not be alone.

The universalism of 49:1-7 is remarkable, given Israel's unhappy and needy state during the exile. One would expect the prophet's attention to be focused entirely on the unfortunate people of God. But the mission to the world does not wait until Israel has become secure. This is because that mission is grounded not in Israel's uncertain condition but in theology, in God's will for the world. Throughout Isaiah 40–55 the theme of God as creator is prominent, and this theme disallows exclusive focus upon Jacob or Israel. The God of Isaiah is the God of the whole creation, so redemption is incomplete until it embraces everyone. Once more then the season of Epiphany compels us to think outside ourselves, to contemplate God's intentions for the whole world, for all peoples. We are to learn the lesson of Jonah, which is that God's grace is neither intended for nor confined to ourselves alone.

THE GOD OF ISAIAH IS THE GOD OF THE WHOLE CREATION, SO REDEMPTION IS INCOMPLETE UNTIL IT EMBRACES EVERYONE. ONCE MORE THEN THE SEASON OF EPIPHANY COMPELS US TO THINK OUTSIDE OURSELVES, TO CONTEMPLATE GOD'S INTENTIONS FOR THE WHOLE WORLD, FOR ALL PEOPLES.

In v. 4 the servant confesses, "I have labored in vain, I have spent my strength for nothing and vanity," and in v. 7 we read that the servant is deeply despised, abhorred by the nations, and the slave of rulers. All this anticipates the final Servant Song in chaps. 52 and 53, in which the servant is marred in his appearance, stricken, crushed, wounded. Further, just as, in Isaiah 53, the servant is eventually vindicated (vv. 10-12), so is it in chap. 49. Verse 7 declares that rulers will prostrate themselves before the servant. We have here the typical biblical pattern of radical reversal—shame now, honor later. One thinks of Prov. 29:23 ("A person's pride will bring humiliation, but one who is lowly in spirit will obtain honor"), which has to do with this world, and of Luke 14:11 (those who humble themselves will be exalted) and Mark 10:31 (the last will be first), which have to do with the world to come. We may not understand why there is anomie and evil in the first place, why God is tardy to undo what God must hate, why "it is through many persecutions that we must enter the kingdom of God" (Acts 14:22); but because God is God, we know that the status quo, full of sin and sorrow, cannot endure forever.

The pattern, shame now, honor later, plays itself out above all in the life of Jesus, who took the form of a slave and humbled himself unto death—wherefore

God has highly exalted him (Phil. 2:6-9). It is altogether natural that Acts 13:47 quotes Isa. 49:6 as having been fulfilled in Jesus. His resurrection comes only after crucifixion, which is not the glorious death of a martyr met with heroic valor but a torment so frightful that he Jesus cries out that God has forsaken him. Before the resurrection, as Jesus hangs on a cross, a man of sorrows, acquainted with grief, his passivity is matched by God's passivity—so much so that the bystanders can jeer and proclaim God's indifference. God does indeed fight for the one who has not fought for himself—but only after he has suffered torment and death. The sequence is our hope. For fight as we might, for ourselves and for others, trouble and horror are all about us, which means that we must look to God to make things right, both in this world and in the world to come.

RESPONSIVE READING
PSALM 40:1–11 (RCL); 40:1–10 (BCP); 40:2, 4, 7-8, 8-9, 10 (RC)

Psalm 40:1-10 is an autobiographical reflection on the psalmist's past, a recounting of his own patient waiting on the Lord (cf. Pss. 25:3; 27:14; 37:34) and the Lord's faithful deliverance. Perhaps the speaker was near death. Verse 2 speaks of being drawn up from "the desolate pit," which may be a reference to the land of death, Sheol (cf. Pss. 30:3; 88:3-4). However that may be, the narrative passes beyond the individual to the communal. Verse 5 declares that "You have multiplied . . . your wondrous deeds and your thoughts toward us" (not "me"). This is probably a glance at the salvific events of Israel's history. And in vv. 9-10 the psalmist depicts himself in the assembly, making known God's righteousness to the whole gathering.

Verse 6 is surprising. A sacrificial offering would be the appropriate response to being delivered from evil, and one does not expect a rejection of sacrifice in a text used in the temple cult. So commentators often assume that we have here what we find also in Isa. 1:12-17; Hos. 6:6; Amos 5:21-24; and Mic. 6:8, namely, the conviction that what matters most of all is the good heart or obedience, and that religious ritual without service to God and neighbor is worse than no ritual at all (cf. Matt. 9:13; 12:7). But what is the meaning of the Hebrew, "but ears you have dug for me," which the NRSV translates as, "but you have given me an open ear"? Probably in mind is heeding God's word (cf. v. 8)—this is what God wants most of all, not empty sacrificial ritual.

Our psalm is taken up in Heb. 10:1-10, which identifies the psalmist with Jesus. (The New Testament also identifies Jesus as the speaker of other psalms, e.g., Psalms 2 [cf. Acts 13:33], 22 [cf. Mark 15:34], and 41 [cf. John 13:18], among others.) Hebrews uses Psalm 40 to interpret Christ's death as the last sac-

rifice: with it the sacrificial system is abolished. The pentateuchal sacrifices, con-
tinually offered year after year, did not make perfect those who drew near; otherwise those sacrifices would no longer have been needed (vv. 1-2). But when
Christ came, he did God's will, and "by that will we have been sanctified through
the offering of the body of Jesus Christ once for all" (Heb.10:10).

Second Reading
1 CORINTHIANS 1:1-9 (RCL, BCP); 1:1-3 (RC)

Interpreting the Text

Corinth is on the isthmus between mainland Greece and the Pelopon-
nesus, or the southern part of Greece. In the first century it was the crossroads of
the Mediterranean world, a bustling city that one recent writer has compared to
San Francisco in the days of the gold rush. Aelius Aristides, a Greek rhetorician
of the second century A.D., wrote that Corinth "receives all cities and sends them
off again and is a common refuge for all, like a kind of route or passage for all
humanity, no matter where one would travel, and it is a common city for all
Greeks, indeed as it were a metropolis and mother in this respect." Paul appears
to have wanted to make Corinth his base of operations. He began by seeking converts from the Jewish synagogue. But his success was with Gentiles (see Acts 18).
Although one often reads about the rampant immorality of Corinth, recent
scholarship has shown that the texts called upon to show this do not really do so.
On the other hand, the city was a hub through which much sea and land traffic
passed, and it is likely enough that Corinth accordingly had more than its quota
of adult entertainment for travelers away from the usual social bonds of home and
family.

Paul's letter to the Corinthians reveals a host of problems. Unlike Galatians,
however, which opens without compliments and moves as quickly as possible to
rebuke, 1 Corinthians begins with thanksgiving. Despite the difficulties Paul must
address, he is sincerely thankful for what has been worked among the Corinthians. Indeed, his words seem overdone—"in every way you have been enriched
in him, in speech and knowledge of every kind" (v. 5) and "you are not lacking
in any spiritual gift" (v. 6).

The salutation (vv. 1-9) subtly prepares in several ways for the following argument. Verse 1 characterizes Paul as an apostle "called" by the will of God, and
this implies grace (cf. Eph. 2:1-10). If some Corinthians have prided themselves
on their spiritual achievements, Paul is content to think of himself as in some
profound sense passive, an object of God's action—something he equally says of

the Corinthians in v. 9 ("by him [God] were you called"). He also, by naming Sosthenes (v. 1), modestly "puts in the same rank with himself one inferior to Apollos, for great was the interval between Paul and Sosthenes" (Chrysostom). Verse 2 presents Jesus as the unifying Lord of all Christians in every place—so how much more ought he to be the unifying Lord of the Christians in one place only? Verse 5, while conceding that the Corinthians have knowledge—something they so much value—grounds this knowledge "in him," that is, Jesus Christ. What the Corinthians have is a gift, not an achievement. There is, moreover, nothing in vv. 3-9 about human teachers or leaders, only God in Christ.

The focus on eschatology in vv. 7-9 is also important. Paul speaks of "the revelation of our Lord Jesus Christ" (v. 7) and of "the day of our Lord Jesus Christ" (v. 8). This takes the eyes of the Corinthians off of their own present, in which they confidently boast, and directs them to God's future. If some in the church believe that they already have all they want, that they have already become rich, that they already reign (4:8), then they have forgotten that eschatology qualifies and relativizes every human present.

Responding to the Text

Paul's attitude in 1 Cor. 1:1-9 is enviable. Before him lies the arduous task of a long letter in which he must correct many mistakes. There is much not to be thankful for—much rather to complain about. The Corinthian church is splintering into rival factions (chaps. 1-4). There is sexual immorality (chap. 5), and some believers are taking others to court (chap. 6). There is additionally confusion regarding both marriage (chap. 7) and the eating of certain foods (chaps. 8-11). Worst of all maybe, there are irregularities at worship, including abuses at the Lord's Supper (chaps. 12–14) and doctrinal confusion about the central tenet of Paul's proclamation, the resurrection (chap. 15). We would not blame the apostle if he were angry or confused or despairing.

What we see, instead, is someone giving thanks. It does not seem to be just rhetorical posturing. Paul appears truly grateful for what has been accomplished among the Corinthians. We should remember that this is the same person who wrote Philippians, in which a prisoner facing the prospect of death goes on and on about rejoicing. The apostle really had learned not just to be content but profoundly joyful in all things. It is presumably such joy and equanimity that move him to open his letter with thanksgiving, to see the good despite the bad, and that further allow him to rebuke his Corinthian converts not as enemies but as children.

Paul's thankful heart is clearly grounded in at least two theological convictions. The first is his faith in an active God who loves human beings. This love Paul sees on display above all in the death and resurrection of Jesus, but also in his own life as a missionary and in the lives of his converts. The second conviction behind what we might call Paul's optimism is that the future belongs to God and will bring to completion what has already been wrought in Jesus Christ. Note how the thanksgiving in 1 Cor. 1:4-9 moves toward eschatology. Paul believes that the present is not the end, that the future is God's future and hence must bring something better. He lives toward the eschaton, which will make the problems of this present time appear as nothing (cf. Rom. 8:18). Paul would have agreed with what Dostoevski memorably said at one point in *The Brothers Karamazov:* "I trust that the wounds will heal, the scars will vanish, that the sorry and ridiculous spectacle of humanity's disagreements and clashes will disappear like a pitiful mirage, like the sordid invention of a puny, microscopic Euclidean, human brain, and that, in the end, in the universal finale, at the moment universal harmony is achieved, something so magnificent will take place that it will satisfy every human heart, allay all indignation, pay for all human crimes, for all the blood we have shed, and enable everyone not only to forgive everything but also to justify everything that has happened to people." In short, Paul sees a God who has acted in the past in Jesus Christ, a God who acts in lives in the present, and a God who will act to redeem the world in the future, when God will be all in all (Rom. 15:28).

THE THANKSGIVING IN 1 COR. 1:4-9 MOVES TOWARD ESCHATOLOGY. PAUL BELIEVES THAT THE PRESENT IS NOT THE END, THAT THE FUTURE IS GOD'S FUTURE AND HENCE MUST BRING SOMETHING BETTER. HE LIVES TOWARD THE ESCHATON.

THE GOSPEL

JOHN 1:29-42 (RCL); 1:29-41 (BCP); 1:29-34 (RC)

Interpreting the Text

Following the prologue (John 1:1-8), which refers to John the Baptist (vv. 6-8), the Fourth Evangelist recounts three episodes involving John that take place on successive days (see vv. 29, 35). The first episode has to do with the Baptist's testimony about himself, that he is not the Messiah, not Elijah, and not "the prophet," but rather only "the voice of one crying out in the wilderness" (Isa. 40:3) who comes before the incomparably greater Word (vv. 19-28). The second episode is John's identification of the coming one with Jesus (vv. 29-34). The third is the story of two of John's disciples leaving him to follow Jesus, from which we learn how Peter met his Lord (vv. 35-42).

John is quizzed in vv. 19-28 by priests and Levites from Jerusalem, experts in purification rites. They seem to approach him with respect, and they do not dispute his answer—which stands in stark contrast to how Jesus is treated by the religious authorities (cf. 5:30-47, where Jesus refers to our episode). John makes three denials. The first is that he is the Messiah, the eschatological Davidic king (cf. the denials in Luke 3:15; Acts 13:25; Justin Martyr, *Dialogue* 88). The second disclaimer is that he is Elijah. There was in Jewish circles an expectation that Elijah would come again (cf. Sir. 48:10; Mark 9:11; *b. 'Erubim* 43a-b). The expectation was based on Mal. 3:23-24, the last two verses in the Old Testament: they proclaim that the prophet Elijah will come before the great and terrible day of the Lord and turn the hearts of parents to their children and the hearts of children to their parents.

John makes yet a third denial, that he is "the prophet." Now the Baptist surely regarded himself as a prophet, but as Origen observed, there is a definite article in the Greek: "Perhaps John would have answered 'Yes' if they had put the question to him without the article, for he was not ignorant that he was a prophet" (cf. Mark 11:32). To what then does the definite article point? Origen and most commentators down through the ages have thought of Deut. 18:15, 18, which promises that God will raise up a prophet like Moses. As Eusebius put it, "John, confessing what was true, did not deny being a prophet, for he was one; but denied that he was the prophet signified by Moses." The expectation of an eschatological prophet like Moses was apparently a lively expectation in antiquity. The Dead Sea Scrolls refer Deut. 18:18 to an eschatological individual (*4QTestimonia*), and Josephus knows of certain prophetic leaders who apparently were thought of in Mosaic terms (see, e.g., *Antiquities* 18.85-87, which tells of the Samaritan who claimed he would recover the sacred vessels that Moses had deposited; 20.97-99, which tells about Theudas, who tried to part the Jordan in imitation of Moses' successor, Joshua; and 20.169-72, which tells of the would-be ruler from Egypt who led his followers from the desert to the Mount of Olives; cf. Acts 21:38).

John's three denials correspond to three Christian affirmations, for believers held Jesus to be the Davidic Messiah, to be like Elijah, and to be the prophet like Moses. John himself has just called Jesus "Christ" (v. 17), and later in our chapter Andrew confesses, "We have found the Messiah" (v. 41), so John's denial of that title is necessary. His denial that he is Elijah has long troubled exegetes, because Matt. 11:14 clearly identifies John with Elijah (cf. Matt. 17:12; Mark 9:13; also Luke 1:17: John will come "in the spirit and power of Elijah"; recall further that John's garments are those

> JOHN'S THREE DENIALS CORRESPOND TO THREE CHRISTIAN AFFIRMATIONS, FOR BELIEVERS HELD JESUS TO BE THE DAVIDIC MESSIAH, TO BE LIKE ELIJAH, AND TO BE THE PROPHET LIKE MOSES.

of Elijah [cf. Mark 1:6 with 2 Kings 1:8]). But whatever one makes of that tension, the Gospels relate that Jesus' ministry reminded some people of the Tishbite (see Mark 6:14-16; 8:27-30). Certainly Jesus himself is sometimes very much like Elijah in the Gospels. In the call stories of Peter and Andrew and James and John, for example, Jesus acts like Elijah (see pp.114-15).

We also know that early Christians thought of Jesus as the prophet like Moses promised in Deut. 18:15, 18. This is clear not only from the multitudinous parallels between the two figures in the Gospels (see above), but also by the clear statement in Acts 3:22-23. As for John's Gospel, Jesus is throughout clearly both like Moses (as in 3:14) as well as greater than Moses (as in 1:17); and when Jesus is called "the prophet" in John 6:14, the Mosaic context implies that here the prophet like Moses is meant (cf. 7:40). When John 1:45 has Philip say, "We have found him about whom Moses in the law and also the prophets wrote," an allusion to Deut. 18:15, 18 is likely. So what John denies is true of himself, the reader will affirm as being true of Jesus.

In vv. 29-34 (which repeats so much of the previous verses) we move from the vague prophecy of a future figure to the identification of that figure with the concrete, historical person Jesus. The narrative assumes a baptismal narrative, but the baptism itself is not recounted. This is not that much different from the Synoptics, for while they tell of a few things that happened immediately before and after the baptism, they do not recount the baptism itself. Also in line with the Synoptics are both the confession of Jesus as "the Son of God" and the Spirit descending like a dove. But John's confession that Jesus is "the Lamb of God who takes away the sin of the world" has no parallel in the Synoptic baptismal narratives. There is continuity even here, however. For we should probably relate the title to Isa. 53:7, where the suffering servant is "like a lamb," and the divine voice at the baptism in the Synoptics alludes to Isa. 42:1 and so also identifies Jesus with Isaiah's servant. (But one should not overlook the possibility that "the Lamb of God" additionally recalls the Passover lamb, even though it was not an atoning sacrifice. For John speaks often of Passover [2:13, 23; 6:4; 11:55; et al.], and in his Gospel Jesus dies as the Passover lamb is being sacrificed [cf. 18:28; 19:14, 31], while the evangelist tells us that not one of Jesus' bones is broken [19:34-36], and the pentateuchal legislation prohibits breaking the bones of the paschal lamb [Exod. 12:46; Num. 9:12].)

"Lamb of God" is one of several christological concepts in 1:19-42. Jesus is also "the Son of God" in v. 34, "rabbi" or "teacher" in v. 38, and the Messiah in v. 41. Earlier in this chapter he is the divine Logos (1:1), and later he is the one written about in Moses and the prophets (v. 45), the Messiah (v. 41), the king of Israel (v. 49), and the Son of Man (v. 51). Obviously one of John's purposes in his opening chapter is to give expression to the fullness of Jesus' person through a fullness of christological expressions. One is reminded of some later Jewish texts that glorify God by piling up as many titles as possible (cf. already Isa. 9:6, where a future ruler is given four different titles).

Just as vv. 29-34 repeat much of vv. 19-28, so vv. 35-42 begin with John reiterating the confession he made in v. 29: "Look, here is the Lamb of God!" (v. 36).

But from this point on John fades into the background. He appears in a dialogue in 3:25-30 and is mentioned also later in the Gospel (4:1; 5:33, 36; 10:40-41), but he is no longer a major actor in the narrative. Some of the later references, like so much of chap. 1, make the most sense if there were, in the evangelist's time, people who continued to believe in John the Baptist but not Jesus (see esp. 1:7-8, 30; 3:30; 5:36; 10:41; people claiming John to be the Messiah appear in the *Pseudo-Clementine Recognitions* 1:54, 60, which may here preserve a second century source).

One of the two disciples of John who, with his blessing, decide to follow Jesus, is Andrew (v. 40). After Andrew introduces his brother, Simon, to Jesus, Jesus looks at him (cf. v. 36) and changes his name to "Cephas," an Aramaic word that means "rock" and comes into Greek as "Peter" (cf. *petros,* the Greek for "rock"). The reason for the name change is not given. Nothing is said here about Peter's character (which John nowhere develops), nor do we have what we find in Matthew 16, where the granting of the name is in response to Peter's confession of Jesus' messiahship and marks the founding of the church. John, like Mark 3:16, leaves the nickname unexplained. But if we leave John's narrative and ask about the history behind it, it is interesting that the other two disciples to get nicknames from Jesus are James and John, "the sons of thunder" (Mark 2:17), and that there are traditions in the Synoptics placing these two and Peter within an inner circle close to Jesus (Mark 5:37; 9:2; 14:33).

Responding to the Text

The three episodes in 1:19-42 create a pattern for discipleship that plays out the sequence in 1:6-8: self-denial, testimony, faith in Christ. The whole section begins with self-denial, with John recognizing that he is not the answer to the questions that the people are asking. John humbly keeps his proper place. He is subordinate to another (v. 27). The next day, self-denial gives way to confession. John recognizes someone else as the answer to the people's questions (vv. 29-34). Finally, confession leads to the hard road of discipleship (vv. 35-42). The right religious

> THE THREE EPISODES IN JOHN 1:19-42 CREATE A PATTERN FOR DISCIPLESHIP THAT PLAYS OUT THE SEQUENCE IN 1:6-8: SELF-DENIAL, TESTIMONY, FAITH IN CHRIST.

confession is no end in itself but only the beginning of a long education whose paths can at this point in no way be anticipated.

The very first words of Jesus in our Gospel appear in v. 38, where he asks two disciples of the Baptist, "What are you looking for?" The Greek is *ti zēteite,* literally: "What do you seek?" The question hangs over all of the Gospel, as well as over all of our lives (cf. John 20:15, where the risen Jesus asks Mary Magdalene, "Whom do you seek?"). In John there are those who seek their own glory (5:30; 7:18), some who seek Jesus because he does miracles (6:24, 26), and some who seek the destruction of Jesus because they perceive him as a threat (5:18; 7:1; 8:37; 18:4). But there are also people who are seeking for meaning, for something more in their lives—people such as the disciples in John 1, Nicodemus in John 3, and the woman at the well in John 4. All these are on a religious quest for the truth. In John they seek and find (cf. Matt. 7:7-11).

We do not have to go seeking for what is in front of our faces. God is no such thing. The source of our meaning rather remains hidden. As Isaiah put it, in a verse Luther especially liked, "Truly, you are a God who hides yourself" (45:15). Much in the world points us to God, and much in the world points us away from God—so much so that, as Pascal said, it is inconceivable that God exists, and it is inconceivable that God does not exist. Pascal himself reflected on this paradox and decided that, were God wholly hidden, we would have no hope, but that if God were wholly revealed, we would be insensible to our own corrupt natures. Before Pascal, Hugh of Saint Victor contemplated the same problem and decided that, if God were so openly manifest as to disallow all doubt, there would be no merit in faith, a virtue God wishes to cultivate in us. God remains hidden that faith might be proved and long for more, and God is sufficiently revealed so that unbelief does not rule all. One might also ask whether the finite can ever see more than shadows of fragments of the Infinite. But however one sorts out this profound issue, why it is that the causes of faith and unbelief are so finely balanced, the hiddenness of the truth means at least two things. First, we are required to quest, to seek that we might find. And God cannot want our search to be easy; otherwise the world would have a wholly different character. Second, we are required to be charitable to all people, because what we believe is in no way obvious. Here is one point at which John's Gospel is deficient, because it too readily ascribes ill will to those the author reckons to be wrong.

The second sentence Jesus utters in John—this time not a question but an imperative—is equally short and equally resonant: "Come and see" (v. 39; cf. 1:46; 11:34). Origen took the twin words to refer to action and contemplation, and ecclesiastical exegetes have often followed him. (The same two concepts are regularly associated also with Mary and Martha of Luke 10.) While this reads too much into the line, both "come" and "see" can indeed be loaded terms in John. The latter is often close to "experience" (cf. 3:3, 36; 8:51) or "truly understand," as at the end of chap. 1, where Jesus tells Nathaniel that he will "see" the angels ascending and descending upon the Son of man. This refers not to a literal vision but to the realization that Jesus is the full revelation of God, the locus at which heaven meets the earth. (In Jewish tradition the angels ascended and descended upon Jacob [Genesis 28] because they recognized his sleeping face as the same as the face on the throne of God in heaven.)

"Come" is also an important term. Not only does Jesus often speak of his having "come" into the world (3:19; 5:43, et al.) and likewise of his "coming" again

(14:3, 28, et al.), but in 7:37 Jesus declares, "Let anyone who is thirsty come to me," and in 6:65, "No one can come to me unless it is granted by the Father." In these two places, "come" connotes conversion. So the "Come and see!" of 1:39 is naturally read as typological: it opens itself up as an invitation to find God in Christ, to understand the identity of Jesus and explore what that identity means for life.

A theological interpretation may also legitimately latch onto the verb repeated in vv. 38 and 39, *menei,* which the NRSV translates with "staying" the first two times it appears and by "remained" the third time. Jesus' word "remains" in believers (5:38); those who eat and drink Jesus' body and blood "remain" in him (6:56); disciples are to "remain" in Jesus' word (8:31); the Father "remains" in the Son (14:10); and the Spirit "remains" with the disciples (14:17). "Remain" is also the key verb in the discourse of Jesus as the true vine (15:1-17—vv. 4, 5, 6, 7, 9, 10, 16). In John "to remain" with Jesus is to be united with him, to do his words and to abide in his love.

> THE "COME AND SEE!" OF 1:39 OPENS ITSELF UP AS AN INVITATION TO FIND GOD IN CHRIST, TO UNDERSTAND THE IDENTITY OF JESUS AND EXPLORE WHAT THAT IDENTITY MEANS FOR LIFE.

One of the more interesting aspects of 1:29-42 is its implicit missionary outlook. John the Baptist does not keep his experience of Jesus to himself but tells others of it (1:34). His witness in turn leads some to find Jesus (1:35-37). And it is the testimony of Andrew that brings Jesus and Peter together (1:41-42). In John 1 Jesus is, so to speak, passed from person to person. The same happens elsewhere in John, as in 4:29-30, where the Samaritan woman asks others to "come and see," and in 20:18, where Mary Magdalene tells the disciples about the risen Lord. So the theme of witnessing, so prominent at the end of the Gospel (20:19-23, 30-31), is already prominent at the beginning. Jesus may be the revelation of God, but that revelation, once given, depends on human messengers who testify to what they have themselves experienced.

> *"This, then, is how from the beginning God has spoken with the few—occasionally, darkly, and in secret. If we study the Scriptures, we shall find that God hardly ever speaks to a crowd of people. Rather, when God's revelation comes, God is revealed not to nations and people but to individuals, or at most to a few, and to them when they were separated from the common ways of people by the silence of the night, maybe, or in the fields, or in deserts and mountains. In this way God spoke with Noah, with Abraham, with Isaac, with Jacob, with Moses, with Samuel, with David, and with all the prophets."*
>
> HUGH OF SAINT VICTOR

THIRD SUNDAY AFTER THE EPIPHANY

JANUARY 27, 2002
THIRD SUNDAY IN ORDINARY TIME; PROPER 3

REVISED COMMON	EPISCOPAL (BCP)	ROMAN CATHOLIC
Isa. 9:1-4	Amos 3:1-8	Isa. 9:1b-4
		(Heb. Bible 8:23b—9:3)
Ps. 27:1, 4-9	Ps. 139:1-17	Ps. 27:1, 4, 13-14
	or 139:1-11	
1 Cor. 1:10-18	1 Cor. 1:10-17	1 Cor. 1:10-13, 17
Matt. 4:12-23	Matt. 4:12-23	Matt. 4:12-23 (4:12-17)

THE LAST TWO SUNDAYS HAVE REFLECTED upon the baptism of Jesus. Today, however, the light of the world moves from the Jordan out into the world, and we learn that command follows illumination. The baptized Jesus demands repentance and calls people to the hard road of discipleship (Matt. 4:17-22). But grace has not gone away. The disciples follow Jesus, which means that he is with them and that we are not alone. The commanding Jesus, moreover, is the healing Jesus (Matt. 4:23); and he is the illumination that brings joy (Isa. 9:2-3) as well as the crucified whose folly is power (1 Cor. 1:17).

FIRST READING
ISAIAH 9:1-4 (RCL); 9:1b-4 (HEB. BIBLE 8:23b—9:3) (RC)

Interpreting the Text

The original setting of this oracle is disputed, some supposing it to be postexilic. But the usual view is that the background is the Assyrian conquest in the eighth century B.C. The darkness, gloom, distress, and contempt of v. 1 and the darkness of v. 2 refer to the terrible state of things after the Northern Kingdom was annexed by Tiglath-pileser. In this context the prophet speaks of sudden victory, of the foreign oppression passing away. Light and joy have indeed come (vv. 2-3), and the yoke and rod of Israel's oppressor have been broken (v. 4).

Commentators have often tried to associate the oracle with this or that historical figure. Maybe our prophet was heartened by the accession of a native king, such as Hezekiah, or by some other encouraging political event (our verses can be understood as a succession oracle full of overblown royal rhetoric). But that can only be speculation. Moreover, and despite the perfect tenses ("has shined," etc.), within its canonical context Isaiah 9 does not celebrate an expectation that has already been realized. The text rather invites an eschatological interpretation. This is of course how Christians have read it when they have thought of its fulfillment in Jesus. Calvin, in his commentary on Matt. 4:13-16, argues that nothing from the Old Testament can reasonably be thought of as fulfilling Isaiah's oracle (and certainly 9:6-7 transcends anything history has seen). He then goes on to contend that the beginning of the "light, its dawning as it were, came at the return of the people from Babylon. At length the fullness of its splendor emerged with Christ the Sun of righteousness, who by his coming utterly scattered the shadows of death."

The rhetorical power of Isa. 9:1-4 derives from its set of strong contrasts. In v. 1 gloom and anguish are contrasted with glory. In v. 2, darkness and light are contrasted—indeed "deep darkness" and "a great light." (Jerome, offering a christological interpretation, commented: "Not a faint light, as the light of the prophets, but a great light, as of him who in the Gospel says, 'I am the light of the world.'") In v. 4 we first see a yoke, then a bar, then a rod—all strong things—and then we see them broken.

Responding to the Text

Christians will respond to Isa. 9:1-4 by reflecting on its transformation in Matt. 4:13-16. Matthew, after remarking upon Jesus' move to Galilee, to the region of Zebulon and Naphtali, cites Isaiah's prophecy. He must have understood the promised child of Isa. 9:6-7 to be Jesus, even though he does not cite that part of the oracle. Obviously he has turned a prophecy about literal destruction and political plight into a text about moral and spiritual darkness, or as Chrysostom had it, "error and ungodliness." Darkness is a symbol of moral and spiritual bankruptcy throughout the New Testament (Luke 1:79; Rom. 2:19; 1 Pet. 2:9; et al.). Moreover, the identity of Jesus as light also appears in John 1:9; 3:19; 8:12; 9:5; and 12:35, 46.

Theophylact, who instead equated the light with the gospel, fittingly observed: "The light has dawned on us, for we were not seeking it, but it appeared to us as if it were pursuing us." Theophylact had read Chrysostom, who similarly wrote: "Implying that they did not of themselves seek and find, but that God was shown from above, he [Matthew] says, 'Light has dawned,' that is, the light of itself sprang up and shone forth; it was not that they first ran to the light. . . . For as persons not even knowing where to put a step forward, so they sat, overtaken by the darkness, not being able so much as to stand anymore."

The Christian imagination has speculated much about light. It has, for example, often distinguished between the created light of day and the uncreated light of Christ. The former is only a sign, the material underside of the eternal light beheld at the transfiguration by three whose eyes for a moment shed their scales. (As Eastern Christian tradition teaches, it was not Jesus, the ever-luminous, who changed, but his disciples, who were otherwise ever-blind.) This is the nimbus or angelic light that appears in stories about St. Francis of Assisi, Seraphim of Serov, and so many other saints. It is the light of the New Jerusalem, which has no need of sun or moon to shine upon it, for the glory of God is its light, and its lamp is the Lamb. It is this supernatural, mystical light that the Hesychast mystics of Byzantium longed to behold, and not just in the world to come. As Boethius wrote of his own experience, the one who "has seen this light will not call the sunbeam bright."

But the New Testament knows that the longing of Boethius and of the Hesychasts is not shared by all. As John 3:19 has it, when the light came into the world, people loved darkness rather than the light because their deeds were evil. And the *Didascalia*, an early church order, when citing Matt. 4:16, says that the people were surrounded by darkness precisely because they were blind, that is, had closed their eyes. Now we are wont to think of ourselves, because we are in the church, as children of the light who walk in the light (Eph. 5:8). But if we are candid, the light of Christ often hurts our eyes. When it beckons us to the uncomfortable tasks of the Gospel, we shrink back, taking solace in our confession while our deeds trumpet our hypocrisy. Isn't today's proclamation of Christ as the great light an opportunity to ask whether we ourselves do not often prefer to sit in darkness? Christ brings the hidden things to light, and we all have things to hide.

> IF WE ARE CANDID, THE LIGHT OF CHRIST OFTEN HURTS OUR EYES. ISN'T TODAY'S PROCLAMATION OF CHRIST AS THE GREAT LIGHT AN OPPORTUNITY TO ASK WHETHER WE OURSELVES DO NOT OFTEN PREFER TO SIT IN DARKNESS?

Matthew's passage about the light dawning is followed immediately by Jesus calling for repentance (4:17) and then in turn by his calling four men to leave work and family (4:18-22). The light that consoles and rescues is equally the light that demands, and if we take away from Isaiah's prophecy nothing but consolation, perhaps we have not heard what we need to.

AMOS 3:1-8 (BCP)

Interpreting the Text

Amos is traditionally dated to the middle of the eighth century, to the reign of Jeroboam II. It was a time of relative prosperity and peace, a time of military confidence when many enjoyed wealth and leisure. Religion also prospered, and people understood their good times as God's reward. But Amos is a book of judgment, and the reason is that the religion of the day did not move enough people to share their good fortune with others. There was immorality and commercial corruption, and the poor suffered injustices. So Amos sounds a discordant note in the midst of affluence and happiness. He proclaims the Day of the Lord, that it will be darkness, not light (Amos probably thought of the Assyrians invading). Israel's only hope is immediate and sincere repentance.

Amos 3:1-8 contains an oracle against Israel. The earlier oracles are all against Israel's neighbors, and they are the foil for what follows: Amos declares that Israel's closeness to God entails special responsibility, more than any other nation (v. 2). That is, here Israel's election (the Hebrew translated "have known" is elsewhere used of marital relations) is not comfort but accountability. The point is underlined through a series of rhetorical questions that have their climax in v. 8, which declares the prophet's authority. The prophet must prophesy because the Lord has spoken.

Responding to the Text

There are at least two themes that emerge from this text. One is the accountability of those who have been given much. This idea also serves as the conclusion of a parable in Luke 12:48: "The one who did not know and did what deserved a beating will receive a light beating. From everyone to whom much has been given, much will be required; and from the one to whom much has been entrusted, even more will be demanded." In Amos the principle is applied to Israel, but Luke applies it equally to the followers of Jesus, which means the church, and especially those in positions of leadership and with special gifts. The application should be obvious; but criticism of others (cf. Amos 1–2) as well as a doctrine of election (cf. Amos 3:2) readily lead to self-satisfaction. They are thus ideas fraught with moral peril. The former tends to nourish complacency—censure of our enemies always makes us feel better about ourselves—while the latter can beget feelings of superiority. Amos and Jesus, however, although they can censure outsiders and hold to Israel's election, know well the illusions those things can foster. This is why Amos in Amos 3–9 and Jesus throughout the Gospels tell insiders to reckon themselves as outsiders, to worry that the judgment of God will fall upon them, even though they belong to the chosen people. There cannot be any self-satisfaction over the condemnation of others. God's judgement is impartial and comes upon all, whether inside or outside Israel or the church. The author of 1 Peter well understood this when he wrote that judgement begins with the household of God (4:17).

A second theme emerges from Amos 3:6, which states that if evil befalls a city, then the Lord has done it. Similar sentiments are expressed elsewhere in the Old Testament (e.g., Job 2:10; Isa. 45:7; Lam. 3:38; cf. Deut. 32:39; 1 Sam. 2:6-7). It is very hard to know what to make of these texts. Most of us nowadays would probably be happier with Homer's *Odyssey,* in which Zeus says at one point, "My word, how mortals take the gods to task! All their afflictions come from us, we hear. And what of their own failings? Greed and folly double the suffering in the lot of humanity," or with Plato, who wrote that "of the good things God and no other must be described as the cause, but of the evil things we must look for many different causes, only not God" (*Republic* 379C). Without presuming to enter into the metaphysical issues, perhaps it can be said that we too readily identify all judgment with evil, just as we equate goodness with niceness. Such equations, however, are shallow. Certainly both Testaments depict the good God as one who demands justice and so must take sides, which means not being perceived by everyone as particularly nice. In the end, we would do well not to exorcise the divine judgment by appealing to the divine goodness.

> AMOS IN AMOS 3–9 AND JESUS THROUGHOUT THE GOSPELS TELL INSIDERS TO RECKON THEMSELVES AS OUTSIDERS, TO WORRY THAT THE JUDGMENT OF GOD WILL FALL UPON THEM, EVEN THOUGH THEY BELONG TO THE CHOSEN PEOPLE.

RESPONSIVE READING
PSALM 27:1, 4-9 (RCL); 27:1, 4, 13-14 (RC)

This psalm falls into three parts. Verses 1-6 proclaim the psalmist's firm trust in God, who is light and salvation (the two words are here nearly synonymous). Verses 7-12 are a prayer for one who has lost father and mother (v. 10; is this just a poetic way of expressing isolation?) and been falsely accused (v. 12; cf. vv. 2, 3, 6). Finally, vv. 13-14—the second of which could be a temple priest's encouragement for the speaker—are an expression of confidence: the prayer will be answered because the Lord is good.

Psalm 27 is remarkable for its declaration of faith despite difficult circumstances. The speaker is in dire straits and can yet declare, "My heart shall not fear" and "I will be confident" (v. 3); and toward the end we read, "I believe" (v. 13).

Such faith is implicitly contrasted not with outright unbelief—hardly our usual temptation—but with fear: "Whom shall I fear?" (v. 1; cf. Mark 5:36: "Do not fear, only believe"). So Psalm 27 invites reflection on the relationship between faith and fear. By imagining the situation of our psalmist who, although threatened by violence (v. 12), yet eschewed fear and stood steadfast in faith in God's goodness, perhaps we can gain some inspiration for our own lives, when we become anxious over far less. Our fight against fear and anxiety should be directed not by Stoicism or commonsense reflections—"What good is worrying?"—but by faith in the God who loves us. We are to be like the troubled child who trusts mother when she says, "Don't be afraid, everything will be OK."

PSALM 139:1-17 or 139:1-11 (BCP)

The last part of Psalm 139 is a prayer for deliverance from the wicked (vv. 19-24). This prayer is prepared for by a lengthy and poetic declaration of God's unsurpassed knowledge (vv. 1-6), of God's presence everywhere (vv. 7-12), and of God's knowledge of the psalmist in particular (vv. 13-16).

The psalm has such majestic power because it takes ideas that can be discussed abstractly as doctrines—God as omniscient, God as omnipresent, and God as creator—and thoroughly personalizes them. That is, Psalm 139 is not about God and the world but about God and the psalmist. God's omniscience means, "You are acquainted with all my ways" (v. 3). God's omnipresence means, "Where can I flee from your presence?" (v. 7). God's status as creator means, "You knit me together in my mother's womb" (v. 13). The intense personal focus means that knowledge of God is knowledge of the self. The self is utterly dependent on God for its origin and its continued existence: it has done and will do nothing apart from the creator.

The psalmist's overwhelming sense of dependency on the divine presence is particularly difficult for us to retrieve in our current culture. It's not just that science has seemingly left little for God to do, but we are surrounded by all sorts of big institutions that function without much use for religion—big business, big education, big media, big entertainment, and of course big government. Up against these giants, the church seems rather puny. But we must nonetheless do our best to keep our people from losing their spiritual sense and intuition. Perhaps we shall not often feel as did the writer of Psalm 139; but when we do, we need to put the experience into well-chosen words, so that we can encourage one another with a faith like that expressed in Psalm 139.

1 CORINTHIANS 1:10-18 (RCL); 1:10-17 (BCP); 1:10-13, 17 (RC)

Interpreting the Text

Paul founded the church in Corinth on his so-called second missionary journey (see Acts 18:1-18; A.D. 49 or 50). After spending two years there, he moved on. Sometime thereafter he wrote the Corinthians a letter, now lost (see 1 Cor. 5:9). The Corinthians in turn wrote a letter to Paul, asking many questions (see 1 Cor. 7:1, 25; 8:1; 12:1; 16:1). It was after receiving this letter and news from "Chloe's people" (1 Cor. 1:11; 16:17; we otherwise know nothing of Chloe) that the apostle then sent 1 Corinthians. Among the many problems the letter deals with is a reported factionalism. Indeed, the first four chapters of 1 Corinthians are largely aimed at addressing this problem. The church, outwardly united, was inwardly divided. Apollos (see Acts 18:24-28) had visited there, and perhaps also Peter, and some people seem to have been more taken with them than with Paul. In any event, the congregation had fallen into groups who thought of themselves as aligned with this leader as opposed to that leader. There were smaller congregations within the larger congregation. Perhaps indeed there were several house-churches, each developing its own identity.

From what Paul says in 1 Corinthians, one cannot outline the beliefs of the different groups (although some identify the Apollos party with people who treasured Alexandrian-like wisdom and rhetoric [cf. Acts 18:24-25], the Peter party with Corinthians attracted to some form of Jewish Christianity [cf. Galatians 2], and the Christ party [v. 12]—if it is not a rhetorical creation of Paul—with people who thought themselves above earthly life [cf. 1 Cor. 7:1] and/or hoped for immortality instead of physical resurrection from the dead [cf. 1 Corinthians 15]). But Paul seems much more concerned with the spirit of division than with party doctrine—certainly he nowhere attacks the teaching of Peter or Apollos—which implies that the problem, at least when 1 Corinthians was written, was less doctrinal than social. Many of the Corinthians probably had Christ but little else in common.

Paul's strategy, which kindly avoids naming offending Corinthians, is to highlight the unity that has not yet been destroyed by the evolving diversity, and he finds it in the cross of the one Christ, who is not cut in pieces (cf. v. 13). Paul even goes so far as to denigrate his own missionary speech, saying that it was not with eloquent wisdom; that is, he invites the Corinthians to recall that he effaced himself even in the act of preaching to them (cf. v. 17). Paul wants the Corinthians to see beyond himself and others to the God who sent Apollos and Peter and himself. His eloquent defense of his ineloquence aims to achieve what we all know from experience, that great good can come when people are "united in the same mind and the same purpose" (v. 10).

Recent scholarship has come to the view that the slogans, "I am of Paul," "I am of Apollos," "I am of Cephas," and "I am of Christ," were probably not self-designations of the various groups. Rather, the formula, personal pronoun + a form of "to be" + proper name in the genitive was usual when describing children or slaves—such people were defined in terms of their parents or masters. So Paul's language here may be a form of mockery. He may have been implying that the Corinthians were acting like slaves or children.

Responding to the Text

The cult of personality does not just dominate the worlds of sports and entertainment; it also clearly dominates our churches. Many of us attend a church or leave it precisely because of the personality and talents of the senior minister. What else could one expect? Like is attracted to like, as we see during every social hour after church. So we all naturally seek out a leader who sees things as we see them; and when the leader sees things differently, it is time to move on. This is how it works in all other areas of life. When we do not have what we want, we change the channel, we buy a new car, we get a new job. We get what pleases us.

Paul, however, has a vision of the Christian community that somehow looks beyond the dominant personalities and what pleases us in particular. This all but impossible way of seeing, which involves commitment to a group even when its leaders change, requires that we think of ourselves as serving Christ's community, not of Christ's community serving us.

In thinking about Paul's remarks in 1 Corinthians 1, we should remember that they are about division, not diversity. Paul nowhere demands homogeneity. In fact, one of the great contributions of 1 Corinthians to ecclesiology is the analogy of church to body in chap. 12. The apostle recognizes that people are different and have different gifts. He does not plead for uniformity but for unity. Hands are different from feet, but the two work together, and when one suffers, all suffer together. In fact, the church is for Paul precisely marked by its inclusivity, its nature as an institution of different sorts, Jews and Gentiles, slaves and free people, males and females (Gal. 3:28).

> PAUL'S REMARKS IN 1 CORINTHIANS ARE ABOUT DIVISION, NOT DIVERSITY. HE DOES NOT PLEAD FOR UNIFORMITY BUT FOR UNITY.

In one of his sermons on 1 Corinthians 1, Chrysostom tries to carry Paul's argument further. Chrysostom charges all "the apostles with want of learning; for this same charge is praise. And when they say that the Apostles were rude, let us follow up the remark and say that they were also untaught and unlettered, and poor, and vile, and stupid, and obscure. It is not a slander on the Apostles to say so, but it is even a glory that, being such, they should have outshone the whole world. For these untrained, rude, and illiterate people, completely vanquished the wise, and powerful, and the tyrants, and those who flourished in wealth and glory and all outward good things. . . ." His conclusion? "It is manifest that great is the power of the cross; and that these things were done by no human strength."

Early Christianity's triumph over the ancient philosophies and religions of its day is indeed an amazing fact, and all the more so given the humble origins of its first leaders.

Chrysostom, however, was not content to rest with this apologetic but went on to explain the true power of the cross, which he found not in words but in deeds. The one unanswerable argument is the argument from conduct. "For though we give ten thousand precepts of philosophy in words, if we do not exhibit a life better than others, the gain is nothing." It is not what is said that draws attention, but actions. The proclamation of the cross triumphed because the proclaimers, such as Paul, lived its truth. So Chrysostom turns 1 Cor. 1:10-18 into an exhortation. "Let us win others by our life. Many, even among the untaught, have in this way astounded the minds of philosophers, as having exhibited in themselves also that philosophy which lies in deeds, and uttered a voice clearer than a trumpet by their mode of life and self-denial. For this is stronger than the tongue."

THE GOSPEL
MATTHEW 4:12-23 (RCL, BCP); 4:12-23 or 4:12-17 (RC)

Interpreting the Text

Matthew 4:12-17, the first half of today's Gospel, marks the beginning of Jesus' public ministry, moves Jesus from Nazareth to Capernaum, and introduces in summary fashion the content of Jesus' proclamation. The verses underline three recurring themes—the fulfillment of Scripture (4:14-16), the salvation of the Gentiles (4:15), and the announcement of the kingdom of God (4:17). This last calls the most attention to itself; for 4:17 not only repeats earlier words of the Baptist (3:2), but the ingressive aorist (*ērxato*, "began") connotes repetition: Jesus evidently utters the words again and again. Matthew 4:17 stands over the entire public ministry.

Jesus, like the Baptist, proclaims the nearness of the kingdom of God (or heaven; the expressions are, despite some, equivalent). In Matthew this kingdom is God's eschatological rule that is even now establishing itself. In fact, it is entering the world through a complex of events, some of which have taken place (e.g., the Messiah's first advent; cf. 11:12: 12:28), some of which are taking place (e.g., the list of trials in 10:16-23), and some of which will take place in the near future (e.g., much of chapters 24 and 25).

Turning to the call of the disciples in 4:18-20 and 21-22, they can be outlined the same way as 9:9 (cf. Mark 1:16-20; 2:14). Each passage has this arrangement:

1. Jesus is passing by
2. He sees a person whose name is given
3. This person is at his place of work
4. Jesus issues a call to discipleship
5. The person obediently responds and follows Jesus.

This common form cannot be naively considered somehow intrinsic to the events it serves to relate. That is, the common structure was not given with the historical events, which could have been told in other ways. One could, for instance, have introduced the first call story by supplying information about Peter's and Andrew's ages and place of birth. Or one could have set the scene by adding picturesque details about the weather or the sea or the boat. Or one could likewise have indicated whether those called had ever before encountered Jesus. Was this their first meeting? Or one could have ordered the elements of the story differently. Why not put the call first and then describe its occasion? The point is clear through comparison with the call of Peter by the shore in Luke 5:1-11, a narrative very different from Matt. 4:18-22. In Luke's longer account, Andrew is not mentioned, but the story of a miraculous catch of fish is. Luke also includes a dialogue between Jesus and Peter.

That Matt. 4:18-20 has precisely the same structure as Matt. 4:21-22 and 9:9 is accounted for by the Hebrew Bible. First Kings 19:19-21 recounts Elijah's call of Elisha:

> So he (Elijah) set out from there, and found Elisha son of Shaphat, who was plowing. There were twelve yoke of oxen ahead of him, and he was with the twelfth. Elijah passed by him and cast his mantle over him. He left the oxen, ran after Elijah, and said, "Let me kiss my father and my mother, and then I will follow you." Then Elijah said to him, "Go back again, for what have I done to you?" He returned from following him, took the yoke of oxen, and slaughtered them; using the equipment from the oxen, he boiled their flesh, and gave it to the people, and they ate. Then he set out and followed Elijah, and became his servant.

This story can be outlined in the following fashion:

1. Elijah is passing by.
2. He finds Elisha.
3. Elisha is at work with a plow.
4. Elijah puts his mantle on Elisha, which is a sign of the call to prophetic office.

5. Elisha, who responds, "I will follow after you," asks to kiss his parents first; and he slaughters oxen for a sacrifice.

6. Elisha follows Elijah.

This outline is, with the exception of the fifth point, exactly the same as that offered above for Matt. 4:18-20, 21-22; and 9:9.

What explains the common pattern? There are two keys—parallelism and contrast. Concerning the former, Jesus is, in Matthew, presented as one who, like Elijah, possesses prophetic authority. That is, Jesus' authority is characterized implicitly through comparison with Elijah's authority. The prophet Elijah called Elisha, and Elisha obediently followed. In like manner, Jesus the prophet calls Peter and others, and they obediently follow. The prophetic word is powerful and effective. It does not invite but rather commands. It requires not consideration but obedience. Jesus, like Elijah, utters the irresistible prophetic word. (More than once in the Gospels Jesus does something reminiscent of Elijah; small wonder then that, according to Matt. 16:14, some people thought Jesus might indeed be Elijah returned.)

Perhaps even more important than the parallels between 1 Kings 19:19-21 and the three Matthean call stories is a major contrast. There is, in Matthew, no element corresponding to 1 Kings 19:20-21a (point 5 on the second outline). When Elijah calls Elisha, the latter asks, "Let me kiss my father and my mother and then I will follow you." Now Elijah's response is ambiguous: "Go back again; for what have I done to you?" It is not clear whether Elijah is turning down the request or whether he is rebuking Elisha, and it is not clear whether Elisha did in fact go back and say farewell to his parents. We do know, however, that in both the Septuagint and Josephus, Elisha does return and kiss his father and mother, and Elijah permits this. Nothing like this, however, is in the Gospels. So Jesus' call is more radical than that of Elijah. Jesus gives no opportunity for anyone to tarry. He demands that his disciples follow him immediately. There can be no preliminary leave-taking. As in the hard saying in Matt. 8:21, where Jesus tells a would-be follower, "Leave the dead to bury their own dead," so too in Matthew 4 and 9 does Jesus demand an immediate break with the past, including family ties. "Immediately they left their nets and followed him" (4:20). "Immediately they left the boat and their father, and followed him" (4:22). "And he got up and followed him" (9:9). Jesus commands a reflex action. His authoritative voice is to be instantly and unquestionably obeyed, no matter how hard and seemingly unreasonable the demand. That, at any rate, appears to be the implication of the implicit contrast with the story of Elijah and Elisha.

Matthew 4:23 forms an inclusion with the very similar 9:35. Between them Jesus first teaches (the Sermon on the Mount) and then secondly acts (chaps. 8–9). Afterwards, in chap. 10, where he instructs and sends out the disciples for mission, he tells them to do and say what he has said and done. This circumstance means that Jesus is the model missionary, and it explains the parallelism not only between 4:23 and 9:35 but also between 4:17 (the proclamation of Jesus) and 10:6 (the similar proclamation of the disciples) and 4:24 (the deeds of Jesus) and 10:1 (the similar deeds of the disciples).

Responding to the Text

If Jesus proclaims what the disciples will later proclaim (cf. 4:17 with 10:6) and if he does what they will later do (cf. 4:23 with 10:1), then he is a model missionary, and implicit is the theme of the imitation of Christ. Such imitation was an important part of early Christianity and should remain so today. Early Christians, in creating a new social entity, had to appeal to new norms and new authorities. Now such norms and authorities are always most persuasively presented when embodied in examples: new fashions must first be modeled. And in the early churches, Jesus himself, through the promulgation of the tradition about him, became the new model par excellence. The fact is often insufficiently appreciated, in part because there has been, since Luther, a reaction against an unimaginative and literalistic *imitatio Christi* (such as that enacted by Francis of Assisi), in part because the notion of the imitation of the canonical Jesus has been condemned as a purely human effort, which, in the event, cannot be achieved, and also in part because many have been eager to preserve Jesus' unique status as a savior whose salvific accomplishments cannot be emulated: the Christian Gospel is not moral imitation of a human hero or fine example (true enough).

But Matthew wrote when it was still possible to think of Jesus as a real model for our emulation (cf. Paul in Rom. 15:1-7). This is why, despite the general silence of the commentators, there is in Matthew a multitude of obvious connections between Jesus' words and his deeds. If Jesus recommended self-denial in the face of evil (5:39), he did not resist the evils done to him (26:67; 27:30). He called for private prayer (6:6) and subsequently withdrew to a mountain to pray alone (14:23). He rejected the service of mammon (6:19) and lived without concern for money (8:20). One could go on and on in this vein, citing instances of Jesus animating his speech. The imperative for us, then, is not just Jesus' words. Rather, his life in its totality is a command, that is, the virtues he embodied as well as the words he spoke must be creatively mirrored by those of us in the church. On the moral level at least Matthew encourages us to identify closely with the main character, whom the evangelist clearly regarded as, to use the words of another first-century Christian, "the pioneer and perfecter of our faith" (Heb. 12:2).

> THE IMPERATIVE FOR US, THEN, IS NOT JUST JESUS' WORDS. RATHER, HIS LIFE IN ITS TOTALITY IS A COMMAND, THAT IS, THE VIRTUES HE EMBODIED AS WELL AS THE WORDS HE SPOKE MUST BE CREATIVELY MIRRORED BY THOSE OF US IN THE CHURCH.

Matthew 4:18-22 also presents the disciples as models to be imitated, as examples of Christian commitment and discipleship. All who follow Jesus, not just Peter and Andrew and James and John, are called to leave behind the past. All must obediently respond to the call, "Follow me."

We must not, however, misunderstand this in an unimaginative way. Matthew's text does not entail that all believers give up home and family and do away with material goods. For one thing, Matthew can call Joseph of Arimathea both a disciple and a rich man (27:57). For another, there are obviously demands made of the immediate group around Jesus that do not hang over the heads of others (e.g., Matt. 10:9-10, which prohibits sandals and staff among other things). In the light of these facts, it is natural to understand the obedience of Peter and his fellows not as a rigid precedent but instead as being illustrative of the nature of discipleship. Matthew 4:18-22, that is, offers an example of wholehearted submission to the cause of Jesus. The implicit demand is to be like the disciples in so far as they were unreservedly obedient to the word that came to them in their situation, even to the point of great sacrifice. There is not, however, any general call to be rid of wealth or to forsake kin.

Matthew 4:23 holds a lesson about grace. Here we read that Jesus went throughout Galilee, curing every disease and every sickness among the people. The important point is that, when Jesus comes to utter the hard demands of the Sermon on the Mount, he is speaking not just to the disciples but to the crowds (see 7:28), and these crowds must include the people that he has healed in 4:23-25. This is crucial for interpreting Jesus' moral demands. Matthew 4:23-25 tells us that, before he made any demands, before Jesus uttered the Sermon on the Mount, he showed compassion by healing the sick among the crowds. The act is pure grace, for the crowds have done nothing. The unspoken lesson is that grace comes before task, succor before demand. Jesus' first act is not the imposition of difficult imperatives but the selfless service of others. Today's command presupposes yesterdays' gift. Matthew's narrative logic is consistent with Barth's declaration that "always and everywhere when the creature works, God is there as the One who has already loved it, who has already undertaken to save and glorify it, who in this sense and to this end has already worked even before the creature itself began to work . . ." (*Church Dogmatics* III/3, p. 119).

> "Jesus left Nazareth that he might enlighten more people by his preaching and miracles. In this way he left an example to all preachers, that they should preach at a time and in places where they may do good, to as many as possible."
>
> REMIGIUS OF AUXERRE

FOURTH SUNDAY
AFTER THE EPIPHANY

FEBRUARY 3, 2002
FOURTH SUNDAY IN ORDINARY TIME; PROPER 4

REVISED COMMON	EPISCOPAL (BCP)	ROMAN CATHOLIC
Mic. 6:1-8	Mic. 6:1-8	Zeph. 2:3; 3:12-13
Psalm 15	Ps. 37:1-18 or 37:1-6	Ps. 146:6-7, 8-9, 9-10
1 Cor. 1:18-31	1 Cor. 1:(18-25), 26-31	1 Cor. 1:26-31
Matt. 5:1-12	Matt. 5:1-12	Matt. 5:1-12a

TODAY WE THINK OF WHAT IS GOOD and what the Lord requires of us—justice, kindness, humility (Mic. 6:8). These social virtues are on memorable display in the Beatitudes, whose beauty should not blind us to their claim upon us. They should indeed comfort and encourage us, but they are not there for our private happiness—otherwise the Beatitudes would not show us the saints being reviled and persecuted. Our virtues are to be cultivated for the sake of others, for the sake of the world, as the verses that follow our passage make plain (Matt. 5:13-16). The salt that has lost its taste is a piety that lives to itself.

FIRST READING
MICAH 6:1-8 (RCL, BCP)

Interpreting the Text

Whether or not this portion of Micah comes from the eighth-century B.C. prophet himself or from a later redactor, it has two parts. The first five verses recount a covenant lawsuit. The prophet calls upon the mountains, ancient witnesses that have seen Israel's history, to serve as a jury and listen to the case against Israel. The prophet's judgment is this: the people have become "wearied" by God (v. 3), which presumably means that they have become tired of following God's moral demands, perhaps because the payoff has been perceived as insufficient. The Lord, however, responds by recounting pentateuchal traditions, a portion of salvation-history. God served the people by bringing them out of Egyptian slavery, by sending as their servants Moses, Aaron, and Miriam, and by thwarting the prophetic curse of Balaam.

God's case breaks off at this point, perhaps because the people are already convicted, or perhaps because we know the rest of the story and can fill it out for ourselves. In either case, the people are in the wrong, and so a representative asks the prophet, in vv. 6-7, what the Lord requires of them. Does God want extravagant offerings, thousands of rams with ten thousand rivers of oil, or even (a clear hyperbole) human sacrifice? The question is rhetorical, for the people know better. God has already declared "what is good" (v. 8), which comes down to this: the many imperatives of the Torah stand upon three things—justice, kindness, and humility.

Mic. 6:1-8 is reminiscent of several other Old Testament texts. Isa. 1:11-17, for example, declares that God is sick of sacrifices and religious ceremonies and instead requires goodness, justice, rescuing the oppressed, defending the orphan, and pleading for the widow. Similar too is Amos 5:21-24: God despises religious festivals and does not accept burnt offerings or grain offerings and hates the noise of songs because there is no justice. In these two places, as in Micah, personal piety divorced from social justice is rejected. Formal religious ceremony certainly has its place, but when it is not integrated with the reordering of society, when it does not raise up the poor and undo injustice, then such ceremony becomes hypocrisy. To be comforted without comforting others is to deny God. The Lord does not perceive the individual apart from the collective or endorse a faith that has no social vision.

As the rabbis noted, Mic. 6:8 reduces the 613 commandments of the Torah to three (cf. Matt. 23:23). They also observed that Isaiah reduces them to two (56:1: "Maintain justice, and do what is right"), and that Habakkuk further boils them down to one: "the righteous shall live by faith" (Heb. 2:4). Such summarizing reductions appear elsewhere in Jewish literature (e.g., the Mishnah, where we are told that the world stands upon three things, Torah, worship, and deeds of loving kindness). But for the Christian the most valuable summary is Matt. 22:37-40, which combines Deut. 6:5 with Lev. 19:18: "You shall love the Lord your God with all your heart, and with all your soul, and with all your mind. This is the greatest and first commandment. And a second is like it: You shall love your neighbor as yourself. On these two commandments hang all the law and the prophets." This twofold imperative falls in line with Mic. 6:8, for in both the religious demand and the social demand are united.

Responding to the Text

What do we make of Micah's three virtues? "Justice" seeks to make right what is wrong, to balance the scales of fortune, to free the oppressed from their oppressors, to enable the poor to gain dignity. By seeking to anticipate eschatological justice and reversal it hopes in the present to make real God's will for those who suffer unjustly.

The Talmud interprets Micah's "kindness" (Hebrew: *hesed*) as "doing loving deeds," which means deeds of charity. Perhaps the best biblical illustration of this is in the Gospels, in Matt. 25:31-46, where the Son of man as judge commends those who feed the hungry, give drink to the thirsty, welcome strangers, clothe the naked, and visit the sick and the imprisoned. The Lord Jesus so much identifies with the oppressed that service to them is service to him.

To "walk humbly with your God" means to recognize our limitations and to check pride in our achievements, which is a leaven that corrupts everything. Such humility is not a contrived, false self-perception but the only right response to the mystery of the Infinite whose demands we fail to live up to again and again. It is worth remembering that, in the Old Testament, Moses is said to be the paragon of this virtue (Num 12:3: "The man Moses was humble, more so than anyone on the face of the earth), and that, in the New Testament, Jesus likewise models this virtue (Matt. 11:29: "I am gentle and humble in heart"). Now Moses delivered a people from political bondage, and Jesus railed against all sorts of error, so humility can have nothing to do with standing in the background or being run over. It is rather the religious courage that comes from a disciplined ego, from knowing one's place over against God, from recognizing one's utter dependence upon Another—and which in this knowledge goes forth to serve the neighbor, even at the expense of its own well-being.

> HUMILITY IS THE RELIGIOUS COURAGE THAT COMES FROM A DISCIPLINED EGO, FROM KNOWING ONE'S PLACE OVER AGAINST GOD, FROM RECOGNIZING ONE'S UTTER DEPENDENCE UPON ANOTHER—AND WHICH IN THIS KNOWLEDGE GOES FORTH TO SERVE THE NEIGHBOR, EVEN AT THE EXPENSE OF ITS OWN WELL-BEING.

Philosophers and theologians have much discussed to what extent moral imperatives require or are strengthened by a religious foundation. However one evaluates their contradictory arguments and conclusions, for the Christian, the fundamental virtues of Micah are embodied in God and Jesus Christ, who stand as models to be emulated (cf. Lev. 19:2; Matt. 5:48; Luke 6:36; Eph. 5:1-2). They are our two chief imperatives, Torah embodied. God, so the Old Testament asserts repeatedly, is a God of justice as well as the dispenser of mercy. In like fashion, Jesus, our incarnate Lord, criticizes those who reject justice (see, e.g., Matt. 23:23), makes right what is wrong through multitudinous acts of compassion, and stands as the supreme example of humility (Matt. 11:28; cf. Phil. 2:5-8).

ZEPHANIAH 2:3; 3:12-13 (RC)

Interpreting the Text

Zephaniah was a seventh-century B.C. prophet who announced divine judgment for the sins of idolatry (1:4, 5, 9), assimilation to foreign ways (1:5), violence and fraud (1:9), and disbelief in God's active involvement in the world (1:12). The prophet painted a dim picture of the awful Day of the Lord, a wrathful day that would bring judgment upon both Israel and Israel's enemies (1:14-3:7). But he punctuated his dire prophecy with today's two readings—first with a call for a humility that might suspend God's wrath and so escape the upcoming disaster (2:3) and, second, with a notice that, on the far side of judgment, God will leave a remnant, "a people humble and lowly" (1:12-13). So there will be salvation in the end. But it is a salvation that appears to be contingent upon humility, which in 2:3 seems to be synonymous with seeking justice and is in 3:12-13 associated with doing no wrong, uttering no lies, and speaking the truth. Thus the future belongs to the humble who seek first not their own selfish gain or honor but the gain and honor of others.

Responding to the Text

Zephaniah 1:12 names a sin we often succumb to—doubt that God is active in our world. This sin once went under the name of Deism, the worldview of Voltaire, Jefferson, and others who thought that God created the world but then in effect went away on vacation, leaving us to fend for ourselves in a world of natural law. Now Christians, wrestling with modern science and comparative religion, can legitimately wonder about this or that miracle, or debate whether Jesus really turned water into wine or was born of a virgin. But what we can never do is to so isolate God from the world that our people are tempted to think that God cannot act for them. Whatever our approach to good old-fashioned miracles, we can never exile divine intervention from the personal sphere—from the conscience, from the mind, from the heart, from the memory. If it really comes to that, then we cannot avoid the sins that Zephaniah denounces, for we will be left with nothing but an old word from an old text. Unless there is an animating Spirit in our lives to give the word power, we are on our own, and to be on our own is to be without hope.

Responsive Reading

PSALM 15 (RCL)

Whether or not this psalm alludes to the Ten Commandments, it depicts the moral characteristics of those who participate in the liturgy of the covenant community. Particularly prominent are virtues of speech—speaking the truth from the heart (v. 2), not slandering with the tongue (v. 3), standing by one's oath even to one's own hurt (v. 4). Now, as the Reformers stressed when commenting on and enlarging the Decalogue's imperative not to bear false witness, lying and hurtful words have always been more than tempting. Human beings have habitually made excuses against the truth and defamed the good names of others. No one is free from the guilt of breaking the commandment "You shall not bear false witness against your neighbor." It is, however, worth asking whether lying and defaming are not a bit easier for us in this modern world, in which hyperbolic and seductive advertising as well as contentious and shallow political debates are ubiquitous.

The church has miserably failed to make parishioners conscious of what happens to language when the culture uses words as instruments to expand our artificial appetites and consumption. We must be called back to the grounding of truth in both theology proper ("The Glory of Israel will not deceive," 1 Sam. 15:29) and in Christology ("I am . . . the truth," John 14:6). Speech is a gift that should be used for love, justice, and fellowship, not manipulation. Words should reveal our hearts and should be the means of repairing and maintaining communion with each other. We would all do well to take another look at James 3 and its warnings against the dangers of speech.

PSALM 37:1–18 (BCP)

This psalm, which contains the scriptural inspiration for Matthew's third beatitude (v. 11; cf. "Blessed are the meek . . ."), concerns itself with the problem of evil. How is it that those who carry out evil devices prosper (v. 7)? How come God allows the wicked to bring down the poor and needy, to kill the upright (v. 14)? The psalm wisely offers no theoretical answer. It does, however, avow that the sad present will not be the lasting reality. One need not fret or be envious of wrongdoers (vv. 1, 7), for whereas the righteous will inherit the land (vv. 9, 11), the wicked will fade away and wither (v. 2), be cut off (v. 9), depart (v. 10).

Like the Beatitudes in today's reading, our psalm, while it does not explain the present or why the divine justice waits to make things right, anticipates an eventual resolution. This admittedly leaves us in mystery, but it does not leave us alone. Faith and hope remain—hope in God's ultimate goodness and faith in God's ability to bring justice to pass (vv. 2, 4, 6). Such faith and hope, moreover, generate the courage to act rightly in the present—to do good (v. 3) and forsake evil (v. 8). That is, God's future becomes the ideal for the here and now, the imperative that one must follow even when justice is tardy and strength seems to belong to those who "bring down the poor and needy" (v. 14).

PSALM 146:6–7, 8–9, 9–10 (RC)

This psalm of praise is the appropriate companion of Matt. 5:1–12 both because it contains a beatitude (v. 5) and because it depicts God as giving food to the hungry (v. 7; cf. Matt. 5:6). The focus is not on the wicked—who are here dismissed in half a sentence (v. 9)—nor on the righteous, but on God, who is to be praised and trusted (vv. 1-4). The God of Jacob is the creator (v. 6) who executes justice for the oppressed, gives food to the hungry, sets prisoners free, opens the eyes of the blind, watches over strangers, upholds the orphans and the widow (vv. 7-9). The psalm, although it contains no explicit imperatives except "Praise the Lord!" (vv. 1, 10), is one large, picturesque imperative. For not only does God always stand as the moral model—we are to be holy because God is holy (Lev. 19:2) and merciful because God is merciful (Luke 6:36)—but God works through us. How is it that orphans and widows are upheld, that strangers are watched over, that the eyes of the blind are opened, that prisoners are set free, that food is given to the hungry, and that the oppressed receive justice? God has chosen to minister to one human being through another. That is just how the world has been set up. So if the vision of Psalm 146 does not match our reality, it is because we have failed to let God minister righteousness through us.

Second Reading

1 CORINTHIANS 1:18-31 (rcl); 1:(18-25), 26-31 (bcp); 1:26-31 (rc)

Interpreting the Text

Those of us who have grown up in church associate crucifixes with salvation. For us the cross is a positive religious symbol, not a heartless reality. Not one of us has ever seen this thing. So for us it is not a special stumbling block. By contrast, crucifixion was a part of everyday life in the ancient world. When the Gospels exhorted believers to take up a cross, and when Paul proclaimed that salvation had been won on a cross, their hearers, unlike us, knew from experience the terror referred to. The sight of crucifixion, a punishment that satisfied the lust for revenge and was thought to be a deterrent, was widespread. It was an obscenity that conjured up the image of a naked body nailed or bound to a stake, a body wounded, bloody, swollen, deformed, covered with insects, and fated for the vultures or other beasts of prey. "The cross" was not a nice theological expression.

The associations of crucifixion were such that to preach Christ crucified was, as Paul says here, to preach folly—perhaps, I like to imagine, a bit like a mad religious sect finding the salvation of the world in poisonous gas or the electric chair. Justin Martyr, the famous Christian apologist of the second century, wrote to the Roman emperor Antonius Pius and his sons that non-Christians "say that our madness (*mania*) consists in the fact that we put a crucified man in second place after the unchangeable and eternal God, creator of the world." Justin goes on to observe that whereas he has heard many miracle stories about pagan gods and heroes, he knows no account of a god or hero being crucified. According to him, then, the crucifixion of Jesus, the divine Savior, distinguishes Christianity. In this particular at least the new faith is without real parallel.

Antiquity shuddered at crucifixion. Outside of Christian texts, it has no positive associations. "The infamous stake" (*Anthologia Latina*) or "the criminal wood" (Seneca) was simply a repulsive, barbarian method of execution—so repulsive that detailed descriptions of what was typically involved are absent. This is why, in Paul's experience, the crucified Jesus is a stumbling block to Jews and foolishness to Gentiles.

Responding to the Text

Paul uses the foolishness of the cross to undercut the wisdom of the wise: God's actions do not correspond to human expectations and cannot be anticipated through logic or reflection. Salvation comes only to the poverty of faith.

In our age, most people think of scientists as the paradigm explorers of reality. With their experimental methods and rational inferences, they are the ones we go to when we want to learn about the way things are. And what is required of scientists? What attributes must they have in order to unlock the secrets of our world? A well-educated mind that will follow the truth wherever it leads, an ability to carry out informed and dispassionate investigation.

Now within the realm of the so-called hard sciences, the idea of unbiased, impersonal inquiry must have its proper place (although it can certainly be exaggerated). But we err if we carry this idea over into Christian faith. Knowledge is a function of being, and when it comes to the ultimate probing of religious reality, what one sees depends on what one is, that is, on one's character. Nothing demands that the biologist making discoveries about a microbe live an upright life. But it is otherwise with the one seeking God. Knowledge of the divine does not come necessarily or especially to the well trained. Such knowledge is rather experiential and comes only to those who can understand what Paul is saying in 1 Corinthians 1, who are aware of their own lack of wisdom and power regarding matters divine. God finds those who know themselves to be lost. As Socrates put it, the wisest are those who know that they do not know. Or, in the idiom of today's Gospel, it is "the poor in spirit" and the "meek," that is, people who are needy and know themselves incomplete, who find themselves embraced by the divine.

One can carry the analogy further. In order to penetrate the secrets of the physical world, scientists must equip themselves properly, thus effectively chang-

> KNOWLEDGE OF THE DIVINE DOES NOT COME NECESSARILY OR ESPECIALLY TO THE WELL TRAINED. SUCH KNOWLEDGE IS RATHER EXPERIENTIAL AND COMES ONLY TO THOSE WHO CAN UNDERSTAND WHAT PAUL IS SAYING IN 1 CORINTHIANS 1.

ing their natures. They must often acquire or invent instruments (such as the microscope) that extend their senses, instruments that make them more than they naturally are, beings of enlarged sensibilities. For nature does not readily give up its mysteries. Everyday life conceals as much as it reveals, and only exceptional methods will make manifest, for instance, the elemental nature of a given substance.

Matters are similar when it comes to genuine knowledge and wisdom about the higher things. Everyday life simply does not render obvious the truth, let us say, of the preaching of the cross or of the Sermon on the Mount. In order to grasp them, or rather to be grasped by them, it is necessary to have our beings changed by God, to be given an extended sensibility. In both Paul and the Beatitudes such enlargement is related to recognition of one's own limitations, with a humility that finds in God's moral demands a door to knowledge. So there is a moral and religious dimension to the knowledge of faith—which is why professional philosophers and academic theologians may often get some things quite wrong while an uneducated individual with a good conscience and a good heart may get some things right. This is one reason we should listen more than we do to the so-called saints, to those who have been equipped by God to see things most of us miss.

The Gospel
MATTHEW 5:1-12

Interpreting the Text

Although Matt. 5:3-12 is often thought of as containing "the Beatitudes," ancient Jewish and Christian writings contain numerous "beatitudes" or blessings. Not only does Luke, in his Sermon on the Plain, have four blessings with close parallels in Matt. 5:3-12, but there are beatitudes elsewhere in Matthew (11:6; 13:16; 16:17; 24:46), and the Old Testament and New Testament are otherwise full of them.

Most biblical beatitudes fall into one of two categories. On the one hand are beatitudes that bless God. Examples include the standard Jewish prayers that begin with, "Blessed art Thou, O Lord our God. . . ." On the other hand, there are beatitudes that bless not God but human beings. Gen. 30:13 ("And Leah said, 'Happy am I! For the women will call me happy'") and Ps. 1:1-2 ("Happy are those who do not follow the advice of the wicked. . .") are illustrations.

Beatitudes addressed to human beings as their object can in turn be divided into two additional classes. One type speaks of people who are blessed because of their present circumstances. Proverbs 3:13 ("Happy are those who find wisdom, and those who get understanding") and Ps. 32:1 ("Happy are those whose transgressions are forgiven, whose sin is covered") supply examples of the first sort. The second sort blesses individuals because of what lies in store for them in the future. Tobit 13:14 ("Blessed are those who grieved over all your [Jerusalem's] afflictions; for they will rejoice for you upon seeing all your glory, and they will be made glad for ever") and *1 Enoch* 58:2-3 ("Blessed are you, righteous and elect ones, for glorious is your portion") are instances of this second class.

The Beatitudes in Matthew belong to this last category. In 5:3-12 Jesus blesses believers because of what lies in store for them. This explains the future tenses— "will be comforted," "will inherit the earth," "will be filled," "will receive mercy." We have here not commonsense wisdom born of experience but eschatological promise that foresees the unprecedented: the evils of the present will be undone and the righteous will be confirmed with reward. The first part of each blessing describes the believer's present whereas the second half anticipates the believer's future:

Present condition	Future condition
poor in spirit	possess kingdom
mourn	obtain comfort
meek	inherit the earth
desire righteousness	obtain satisfaction
merciful	obtain mercy
pure in heart	see God
peacemakers	sons of God
persecuted	possess kingdom
oppressed	great reward

The right-hand column in its entirety is a picture of the blessed future, which can be summarily characterized as experiencing in its fullness "the kingdom of heaven."

It is true that we find a present tense in both the first and eighth beatitudes ("for theirs *is* [*estin*] the kingdom of heaven"). The emphasis, however, obviously lies upon things to come. So we should probably explain the two present tenses as expressions of certainty: the surety of the saints' possession of the kingdom is underlined by use of a proleptic present. Greek can use a present tense to indicate a circumstance, which, although it has not yet occurred, is regarded as so certain that it is spoken of as having already happened—as in Matt. 26:2: "the Son of man is handed over to be crucified." The very last line in Matthew's Beatitudes—"for your reward is great in heaven, for in the same way they persecuted the prophets who were before you"—illustrates the point nicely. Although reward is yet to be bestowed, its secure reality is here conveyed through a present tense. This is probably how we should interpret "theirs is the kingdom of heaven."

If the second half of each beatitude sees a wrong undone or a good rewarded, it often does this through a reversal of ordinary values. Although few in the ancient world would have opposed mercy or peacemaking, it was obviously no good thing to mourn. Nor did "poor" or "meek" or "thirst" or "hunger" have better connotations then than now, and in no time or place do normal people wish to be persecuted or reviled. So in 5:3-12 Jesus takes up words with negative connotations and associates them with the saints. Chrysostom saw the truth: "What could be newer than these injunctions wherein the very things that all others avoid, these he declares to be desirable? I mean being poor, mourning, persecution, and evil reputation. . . . And hearing things so grievous and galling, so contrary to the accustomed ways of human beings, the multitudes were astonished."

Responding to the Text

We are so used to hearing the Beatitudes that we often miss their paradoxical dimension. Originally the Beatitudes were intended to startle. Simple observation of the world as it is informs us that the rich, not the poor, are blessed, that those who rejoice, not those who mourn, are blessed, that those who have power, not the meek, are blessed, that those who are filled, not the hungry and thirsty, are blessed, and that those who are well treated, not those who are persecuted, are blessed. So the Beatitudes have things backward. To take them seriously is to call in question our ordinary values, which for us must mean, among other things, our economics of consumption and our hedonistic ethic.

Insofar as the promises connected with the kingdom bring consolation and comfort, they function as a practical theodicy. The Beatitudes, no more than Psalm 37, hardly explain evil or human suffering. They do, however, lessen pain and anguish by putting into perspective the difficulties of the present. This happens through an exercise of the imagination. Eschatological promises for those on the bottom reveal that all is not what it seems to be. That is, the truth, like the kingdom, is hidden. Only the future, with its rewards and punishments, will bring to light the true condition of the world and those in it (cf. 25:31-46). Those who use the eye of the mind in order to foresee and live for the future promised by the Beatitudes will, with their faith, possess a secret vision and hope that makes powerlessness and suffering more bearable.

> THE BEATITUDES HAVE THINGS BACKWARD. TO TAKE THEM SERIOUSLY IS TO CALL IN QUESTION OUR ORDINARY VALUES, WHICH FOR US MUST MEAN, AMONG OTHER THINGS, OUR ECONOMICS OF CONSUMPTION AND OUR HEDONISTIC ETHIC.

In Matthew's Beatitudes the ethical thrust does not eliminate or even overshadow the elements of consolation and promise. This is evident above all in 5:10-12, verses that bless the persecuted. Being persecuted is hardly a virtue in and of itself, nor can it be obtained on one's own, nor is it normally something to be exhorted to. So in 5:10-12 the faithful are not being called to behave any differently than they are now; rather, are they being offered consolation in their present trying circumstance.

"The poor in spirit" (5:3) are not the "poor spirited," "fainthearted," or "despondent." Nor are they necessarily literally impoverished—although Luke's parallel (which is generally the preferred version of those battling the evils of poverty) has such in mind (6:20). "Poor in spirit" rather refers to those who acknowledge their spiritual need. They are, whatever their socio-economic situation, beggars before God and have accordingly abandoned human ambition. The meaning is close to "humble," and 5:5 is just a poetic variant of 5:3.

This beatitude is difficult for us today because of our concern for "self-esteem." By contrast, throughout exegetical history, the idea that God calls people to recognize their spiritual poverty, their inner need for the transcendent, has been enthusiastically promoted. For although monastic texts often take 5:3 to praise the life of literal poverty, most interpreters, including most of the early Fathers and later the Reformers, have instead rightly found in our text an acclamation of humility. They have often done so with the observation that the beatitude with "poor in spirit" heads its list and so names the fundamental virtue. Theophylact is typical: Jesus "lays down humility as a foundation. Since Adam fell through pride, Christ raises us up by humility; for Adam had aspired to become God. The 'poor in spirit' are those whose pride is crushed and who are contrite in soul." This is right interpretation.

Although "the poor" has a "spiritual" meaning in 5:3, it has a more literal sense everywhere else in Matthew, in 11:5; 19:21; 26:9, 11. So while one hesitates to cite 5:3 in support of what we now call a preferential option for the poor, such an option can appeal to other texts in Matthew, where Jesus preaches good news to the poor (11:5) and commends giving to them (19:21). Moreover, when one takes into account that the faithful hearers of the Sermon on the Mount suffer persecution (5:11-2), missionize and witness to God (5:13-16), pray for daily bread (6:11), do not serve mammon (6:24), and must trust God for basic necessities (6:25-33), so that the image we have of them is of marginal missionaries with few possessions, we can begin to imagine the needy as not just the objects of compassion but as people of power who can change things.

"Blessed are those who mourn, for they will be comforted" (5:4) is obviously false as a statement about this life: many sad people die without consolation. But Jesus here uses eschatology to encourage those who mourn: God will indeed bring them comfort. One thinks of Rev. 21:4, where it says that God will wipe away every tear from their eyes: "neither shall there be mourning nor crying nor pain any more, for the former things have passed away."

Why do the saints mourn? The dominant answer in exegetical history is sin. But the tradition is here likely wrong. The key to mourning is probably to be found in the scriptural allusion. Matthew 5:4 draws upon Isa. 61:2: "to proclaim the year of the Lord's favor, and the day of vengeance of our God: to comfort all who mourn." In Isaiah Israel is oppressed at the hands of heathen captors; cities are in ruins; the people know shame and dishonor. So God's own are on the bottom, their enemies on top. Mourning is heard because the righteous suffer, the wicked prosper, and God has not yet righted the situation (cf. Rev. 6:9-11). It is the same in Matthew. The saints are reviled and persecuted (5:10-12). The meek have not yet inherited the earth (5:5). The righteous still have enemies (5:43-48) who misuse them (5:38-42). In short, God's will is not yet done on earth as it is in heaven (6:10), and that can only mean mourning for God's people. To those who understand the truth about the present age, grief cannot be eliminated. There is no room for triumphalism. Our worship must be mingled with lamentation.

The big question regarding "Blessed are those who hunger and thirst for righteousness for they will be filled" (5:6) is the meaning of "righteousness." Two interpretations dominate the commentaries. The usual interpretation in patristic and Roman Catholic writings is that "righteousness" is behavior according to God's will—"the whole of virtue" in Chrysostom's words. Matthew 5:6 blesses those who, like Joseph, are "righteous" (1:19). Protestants, however, have typically found here God's action: the reference is either to justification (cf. Paul's use of "righteousness") or to God's eschatological bringing of justice.

The Catholic interpretation is probably more in line with Matthew's intention. For if the "righteousness" of 5:6 is equivocal, this is not the case when the word appears in 5:10, 20; and 6:1, where "righteousness" has little or nothing to do with God's gift. So if we interpret the uncertain (5:6) by way of the certain (5:10, 20; 6:1), the fourth beatitude means that God will satisfy those who earnestly and habitually seek to do the divine will as though it were meat and drink.

In appropriating this line, it is helpful to recognize that 5:6 does not congratulate those who are as a matter of fact righteous. Instead, it encourages those who are hungering and thirsting for conformity to the will of God. "Righteousness," it is implied, must be ever sought, must always be a goal that lies ahead. One is reminded of Phil. 3:12-16, where Paul says he has not already obtained his goal but presses on. Those who think themselves to be righteous are not (Luke 18:9-14).

The fifth beatitude promises like for like: "Blessed are the merciful, for they will [at the last judgment] receive mercy" (5:7; cf. 2 Tim. 1:18). Matthew has a great deal to say about the virtue of mercy, which is typically the external manifestation of an internal feeling of compassion for the unfortunate. It is a fundamental demand (9:13; 12:7), on a par in importance with love and faith (23:23). Jesus himself enjoins it (18:21-35), even when the word itself does not appear (25:31-46). And he himself embodies it (9:27-31; 15:21-28; 17:14-18; 20:29-34). In 25:31-46 it appears to be the criterion for salvation at the final judgment, and 18:23-35 teaches that those who do not show mercy cannot receive it from God. Would we not do well to listen to this side of Scripture and not prematurely subordinate it to Paul's emphasis on justification by faith?

Matthew 5:7 does not specify the means of mercy. This allowed Chrysostom to write: "Here he seems to me to speak not of those only who show mercy in giving of money, but those likewise who are merciful in their actions. For the way of showing mercy is manifold, and this commandment is broad." Chrysostom also helpfully commented that despite the reciprocal formulation in our verse, there is here no "equal recompense," for human mercy and divine mercy are not on the same level: "as wide as is the interval between wickedness and goodness, so far is the one of these removed from the other."

Matthew 5:8 says that "the pure in heart"—the expression refers to what Augustine called a "simple heart," that is, a heart undivided in allegiance and so rightly directed—will "see God." All sorts of interpretations have been given to this. Some Christians have believed that God has a body and that someday we will behold it. The old apocryphal text *Pseudo-Clementine Homilies* 17:7 claims that God "has shape, and he has every limb primarily and solely for beauty's sake, and not for use. For he has not eyes that he may see with them, for he sees on every side. . . . [God] has the most beautiful shape on account of the human being, that the pure in heart may be able to see him." Those of us who think rather of God as a Spirit may prefer a christological interpretation (one will someday see Jesus, "the visible image of the invisible God," Col 1:14; cf. John 14:9: "the one who has seen me has seen the Father") or, alternately, imagine some special vision that does not encompass God but is nonetheless a manifestation of the divine reality (like that of Moses at the burning bush). One might also think, with Origen and Schleiermacher, that the sixth beatitude refers not to physical sight but to spiritual and intellectual apprehension—sort of like, "I see the point," which is usually not about dots. Augustine took still a different path. He contended that in the new world the perfected saints will be able to perceive God directly through a perfected creation. The thought seems to be that we can sometimes perceive things through their effects, and that in the world to come God will be plainly perceived constantly through God's effects. One might also wish to identify seeing God with perceiving the image of God in the perfected saints, as some Eastern theologians have done.

Because, in Matthew and throughout the New Testament, the kingdom does not just belong to the future, one might ask how the different ideas of seeing God can be related to our present life. Is not the study of the historical Jesus one way of seeing Jesus? Do we ever have visionary experiences of the divine, and what do we make of them? Are we not always seeing some point as if for the first time and constantly learning about God? How have we experienced the reality of God in the natural world? And how do we recognize the image of God in our neighbor?

Matthew's seventh beatitude, which blesses the peacemakers (5:9), raises the question of what it means to be a peacemaker. Pacifists have thought it refers to the healing and prevention of political and military conflicts (and it has occasionally been suggested that our beatitude may have been composed not by Jesus but by someone during or immediately after the Jewish War of A.D. 66–70). Others have thought more in terms of personal relationships: one should make strenuous efforts to be reconciled to others both within and without the community. Given Matthew's keen interest in the subject of reconciliation (18:21-35), especially within the Sermon on the Mount itself (5:21-26; 6:14-15), one suspects that the interpretation that puts the emphasis upon interpersonal relationships comes closer to the authorial intention. Yet it would perhaps be unwise to restrict the application to this. For there is after all no qualification after "peacemakers," and one can find ancient texts that juxtapose social and interpersonal peace. Further, peace in interpersonal relationships should naturally lead to enlarging itself as much as possible, for the Gospel does not allow one to love neighbor but not enemy.

The eighth beatitude speaks of persecution. The reference is to physical violence or verbal abuse or both. What is envisioned is all hostility brought on because of "righteousness," that is, because of faithful obedience to God's will. God's ways are not our ways, which means they are not always pleasant ways, so those who demand and live obedience to them will meet opposition. Matthew's story of John the Baptist illustrates this fact. But the preeminent illustration is Jesus, who is reviled and spoken against again and again. Opponents claim that he blasphemes (9:2; 26:65) and acts unlawfully on the Sabbath (12:1-14). The Pharisees accuse him of consorting with sinners (9:11) and of casting out demons by the power of Satan (9:34; 12:24). Crowds laugh at him (9:24) and mock him (27:30, 38-44). Others call him Beelzebul (10:25) and accuse him of being a glutton and drunkard (11:19). And in the end, the one who proclaims the truth, makes hard moral demands, and alienates the powerful by serving the powerless ends up hanging on a cross. As so often, the best illustration of Jesus' speech is his own story.

"All the beatitudes that Jesus uttered in the Gospel, he confirms by his example, exemplifying what he taught. So he says, 'Blessed are the meek' and again of himself, 'Learn of me, for I am meek.' He says, 'Blessed are the peacemakers,' and who is such a peacemaker as my Lord Jesus, who is our peace, who did away with the enmity and destroyed it in his flesh? 'Blessed are those who suffer persecution for righteousness' sake'—no one so endured persecution for righteousness' sake as the Lord Jesus, who was crucified for our sins. So the Lord displayed all the beatitudes in himself. Thus having said 'Blessed are they that weep,' he himself wept over Jerusalem, to lay the foundation of the beatitude also."

ORIGEN

THE TRANSFIGURATION OF OUR LORD / LAST SUNDAY AFTER THE EPIPHANY

FEBRUARY 10, 2002
FIFTH SUNDAY IN ORDINARY TIME

REVISED COMMON	EPISCOPAL (BCP)	ROMAN CATHOLIC
Exod. 24:12-18	Exod. 24:12 (13-14), 15-18	Isa. 58:7-10
Ps. 2 or 99	Ps. 99	Ps. 112:4-5, 6-7, 8-9
2 Pet. 1:16-21	Phil. 3:7-14	1 Cor. 2:1-5
Matt. 17:1-9	Matt. 17:1-9	Matt. 5:13-16

THE SEASON OF EPIPHANY ENDS AS IT BEGAN, with light. In the reading from the Pentateuch, Mount Sinai is covered with the glory of the Lord and a devouring fire. In Isa. 58:7-10, light is about to break forth like the dawn. In 2 Peter 1 and Matthew 17, we read of the transfiguration of Jesus into light. Finally, Matt. 5:13-16 commands us to be the light of the world. So the divine light that suffuses our season serves to unite the two testaments; it is also both testimony to God and imperative for us. God's radiance, which typically comes unexpected to the darkness, is always a disclosure that commands.

FIRST READING

EXODUS 24:12-18 (RCL); 24:12 (13-14), 15-18 (BCP)

Interpreting the Text

Here God commands Moses to ascend Sinai so that he can receive the tablets of stone with the Ten Commandments. A cloud descends and covers the mountain as the glory of the Lord comes down. This lasts six days, after which God calls from the cloud to Moses. He then enters the cloud and remains there forty days and forty nights. To the people below, the mountain appears to be on fire.

Jewish legend underlined the momentous occasion of Moses climbing Sinai and receiving the Torah by adding additional supernatural signs to Exodus's cloud and fire. One first-century source says that, when God gave the law to Moses, "the mountains burned with fire and the earth shook and the hills were removed and the mountains overthrown; the depths boiled, and all the habitable places were shaken; and the heavens were folded up and the clouds drew up water. And flames of fire shone forth and thunderings and lightnings were multiplied and winds and tempests made a roaring; the stars were gathered together and the angels ran before, until God established the law of an everlasting covenant with the children of Israel and gave unto them an eternal commandment which should not pass away" (4 Ezra 3:18-19). A later legend went so far as to understand Exod. 19:17 and Deut. 4:11 to mean not "at the foot of the mountain" but "under the mountain," so that the picture is of Israel standing under a mountain that has levitated; and the mountain itself was said to have become as clear as glass—otherwise how could the Israelites have seen the fire above it? With such elaborations as these, Jewish storytellers and rabbis underlined the seriousness of what was happening: if the people had not accepted the commandments, the mountain would have dropped down upon them!

But even without the later legends the scene in Exodus is full of meaning. For one thing, the text stresses that God, not Moses, is the giver of the law: "I will give you the tablets of stone" (v. 12). One understands the psychology. All traditional cultures root moral imperatives in the transcendent, not in the purely human. There is a world of difference between "Moses says" and "God says." Our narrative also contains a lesson about grace. For at this point in the larger narrative, Israel has not done anything to merit receiving the gift of Torah. Indeed, at this juncture, the people have simply been rescued from the bitter bondage of slavery and shown ingratitude by complaining about their new situation (see Exodus 16–17). So the law is a sheer gift, unearned.

Responding to the Text

Today's Old Testament reading is the intertext for today's Gospel, Matt. 17:1-9 (see further below). That is, the story of Jesus' transfiguration in Matthew is intended to recall the story of Moses on Sinai. Now this correlation of Jesus and Moses is something that appears often in the New Testament. It is particularly obvious in Matthew's birth narrative, where Herod the Great reprises the role of Pharaoh and seeks to kill the Jewish infants. In fact, Matthew's first several chapters appear to contain an extensive Moses typology:

Exodus	*Matthew*
slaughter of infants	slaughter of infants
return of hero	return of hero
passage through water	passage through water
temptation	temptation
mountain of lawgiving	mountain of lawgiving

It is pleasant to observe these and other literary links, but what do they mean theologically?

Matthew did not share the modern disdain for imitation, which grows out of our love for novelty and our respect for all things new. In his Jewish world, the new was less authoritative than the old. This is one of the reasons why the story of a crucified and resurrected Messiah was offensive—it was unexpected, unprecedented, a novelty. So Matthew had to show that the new was not wholly unfamiliar. This is why he opened his book by relating Jesus to David and Abraham, why he immediately followed with a genealogy full of old Jewish names, why he sprinkled quotations from the Old Testament throughout, and why he constructed a Moses typology. He wanted both the new wine and the old wine to be preserved together (Matt. 9:17). Thus Jesus' newness becomes that of completion, and Matthew always gives us déjà vu: there is repetition and the past lives on. Indeed, the old vindicates the new, through the resemblance of the two. Had Matthew been around in the second century, he would have made Marcion and others who thought the Jewish Scriptures passé his bitter enemies.

Matthew, like the rest of the New Testament, contains a defining dialectic: the past informs the present, and the present informs the past. In accord with this, the typological lines between Jesus and Moses are bi-directional: informed understanding of Jesus requires true understanding of Moses, and true understanding of Moses requires informed understanding of Jesus.

Writing in the first century, Matthew must have been anxious about the preservation of his Jewish heritage in a church fast becoming Gentile. And he clearly sought to preserve that heritage, to bind the story of Jesus inextricably to Judaism. Living as he did after the fall of Jerusalem, in a period of successful Gentile missions, he did not need to be a prophet to foresee whither things were tending: Christianity was fast becoming a Gentile religion. And however much our evangelist endorsed the evangelism of non-Jews (28:16-20), he cannot have been oblivious to the danger that the originally Hebrew gospel would be misconstrued by persons outside the orbit of Judaism, that a Gentile Christianity might define itself in opposition to its origin and then cease watering its scriptural roots, thus becoming fertile ground for the weeds of

> MATTHEW MUST HAVE BEEN ANXIOUS ABOUT THE PRESERVATION OF HIS JEWISH HERITAGE IN A CHURCH FAST BECOMING GENTILE. AND HE CLEARLY SOUGHT TO PRESERVE THAT HERITAGE, TO BIND THE STORY OF JESUS INEXTRICABLY TO JUDAISM.

error. This happened with Marcion and other groups in the second century. The same sad evolution later led to the anti-Semitism of so much of Christian history. In this time after the Holocaust, a renewed appreciation of Matthew's Jewishness should help us to unlearn our prejudices and to repent of our past sins. If we are reading and proclaiming a book that was designed to prohibit the disassociation of Christianity from Judaism, a book that demonstrates that to abandon Moses is to abandon Jesus, perhaps we can, with all this in mind, learn to treat our Jewish neighbors as we ought, with gratitude for all we owe them and their tradition.

ISAIAH 58:7-10 (RC)

Interpreting the Text

These verses are part of a remarkable chapter that, like Amos 6:6–8 and Matt. 25:31-46, sticks in the memory and pricks the conscience. The people, so the text leads us to believe, fast; they are indeed very religious. But the prophet, sounding here much like Jesus complaining about some of the Pharisees, thinks that meticulous religious observance can be a trap when it becomes isolated from the rest of society. When piety does not entail compassion and justice, then piety is bankrupt. Reconciliation with God requires reconciliation with human beings. God's demand is holistic, it embraces all of life. So the prophet takes to task the religious who have not shared their bread with the hungry, have not clothed the naked, have not refrained from speaking evil of others, have not met the needs of the afflicted.

The original context for this oracle was the return from exile. Israel had come back to the land, and in some ways religion was prospering. Rituals were being observed, the Torah was being studied, and people were fasting, seeking God's favor. But the prophet interpreted all this as self-serving because it was not inclusive. As long as there are unfortunates who can be helped and are not being helped, as long as religion remains a sphere unto itself, then God's blessing is withheld.

Responding to the Text

This is a text one hesitates to paraphrase or even interpret. The words as they stand are so powerful and clear that one would hope nothing more than reading them would be necessary. But we all know this is not the case. We also know that no amount of interpretation will move people who are satisfied with their religiosity to move outside themselves and their own circle of friends to perform the sorts of acts of charity Isaiah requires. Words cannot do everything.

Preachers of the Word should never forget the old maxim: the greatest influence on our conduct is the conduct of others. From this undoubted truth of psychology, that we emulate what appears before us, it follows that if we wish to shape behavior and impact morality, we will be well advised to put forward what Milton termed "the salutary influence of example." We must appeal to sight as well as to sound. This is why the Talmud observes that the Torah is learned not just through study of a book but also through sitting at the feet of the rabbi: see what the master does and go and do likewise. As Seneca noted: "The way is long if one follows precept . . . but short and helpful if one follows patterns."

This truth should be obvious, and it was once proverbial; but times change. We live in a culture in which moral models or heroes play little role in learning. They have been supplanted by an uncritical faith in the possibilities of formal education. Many teachers now seem to believe that moral education can be equated with verbal discourse. We now feel that people can be guided, their behavior altered, through classroom instruction or a sermon. But people are not computers whose output is determined by programs. Words and ideas are not our sovereigns. We are animals, which means we are creatures of habit; and our habits are formed by the repeated imitation of others of the same species, others close at hand. This is why family life is inescapably formative: behavior is molded most by observation. Here the behaviorists were right. "Imprinting" is fundamental: the eyes paint the soul. Example is better than precept because example is stronger than precept. As experience proves, the catechism communicates nothing if not incarnated in a community or a person. And the same is true of today's reading. Moving as it is, and as dramatic as our preaching of it may be, unless it is incarnated somehow in our immediate environment, the word will probably return empty.

RESPONSIVE READING
PSALM 2 (RCL)

This is a royal psalm presumably composed for the accession of a new king (or the annual reenactment of his accession). When a new king took office, it was often the occasion for vassals to revolt. Our psalm, which equates the rule of God with the rule of the king, declares such revolt to be vain (vv. 1-6). If God has determined to do something—in this case to rule through the new king— then nothing can stand in the way.

Verses 7-9 preserve the first-person speech of the king himself. He declares himself to be God's "son," who is destined to rule the ends of the earth. His confidence is matched by vv. 9-11, where the psalmist addresses the vassals directly. If they are wise, they will serve the Lord with fear and submit to his anointed.

Because Psalm 2 speaks of a universal rule (v. 8), Jewish interpreters came to view it as messianic, and the New Testament cites it and alludes to it often in connection with Jesus (Matt. 3:17; Acts 4:25-26; Heb. 1:5; et al.). It is of particular interest that the divine voice at both the baptism and transfiguration alludes to it, with the implication that Jesus is the fulfillment of the old hope that God, through a chosen human being, will rule the world.

One of the prominent features of our psalm is the emotional character of the deity. In v. 4 God laughs, in v. 5 God is furious, and in v. 6 God is angry. This raises the question of God's nature. Much of our tradition, citing James 1:17 among other texts, has asserted that God is immutable, without change, and that this entails that God is not subject to shifting emotions arising from external circumstances. Modern theology, however, has found itself more and more attracted to a passible God, a God who can feel. Not only has process theology popularized the notion of God's becoming, but even more traditional theists have recently speculated about the passibility of God's nature in the incarnation, about the passibility of God's knowledge in response to the world, and about the passibility of God's feelings in the suffering of the Son of God as well as in human beings in general. While Psalm 2 speaks of responsive anger rather than sympathetic suffering, it nonetheless presents us with an opportunity to think about God's responsive nature and relationship to our world.

PSALM 99 (BCP, RCL alt.)

This hymn celebrates the Lord's kingship. It envisions a holy God as enthroned upon the cherubim in heaven (vv. 1-3), a God who loves justice and equity upon the earth (v. 5). The response to this God should be fear (v. 1), worship (vv. 5, 9), and praise (v. 9). In order to promote these acts, the psalmist calls upon Israel's collective memory—upon the stories of Moses and Aaron and Samuel (vv. 7-8).

Perhaps we should appropriate this psalm today by considering either the collective memory of the church through the ages or the collective memory of one's particular or local Christian community. Should we not be able to recite our psalm by inserting into it Francis of Assisi, Dietrich Bonhoeffer, and Martin Luther King Jr., or by inserting into it people we have known personally whose lives testify to the continuing work of God in our midst?

This sort of exercise is much needed. As the psychologists and sociologists have taught us, we now more than ever live in the present. We have devalued our past (under the technological illusion that the new always supercedes what has been) and are afraid of the future (which looms up as an ecological or nuclear nightmare). The upshot is that we have isolated ourselves in the present.

PSALM 112:4-5, 6-7, 8-9 (RC)

This is a wisdom psalm in acrostic form, that is, the first line begins with the Hebrew equivalent of A, the second with the Hebrew equivalent of B, and so forth (there are twenty-two letters corresponding to the twenty-two lines of our Psalm). It opens with a beatitude that states a condition and its cause: delight in God's commandments and fear of the Lord bring blessedness (v. 1). The rest of the psalm then makes extravagant promises to those who are righteous, gracious, merciful, generous, just, unafraid, and firm.

This psalm readily lends itself to reflection upon issues of social justice. But it also makes an important statement about human desire. Here those who prosper are those who desire to do the divine commandments (v. 1) and serve those less fortunate than themselves. But there is another desire, that of the wicked, that comes to nothing. From the fact that they look on the prosperity of the righteous and become angry (v. 10), it would seem that the wicked are seeking prosperity for themselves and do not get it whereas the righteous, who are not seeking prosperity for themselves, are given it anyway. Now the book of Job and too much sad experience teach us unquestioningly that such a generalization does not hold in this world. The faithful, however, must continue to believe that somehow, in the long run, this view remains correct. "The desire of the wicked must come to nothing" (v. 10), if not in this world, then in the world to come; and the contrary holds for those who delight to serve others instead of themselves.

SECOND READING
2 PETER 1:16-21 (RCL)

In 2 Pet. 1:16-21, the story of Jesus' transfiguration functions as an apologetic. It vindicates belief in Jesus as God's beloved Son and as the recipient of divine honor and glory. It also serves to uphold what 2 Pet. 1:19 calls "the prophetic word," which probably refers to the promises of the second advent or, more precisely, to the transfiguration as an anticipation of and so prophecy of that advent. Christ's glory at his first coming assures believers that his promise of a second advent is sure.

It seems very difficult to appropriate this text without pondering the problem of miracles. Before the Enlightenment, most people had no difficulty believing in supernatural stories. Since then many—including many in the church—have become skeptical, others uncertain. Now when Peter appeals to the transfiguration of Jesus as a sort of proof of the Christian proclamation, one can only ask, Well, did the transfiguration happen, or is it a myth? David Friedrich Strauss took the parallels between the Gospel accounts and Exodus to be signs of fictional creativity: the early Christians believed that Jesus was at least as great as Moses, so they invented a story in which their Lord is transfigured like the lawgiver. But the parallels were already noted long before by Eusebius, who took them to be due to the activity of Providence. Even if one instead sympathizes with Strauss, there always remains the possibility that the transfiguration is a mixture of history and theology. Maybe, for example, it is the legendary expansion of a vision that came to one or more disciples.

It is, in the end, all but impossible for the historian to know what to make of a story such as the transfiguration. If there are many legends from around the world in which people glow, there are also some stories, such as those about Seraphim of Sarov and Sai Baba, which, because they are attested by sincere firsthand witnesses, make one wonder. I remember once being told by a sane and sober friend that, when he sat in a room alone with his Sufi master, the master became transfigured in a light so bright it hurt the eyes. What should I make of this? Even if I were to decide that, on rare occasions, saintly human beings may be perceived as surrounded by light, do not the narratives of Jesus' transfiguration want to stress his uniqueness? Is he not presented as God's "Son" in a unique sense? If analogous stories might help some to entertain the possibility of a historical event behind Matt. 17:1-9, would they not at the same time lead to a diminution of the theological content, which associates the experience with Jesus' unique sonship?

If trying to find the history behind the transfiguration seems to be a dead end, so too must be use of it as an apologetic. But the instinct of the author of 2 Peter remains that of many of us. For in trying to validate his own faith, the letter writer appeals to the historical Jesus. We may have trouble knowing how to evaluate the miracle stories in general or the transfiguration in particular, but there is much about Jesus that, even with a critical eye, one may affirm with some degree of confidence; and whatever else Christian faith is, surely it must somehow be congruent with the concerns and activities of Jesus himself. So while we may find the appeal to the transfiguration in our modern context question-begging, we may find ourselves doing something not that much different than 2 Peter 1, that is, we may find ourselves defending our faith by looking at the words of and stories about our Lord. Is this not much of the motivation behind the modern quest for the historical Jesus?

PHILIPPIANS 3:7-14 (BCP)

Interpretation of the Text

Paul, writing from prison (1:7, 13) to suffering Christians (1:29-30), seeks to inform them of his present state (1:12-30), to pass on news about Timothy and Epaphroditus (1:19-30), and to encourage and exhort the Philippians on their way (2:1-18; 3:1—4:23). Much of the encouragement and exhortation comes by way of autobiography: Paul holds up his own experience as something with which his hearers can identify. In 3:7-14 this takes the form of focusing on the three tenses of all existence—the past, present, future.

In retrospect, Paul views his pre-Christian history as loss; indeed, he considers his past to be rubbish. This is because the former things did not bring him what he now finds to be of utmost value, his life in Christ. Paul's view is akin to the parable in Matt. 13:44, in which an individual sells everything in order to own the one true treasure. But Paul's sacrifices do not just belong to the past. He continues in the present to regard everything beside Christ as rubbish. Even now he knows "the loss of all things" and suffering (Phil. 3:8, 10; one should recall here Paul's account of his trials in 2 Cor. 11:16-33). One wonders, then, how Christ can be the treasure Paul takes him to be. The answer is many-sided, but part of the answer lies in the future, which Paul pursues like an athlete (3:14). Paul hopes for a resurrection on the other side of death, which will bring a prize that makes the sufferings of the present seem as nothing (cf. Rom. 8:18).

Responding to the Text

In 3:15 Paul labels himself "perfect" (*teleios*). Yet in v. 12 he declares that he has not yet obtained "perfection" (*teteleiōmai*). It appears that, for Paul, perfection consists precisely in pressing ever onward toward perfection. This reminds one of Gregory of Nyssa's innovative idea of perpetual progress. Gregory rejected the Platonic notion that change is a defect and affirmed that "the one definition of perfection is its not having any limit. . . . Why? Because every good is by its very nature unlimited." Gregory argued that everything is always changing and that the spiritual quest never ends in any sort of stasis but goes on forever, even in the world to come, where we eternally move forward into God. Christians should "change in such a way that we may constantly evolve toward what is better, being transformed from glory to glory, and thus always improving and ever becoming perfect by daily growth, and never arriving at any limit of perfection. For that perfection consists in our never stopping in our growth in good, never circumscribing our perfection by any limitation." From this point of view the moral demands on the Christian become a constant challenge that can become ever more effective over the course of time. As the Flemish mystic Jan

Van Ruysbroeck (1293–1381) would later write, the perfect Christian "will constantly grow and increase in grace, in all the virtues, and in knowledge of the truth before God and all upright people." If God is infinite and so can never be exhausted, and if the virtues embodied in God are likewise incapable of being exhausted, then there is never any boundary to virtue, nor any end to our growing into likeness to God.

FIRST CORINTHIANS 2:1-5 (RC)

Interpreting the Text

In his attempt to heal divisions within the Corinthian church (1:10-17), Paul turns to the proclamation of Christ crucified. This was the foundation of the community and it should therefore constitute its continuing unity. If that unity has instead been fractured, it is because focus has turned elsewhere.

From Paul's disparagement of rhetoric and wisdom, we may infer that those two things had somehow come to be a cause of disunity. Perhaps Apollos's speech and methods captured the imagination of certain Corinthians, who found Paul inferior by comparison and so came to have second thoughts about Paul's authority. However that may be, Paul makes the most of his weakness (2:3) and his rhetorical deficiencies (2:1)—the latter strikes us as hyperbole given the rhetorical heights his letters sometimes reach—by turning them into positives: the apostle's deficiencies made room for God's working.

Responding to the Text

In this case it is more needful to oppose a common misuse of the text than it is to set forth its proper exegesis. Paul's words can be dangerous in our present context, when the church is in so many ways separated from the secularized academy, a fact that seemingly moves many to turn a deaf ear to that academy. It may be true that spiritual things are only discerned by the spiritual and that only those who love God can truly know God. It is also often true that knowledge, like wealth, can "puff up" (1 Cor. 8:1), and certainly true that, "if you understand it, it is not God" (Augustine). None of this, however, should be an excuse for Christians not to use their minds to the utmost or to learn as much as possible about as many things as possible. Often, as sad experience teaching future ministers constantly reminds me, a pietistic focus on the heart has misled the faithful into feeling that God somehow does not require them to use their minds to the utmost. But this is to return to the old Gnosticism, which held that only a part of the human being comes from the highest God and can be redeemed. Such disrespect of human reason is a denial of the doctrine of creation. God made our minds as well as our hearts.

Paul himself, it should be obvious, had some kind of education that he put to very good use. His rhetoric, despite what he says here, sometimes soars (e.g., in 1 Corinthians 13), and he clearly gave himself successfully to thinking deeply about many things. And so it has been with so many others throughout church history. For every Francis of Assisi, who seems to have done quite well without book learning, the church has been edified by those who have set themselves to thinking—by Origen, Augustine, Aquinas, Calvin, and Karl Barth. These luminaries all show us that God wishes to capture and redeem the mind no less than the heart. A church that imagines that it can get by with only the later will, in the long run, wither and die: the gates of Hades will prevail against it.

The Gospel
MATTHEW 17:1-9 (RCL, BCP)

Interpreting the Text

Matthew's transfiguration narrative is designed to recall Exodus 24 and 34 and the story of Moses on Sinai. After "six days" Jesus' face shines like the sun, a circumstance that reminds one of what happens to Moses' face in Exod. 34:29-35 (cf. Exod. 24:16, where God calls to Moses out of the cloud on the seventh day). Further, as in Exod. 24:15-18 and 34:5, a bright cloud appears, and a voice speaks from it. And the onlookers—a special group of three (cf. Exod. 24:1)—are afraid (cf. Exod. 34:29-30). All this, moreover, takes place on a mountain (cf. Exod. 24:12, 15-18; 34:3); and Moses and Elijah, who converse with the transfigured Jesus, are the only figures in the Old Testament who speak with God on Mount Sinai (called Horeb in Kings), so their presence together makes us think of that mountain and the epiphanies that took place there. As so often in Matthew, then, Jesus is like Moses, and his history is something like a new exodus. In the early part of the fourth century Eusebius wrote: "When Moses descended from the Mount, his face was seen full of glory, for it is written . . . [Eusebius quotes Exod. 24:19]. In the same way only more grandly our savior led his disciples 'to a very high mountain, and he was transfigured before them, and his face did shine as the sun, and his garments were white like the light.'"

The heavenly voice, which, like the voice at the baptism, seems to mix Ps. 2:7 ("I will tell of the decree of the LORD: He said to me, 'You are my son; today I have begotten you'") and Isa. 42:1 ("Here is my servant, whom I uphold, my chosen, in whom my soul is well pleased"), is probably designed to reinforce this idea that Jesus is here like Moses. For Deut. 18:15 and 18, which Acts 3:22-23 sees as fulfilled in Jesus, foretell the coming of one like Moses, to whom the people should "listen."

If Matt. 17:1-9 sends thoughts back to several Old Testament texts, it also recalls texts within Matthew itself. There is, for example, an obvious connection with the baptismal narrative. "This is my Son, the Beloved; with him I am well pleased" (17:6) is a verbatim repetition of the voice of the baptism (3:17). So the transfiguration, in the middle of the story, confirms a declaration made at the beginning of Jesus' public ministry.

But the most interesting links for theological and homiletical explication are with the passion narrative. For the transfiguration has a twin of sorts in 27:32-54. After the centurion and those with him see the miraculous signs attendant upon the crucifixion, they too fear exceedingly (27:54), just as the disciples do in 17:6. Only in these two places does Matthew say that people were "exceedingly afraid" (the Greek is exactly the same). The link is small, but it prods one to observe that also common to the transfiguration and the crucifixion are the confession of Jesus as God's "Son" (17:6; 27:54), the presence of three named onlookers (17:1, three male disciples: Peter, James, and John; 27:55-56, three female disciples: Mary Magdalene, Mary of James and Joseph, the mother of the sons of Zebedee), and the number six ("after six days," 17:1; "from the sixth hour," 27:54). Moreover, these shared features exist in the midst of dramatic contrasts:

The transfiguration	The crucifixion
Jesus takes others (17:1)	(27:31) Jesus is taken by others
elevation on mountain (17:1)	(27:35) elevation on cross
private epiphany (17:1)	(27:39) public spectacle
light (17:2	(27:45) darkness
garments illumined (17:2)	(27: 28, 35) garments stripped off
Jesus is glorified (17:2ff.)	(27:27ff.) Jesus is shamed
Elijah appears (17:3)	(27:45-50) Elijah does not appear
two saints beside Jesus (17:3)	(27:38) two criminals beside Jesus
God confesses Jesus (17:5)	(27:46) God abandons Jesus
reverent prostration (17:6)	(27:29) mocking prostration

Between Matt. 17:1-8 and 27:27-56 there is a curious confluence of similar motifs and contrasting images. We have here pictorial antithetical parallelism, something like a diptych in which the two plates have similar outlines but different colors. If one scene were sketched on a transparency and placed over the other, many of its lines would disappear.

One part of the story of the transfiguration remains intractable. What is the significance of the three booths that Peter wants to build (17:4)? Some think that there might be a connection with the feast of booths, which Jewish tradition sometimes associated with eschatological expectation. Is Peter then expressing his conviction that the transfiguration is a harbinger of the end of the world? Cyril of Jerusalem wrote: "Peter, thinking perchance that the time of the kingdom of

God was even now come, proposes dwellings on the mountain, and says that it is fitting there should be three tabernacles. . . . But he knew not, it says, what he was saying, for it was not the time of the consummation of the world, nor for the saints to take possession of the hope promised to them." Others have simply surmised that Peter wishes to prolong the blessed moment, or that his request comes from a desire to observe the feast that is at hand, or that he assumes that the saints in heaven have dwellings and so will need them when or earth. Whatever Peter has in mind, and whatever his mistake might be—Is it that he wants to linger when he cannot? Is it that he wants to build the booths instead of letting God take things in hand? Is it that "One for you and one for Moses and one for Elijah" implies the parity of the three named?—the cloud and its voice interrupt him. His job is not at this point to do or to teach but to listen.

The final verse of today's reading has Jesus enjoining secrecy: the disciples are not supposed to tell what they have seen until the Son of man is resurrected (v. 9). The command presupposes that some things should be proclaimed only in the light of Easter, because some things can only be rightly understood in the light of Easter.

How does Matt. 17:1-9 fit into its immediate context? Jesus' appearance in glory anticipates or foreshadows both his resurrection and his second advent—maybe one could liken the transfiguration to a movie preview—and so helps to confirm the prophecy of his resurrection in 16:21 and his prophecy of the second coming in 16:28. There is also a close connection with the confession at Caesarea Philippi (16:13-20), for both there and on the mount of transfiguration Jesus is proclaimed to be the Son of God. There is, to be sure, a major difference in that in the earlier story the confession of Jesus as Son of God comes from Peter, whereas in the latter God speaks. But this only makes 17:1-9 set the divine seal of approval upon Peter's pronouncement. Further, the two passages are related in so far as both qualify sonship with suffering service. Just as 16:13-30 is followed by 16:21-23, which holds forth the necessity for suffering, so 17:1-8 interprets Jesus' sonship in terms of Isaiah's servant ("in whom I am well pleased," cf. Isa. 42:12).

Responding to the Text

What is the significance of the parallels between the transfiguration and the crucifixion? The two scenes represent the extremities of human experience. One tells of spit and mockery, nails and nakedness, blood and loneliness, torture and death. The other makes visible the presence of God and depicts the divinization of human nature. So Jesus embodies the gamut of human possibilities; he is the coincidence of opposites in one person. Perhaps this is one of the reasons he has always been so attractive and inspiring. He shows forth in his own person both the depths of pain and anguish that human beings have known as well as what we all long for—transfiguration into some state beyond such pain and anguish. Jesus is the great illustration of both despair and hope; he is humanity exalted and humanity glorified.

Despite the dialectic just observed, the church has always identified the moment of crucifixion, not the moment of transfiguration, as the saving event. It is the former, not the latter, that stands as the climax of Matthew's book. This is part of the humanity of the Gospel. While fallen humanity needs the vision of future glory exhibited by the transfiguration, it even more perhaps needs the spectacle of the suffering God, the Lord who identifies with us in our brokenness and anguish. Pascal once asserted that Jesus remains on the cross until the end of time. Our Lord is not just our hope but our sympathy. He is the one who understands and feels with us, the one who suffered and still suffers for the sins of this world that yet groans for redemption.

The history of the interpretation of the transfiguration leads to fruitful reflections. In 2 Pet. 1:16-21, the story functions as an apologetic, as we have seen. But in the second-century *Apocalypse of Peter* 16, the transfiguration is recounted in response to the disciples' request that they behold the fate of the righteous after death. Furthermore, when Peter asks where the righteous ones dwell and inquires about their world, the scene expands to include the paradise of God, with its lights and flowers and trees and fragrances and fruits. So here the transfiguration is a preview of what heaven will be like and an illustration of what awaits Christians.

Perhaps the most common interpretation in Christian history is that found in the apocryphal *Acts of Peter* 20 and *Acts of Thomas* 143: the transfiguration is a revelation of Christ's heavenly or divine nature, a revelation of Jesus as he always was and is. On this view, Jesus was not really changed. Rather, the disciples were enabled to perceive what was always the case. On this reading, Matt. 17:1-8 reminds one of the story in 2 Kings 6:15-17, where the eyes of Elisha's servant are opened so he can see the invisible horses and chariots of fire around Elijah.

MATTHEW 5:13–16 (RC)

Between the introductory eschatological blessings (5:3-12) and the concluding eschatological warnings (7:13-27) of the Sermon on the Mount are three major sections, each one primarily a compilation of imperatives. In 5:17-42 Jesus engages Moses and the Torah. In 6:1-18 he talks about properly cultic issues, almsgiving, prayer, and fasting. Finally, in 6:19—7:12, he addresses social issues, such as what to do with or about wealth (6:19-34) and what to do about judging others (7:1-6). But preceding these segments are the prefatory parables about salt, light, and lamp (5:13-16). It is not the Torah or the temple or Jerusalem or

Israel that is said to be the salt or light of the world (as in Isa. 60:1-3 and Bar. 4:2) but Jesus' followers. As the second-century *Epistle of Diognetus* has it, "What the soul is in a body, this the Christians are in the world."

Matthew's words do not tell us how to become salt or light or lamp, nor exactly what those things mean. This is because the sayings together constitute a transitional passage that functions as a general heading for 5:17—7:12, where those issues are addressed. Matthew 5:13-16 moves readers from the life of the blessed future (depicted in 5:3-12) to the demands of the present, and so the theme switches from gift to task.

Responding to the Text

Some have detected a tension between 5:13-16, where disciples are to be light to the world and let their good works be seen, and 6:1-18, where Jesus enjoins a private piety: Do not let the left hand know what the right hand is doing, go into your closet when you pray, do not display your fasting. The tension is undeniable. But it is also unavoidable, part of living with others. For if Christians are not to call attention to themselves, they are also called to a piety that manifests itself in the world, to a faith that visits prisoners and feeds the hungry, a faith that lives in the world for the sake of the world. Perhaps the difference between 5:13-16 and 6:1-18 is not, so to speak, location but motivation. 6:1-18 warns us that acts of piety can be done to make ourselves look better in the eyes of others while 5:13-16 tells us that the goal of our activities is the glorification of God (5:16). Putting the two texts together, we are to be motivated by a passion for God and neighbor, not a passion for ourselves.

Theophylact observed that if Christians are the light of the world, then they must be in view of all. Jesus is telling us that we cannot be hidden away in a corner but are in fact most visible. From this it follows that we must live blamelessly, lest we become a stumbling block for others. Some rabbinic texts say that to sin against a Gentile is worse than sinning against a Jew, for in the former case people will be encouraged to dismiss the God of Israel. So here too. When the light of the world fades, when the church fails in its testimony, the world is encouraged to turn from God.

Calvin, like some patristic writers, found in 5:13-16 a stern warning especially for all ministers of the gospel. Once Jesus tells the apostles their vocation, he "announces the heavy and appalling sentence that befalls them if they do not come up to their duty. The teaching which is put in their hands he shows to be so attached to the good of our conscience, and the life of godliness and integrity, that the wastage which might in others be tolerable, is in them detestable and indeed monstrous. . . . It is an incurable disease when ministers and teachers of the Word waste themselves and render themselves without savor, for it is their savor that should season the rest of the world. . . . Certainly the higher people stand, the worse the effects of their bad example if they misbehave. Christ wishes his disciples to be more keenly concerned to live in a godly and holy way, than the nondescript members of the crowd, for the eyes of all are turned upon them as upon a beacon. They cannot be tolerated, if their decent behavior and integrity of life do not correspond to the teaching of which they are the ministers."

"When you were transfigured before your crucifixion, O Lord, the mount resembled heaven, and a cloud spread out like a canopy, and the Father bore witness to you. And there were present Peter, James, and John, since they were to be with you at your betrayal; so that seeing your wonders they might not be dismayed at your sufferings. Make us, therefore, to worship the same in peace for your great mercy."

COZMA THE ANCHORITE

THE SEASON
OF LENT

CHRISTINE
ROY YODER

L ENT IS "IN BETWEEN" TIME. It is that season between Epiphany and Holy
Week, between Jesus' transfiguration and our shouts of "Hosanna!" and
"Crucify him!" as we strain our necks and push our way through the crowds to
see Jesus coming into Jerusalem. It is "in-between" time, forty days in which we,
like Israel and Jesus before us, are called into the wilderness to prepare for something new. We may be reluctant to go. The wilderness can be a disconcerting
place of blinding sands, heightened senses, and heavy thoughts. Dry bones dot
the landscape. The tempter awaits us. And
our feet sink like lead into shifting dunes.
But it is there, to that risky, sacred ground
that God leads us in these days. There, on

THE JOURNEY FROM ASHES TO PALM BRANCHES IS
NOT EASY, BUT WE DO NOT MAKE IT ALONE.

that risky, sacred ground, Jesus meets us. The wilderness is, during Lent, our destination *and* our way ahead. It is the stark landscape where we confront the most
painful parts of ourselves, where we face our weaknesses, limitations, and failures.
It is the respite where we listen to the beating of our hearts away from the noise
and business of our lives. It is the path to newness, our way to the Promised Land.
The journey from ashes to palm branches is not easy, but we do not make it alone.
Barren wastes become green pastures, rocks release cascades of fresh water, and
winds stir dry bones to dancing.

ASH WEDNESDAY

FEBRUARY 13, 2002

REVISED COMMON	EPISCOPAL (BCP)	ROMAN CATHOLIC
Joel 2:1-2, 12-17	Joel 2:1-2, 12-17	Joel 2:12-18
or Isa. 58:1-12	or Isa. 58:1-12	
Ps. 51:1-17	Ps. 103 or 103:8-14	Ps. 51:3-6, 12-14, 17
2 Cor. 5:20b—6:10	2 Cor. 5:20b—6:10	2 Cor. 5:20—6:2
Matt. 6:1-6, 16-21	Matt. 6:1-6, 16-21	Matt. 6:1-6, 16-18

L ENT BEGINS WITH A CROSS OF ASHES. Paradoxically, that which signifies grief, the pervasiveness of sin, and human mortality at the same time symbolizes joy, forgiveness, and victory over death. The texts for today set us firmly amid the ashes, calling us to return, to repent, and pointing us ahead to the redemptive power of God.

FIRST READING

JOEL 2:1-2, 12-17 (RCL, BCP); 2:12-18 (RC)

Interpreting the Text

The fields were devastated, the vines withered, and the crops ruined. Gnarled white tree branches, stripped of their bark, scratched the skies. The scorched earth wept. It was the work of locusts—an invading army unlike any seen before (1:2)—and, for Joel, the foretaste of an approaching, terrifying "day of the Lord" (1:15; 2:1-2; cf. Amos 5:18-20; Zeph. 1). At God's command ("my holy mountain"; 2:1), the blast of a watchman's trumpet heralds the gravity of the people's situation. A day that ought to mark the salvation of Israel (cf. 2:31-32; 3:14-21) promises instead gloom and darkness (2:1). An army of unprecedented power draws near, thundering over the mountaintops and charging up the city walls. Joel masterfully describes its relentless movement, its unstoppable advance (2:2b-10), before he announces the most horrifying news of all. The commander-in-chief of this numberless legion is none other than God (2:11).

Joel is clear that the people face imminent defeat. He orders that the trumpet blast again (2:15), this time to summon *everyone* to gather and together repent and fast. The people's only hope is the very God who leads the enemy forces against them, who sounds the alarm (2:1), and "even now" (2:12) urges them to return. Joel cries out for a "return" to God, reminding the community with an age-old creed that "your God" (2:13, 14) is gracious, merciful, and may relent from exacting the punishment already unleashed (2:13; cf. Exod. 34:6-7; John 4:2; Ps. 103:8). At the same time, Joel instructs the priests to call on God's vested interest in the community ("your people," "your heritage," 2:17).

The people's return must be a matter of practice *and* purpose. Worship conducted without right motives, without a rending of the heart and mind (2:12), is a hollow performance. There can be no disjunction between intentions and conduct, attitude and action. If this community in crisis dares to hope that God will "turn and relent," its own return must be genuine (see "Responding to the Texts" below).

ISAIAH 58:1-12 (RCL, BCP, alt.)

Interpreting the Text

As God commands the watchman to trumpet the alarm in Joel 2:1, God here charges the speaker to "lift up your voice like a trumpet" and announce that just such a dichotomy between intentions and conduct exists in the early post-exilic community, the presumed audience of Third Isaiah (58:1-2). The people sin and rebel (58:1) and "yet" continue to delight in their piety, acting "as if" they are righteous (58:2). They fast and, when their worship does not yield any apparent advantage, they cry out that God does not see and take notice (58:3). In a dramatic reversal, God commands twice that the people look instead at the dissonance between the intent of a fast and their ongoing self-serving, oppressive, and contentious practices. Even as they fast, they exploit others. Even as they humble themselves, they fail to do justice and to be compassionate. In short, the people "bow down the head like a bulrush and . . . lie in sackcloth and ashes" not to worship God, but to serve their own purposes (58:3b-5). Their piety is contrived, separated from and inconsequential to their lives. As such, God refuses to hear them (58:4).

The two rhetorical questions in the first person that follow describe the "fast" that God chooses (58:6-7). In contrast to that of the people, God's is one of *liberating action:* to loose the bonds of injustice, to break every yoke (likely a reference to debts), to let the oppressed go free. It is one of *self-giving and compassion:* to share bread, to house the homeless, and to clothe the naked. Worshiping God is thus inseparable from the practice of social solidarity. The people cannot worship rightly and at the same time hide themselves from the needs of their neighbors (58:7).

The text ends with a series of conditional ("if . . . then") statements in which the speaker testifies to what will happen *if* the people can find a way to practice what they preach (58:8-14). They will live again in the presence of God. God will hear them and answer their cries, lead them forward and protect them from behind. There will be light in darkness, waters in a parched wilderness, and, quite significantly for this early postexilic community, a thriving city where ruins now stand. When people abandon self-interest and go about the work of liberation and compassion, they find restored community and true "delight" in God (58:14).

Responding to the Texts

On Ash Wednesday, when the trumpets blast in Joel and Third Isaiah, I suspect that many of us wish we could cover our ears. Their sound pierces through our complacency, startles us in our apathy, and calls attention to our hypocrisy. Their tone reverberates through every fiber of our lives and our worship. It demands that we face God and take stock of the seriousness of our situation. We see God approaching as warrior, prepared to battle in judgment against us. We hear God refusing our worship for its emptiness and insincerity. We see God turning toward us, but God does not fit our descriptions and our self-assured understandings. Our feet set now on the Lenten path, we dare not miss the trumpets' blast, the prophetic alarm that wakens us and makes clear our predicament.

We dare not, because with clarity comes the awareness that all is not finished. Even now, with the dark "day of the Lord" advancing, the prophets proclaim that God calls out to us, urging us to return. God holds out the way for renewal and reconciliation. God summons us to a radical reorientation, a turning of our full devotion to God, a commitment to live and serve worshipfully on God's terms and for God's purposes. Repent, cry the prophets, as individuals and as communities. If we do, God, too, may turn and we may find delight and blessings (Joel 2:14).

THE PROPHETS PROCLAIM THAT GOD CALLS OUT TO US, URGING US TO RETURN. GOD HOLDS OUT THE WAY FOR RENEWAL AND RECONCILIATION.

PSALM 51:1-17 (RCL); 51:3-6, 12-14, 17 (RC)

The rending of a heart is given poignant expression in this well-known penitential psalm, ascribed by tradition to David after Nathan confronts him about the rape of Bathsheba (cf. 2 Sam. 11-12). Before God, the arbiter of human life, the psalmist confesses not one or a few sins, but an existence marked by "what is evil in your sight" (51:4; cf. repeated references to "my transgressions," 51:1, 3; "my iniquity," 51:2, 9; and "my sin," 51:2, 3, 9). This recognition of the pervasiveness of sin prompts the penitent to acknowledge that God's sentence is justified (51:4-5), to plead for mercy, and to request that God intervene and effect change. The psalmist unleashes a torrent of petitions for God to act—to teach (51:6), to purge, clean, and wash (51:2, 7), to blot out (51:1, 9), to let hear (51:8), to create (5:10, 12), to restore (51:12), to deliver (51:14), and to open (51:15). The penitent offers a broken, contrite self as sacrifice (51:17) and holds out hope that God will make what is so broken wholly new, that God will let crushed bones rise up and, with joy, again declare God's praise, teach God's ways, and sing of God's deliverance (51:8, 13-17).

PSALM 103 or 103:8-14 (BCP)

Framed with the imperative "bless the Lord" (103:1-2, 20-22), this is a litany of thanksgiving, remembrance, and a reminder that the steadfast love of God prevails over God's anger at human sinfulness. Its testimony to God's mercy is comprehensive, moving from the personal (103:1-5) to the communal (103:6-18) to the cosmic (103:19-22) in twenty-two lines (the number of letters in the Hebrew alphabet). Repetition of the word "all" five times in the first six verses and four times in the last four further signals its inclusive scope. Throughout the poem, the psalmist professes that God's nature and ways are marked by steadfast love and compassion. God's mercy fills the heavens and earth (103:11-12) and persists well beyond the fleeting moments of human life (103:15-17). The psalmist recognizes this is true from the "benefits" that renew life: forgiveness, healing, redemption from the Pit, and the capacity to experience life as good (103:1-5). So, too, the Israelites knew God's justice by their liberation from slavery and God's mercy after the incident with the golden calf (103:6-8; cf. Exod. 34:6-7). The psalmist thereby urges "those who fear God" to remember that they are forgiven, to trust in the gospel of God's steadfast love, and to persevere in obedience (103:17-18).

2 CORINTHIANS 5:20b—6:10

Interpreting the Text

Paul's urgent call for Christians to "be reconciled to God" reverberates like the trumpet blasts of the prophets. Paul begins with the appeal proper (5:20b—6:2), emphasizing that "for our sake" God made Christ "to be sin" so that, through his death and resurrection, believers might know an existence not formerly theirs, "the righteousness of God" (5:21). God acted decisively in Christ to be reconciled with the world (5:19). Paul then implores the Corinthian community not to receive this divine grace in vain. Quoting from Second Isaiah (49:8a), Paul proclaims that *now* is the "acceptable time" and the "day of salvation" (6:2-3). The need for reconciliation is *now* in Christian life. Christians have been forgiven. Paul urges them to see *now* that they continue to need that forgiveness (6:2).

As support for his appeal, Paul defends his ministry, insisting that he and his associates are servants of God (6:4; cf. 6:1), people who have experienced God's reconciliation and now work together to persuade others of its transforming reality (cf. 5:11). He introduces (6:3-4a) and enumerates their credentials (6:4b-10): *endurance in hardship* (4b-5), *genuine and Spirit-filled lives* (6-7a), and *possession of the weapons of righteousness* (7b-8). Moreover, their existence in Christ is markedly different from how those who see "according to the human point of view" perceive it (6:8-10; cf. 5:16). According to Paul, therefore, service in the name of God means experiencing and enduring hardships, testifying to the power of God by one's nature and conduct, and continuing to affirm the gospel in the face of outright denial.

Responding to the Text

It is important to remember that Paul addresses these words to the Corinthian Christians, people with whom he has had a strained relationship. His letter testifies to the severity of this alienation, to how difficult it is to live together in community. Paul declares at once the good news of God's reconciliation with the world accomplished in Christ and the ongoing need that Christians have for reconciliation. We have become the "righteousness of God," but this new existence cannot be taken for granted. We continue to need forgiveness. We continue to find ourselves, as individuals and communities, in situations that cry out for reconciliation.

> WE HAVE BECOME THE "RIGHTEOUSNESS OF GOD," BUT THIS NEW EXISTENCE CANNOT BE TAKEN FOR GRANTED. WE CONTINUE TO FIND OURSELVES, AS INDIVIDUALS AND COMMUNITIES, IN SITUATIONS THAT CRY OUT FOR RECONCILIATION.

Reconciliation, therefore, is a continual work of life. To think otherwise is to risk accepting the grace of God "in vain" (6:1).

Paul emphasizes that because God acted definitively for our sake, because we have experienced God's redemptive power, we are compelled to act *now* for God's sake. Our experience of God encourages us to serve as coworkers with God in the world. On this Ash Wednesday, Paul's defense of his ministry invites us to reflect on our own. And he challenges us with eschatological urgency not to postpone the work of our servanthood.

THE GOSPEL
MATTHEW 6:1-6, 16-21

Interpreting the Text

After reinterpreting laws (5:21-48), Jesus turns his attention in this sermon to three religious practices: charity, prayer, and fasting (6:1-6, 16-18). As 6:1 indicates, his concern is not the practices themselves, but rather the motivation underlying them. For whose eyes—human or divine—does one practice one's piety? Jesus points to the hypocrites, those who perform their piety in front of others. Hypocrites act out an *ostentatious, manipulative piety,* blasting trumpets as they take their offerings to the synagogue, standing in prayer for hours at bustling street corners, and distorting their faces so that people will know they are fasting. Because they seek a human audience, Jesus says, their full and only reward is whatever recognition they may receive from onlookers. In contrast, Jesus encourages the practice of an *inconspicuous piety*, to give without one hand knowing what the other is doing, to pray in a private room with the door closed, and to fast with an anointed and joyful face. Such deeds done "in secret" will not escape the attention of God "who sees in secret."

JESUS ENCOURAGES THE PRACTICE OF AN INCONSPICUOUS PIETY. SUCH DEEDS DONE "IN SECRET" WILL NOT ESCAPE THE ATTENTION OF GOD.

In 6:19-21, Jesus talks about money to teach about the nature of discipleship. The choice between the pursuit of earthly wealth and the treasures of heaven, he argues, is an "either-or" proposition. Only one treasure can ultimately command one's commitment and energy. Those who choose money, like the hypocrites who seek public admiration, pursue a precarious reward. Though money may be pleasing, it is fleeting, vulnerable to decay, theft, and destruction. Those who choose heavenly treasures, in contrast, pursue a wealth that endures.

Responding to the Text

On this day when many worship services will include the imposition of ashes, Jesus' warning may seem to us ironic. The sooty smudges on our foreheads testify to the world that we have been in church even as Jesus charges us to avoid outward signs of our piety. Jesus' concern is not the rituals themselves, however. He assumes, even advocates, the giving of alms, praying, fasting ("whenever you," 6:2, 3, 5, 6, 16, 17). Rather, Jesus cautions us about the ever-present danger of hypocritical worship. It is difficult to imagine that anyone would set out to be a hypocrite. Indeed, most of us are often not even aware when we cross the line, when we begin to worship more for public recognition, even accolades, than for giving proper praise to God. Public acclaim can be quite a seductive, slippery slope. Over time, the sanctuary can become a theater, a place of performers and audience where what ultimately matters are the reviews, not the integrity of what we are doing. In this season of self-examination, Jesus urges us to beware that we worship not to be seen by others but to be seen by God. Our piety is not a performance but the response to our relationship to God.

Jesus' warning comes with the promise that God will reward those who try to live faithfully. He does not specify the nature of the reward but implies that its worth far exceeds that of the hypocrites. Such a promise is a reassuring word for those trying to pursue "heavenly treasures" in a culture consumed by the pursuit of earthly ones. At a time when there is often little regard for efforts to work and serve worshipfully, Jesus declares that God takes note and will respond generously.

FIRST SUNDAY IN LENT

FEBRUARY 17, 2002

REVISED COMMON	EPISCOPAL (BCP)	ROMAN CATHOLIC
Gen. 2:15-17; 3:1-7	Gen. 2:4b-9, 15-17, 25—3:7	Gen. 2:7-9; 3:1-7
Ps. 32	Ps. 51 or 51:1-13	Ps. 51:3-4, 5-6, 12-13, 17
Rom. 5:12-19	Rom. 5:12-19 (20-21)	Rom. 5:12-19
Matt. 4:1-11	Matt. 4:1-11	Matt. 4:1-11

THE TEXTS FOR THIS SUNDAY NAME, in no uncertain terms, the realities of temptation, sin, and the effects of sin in the human story. The Genesis text tells that, from the very beginning, humans have struggled against God's ordering of life. In the epistolary reading, Paul draws on the Genesis narrative to proclaim the radical, life-giving, grace-abounding age ushered in by Christ. The psalm is a prayer of lament that calls on the hearers to confess their sins out loud, to trust that God forgives. Finally, Matthew recounts the temptations of Jesus in the wilderness.

FIRST LESSON

GENESIS 2:15-17; 3:1-7 (RCL); 2:4b-9, 15-17, 25—3:7 (BCP); 2:7-9; 3:1-7 (RC)

Interpreting the Text

The opening verses of this text (2:4b-9, 15-17) speak to the relationship between God and the human. God is the subject who acts, the one who makes earth and heaven (2:4b), forms the human from dust of the ground (2:7, 8), breathes the breath of life (2:7), plants a garden (2:8), puts the human there (2:8), and makes trees to grow (2:9). The human is utterly dependent, a beneficiary of God's work. Just as plants and herbs wait to spring up until God provides rain and a tiller (2:5), the human is lifeless clay until God exhales into it (2:7). The human lives—and in the midst of abundance (2:9)—because God wants it so. God then defines clearly the terms of this existence: the human has the task of tending the garden and may eat from all of its trees except one, the tree of knowledge (2:15-17). There is extravagant provision and an appointed limit.

God's prohibition of one tree sets the stage for humanity's first struggle with temptation (3:1-7). The tempter here is just another creature in the garden, a serpent, but one distinguished by his craftiness. The serpent asks a question that distorts God's command, denies that they will be punished, and offers the woman an alternative to obedience: "you will not die," he asserts, "you will be like God, knowing good and evil" (3:5). His clever words invite her to step outside the bounds of human existence as defined by God, to be suspect of divine motives. From this point of view, the woman sees that the prohibited tree is desirable not only as "good for food and . . . a delight to the eyes" like all the others (3:6; cf. 2:9), but even more for its ability to make the two humans wise. Their decision to disobey, to try to be like God, does in fact open their eyes, but to a self-focused, fear-filled distortion of the existence God intends for them.

Responding to the Text

From the very beginning, this story claims, humans have struggled with what it means to live in the world as creatures of God. Set in a garden beyond imagining and entrusted with good work to do, their attention soon turns to the one thing they could not have. It does not take very much. A few questions. A suggestion or two that the world might be different, that God might not be who they think.

A SIMPLE ACT OF DISOBEDIENCE HAS PROFOUND CONSEQUENCES. IT THROWS WHAT WAS ORDERED INTO DISARRAY, TURNS CONFIDENCE INTO FEAR, MUTUALITY INTO SELF-PRESERVATION.

And soon their desire to know more, to test the boundaries, overwhelms their trust in God's ordering of life. Just a taste of the fruit, a simple act of disobedience, has profound consequences. It throws what was ordered into disarray, turns innocence into (distorted) knowledge, confidence into fear, mutuality into self-preservation and the casting of blame. From this new perspective, the garden is no longer a haven, the Creator no longer a gracious host. What begins as a story about God's power and extravagant provision, ends with the two humans hiding in the bushes, eyes open yet strangely blinded, and trembling as God approaches with the evening breeze. God renders judgment, driving them out of the garden (3:23-24), but they do not die. God makes a way for life even when death is warranted.

PSALM 32 (RCL)

Psalm 32 teaches about the practice and necessity of penitence. The psalmist begins with the wisdom principle that those who are "happy" are so because they have been forgiven by God (32:1-2; cf. Prov. 28:13). God's pardon is required for well-being. Drawing on personal experience, the psalmist then testifies to the validity of this principle (32:3-4). When she was *silent* and did not confess her iniquities, the unspoken wrongs withered her very being: her bones aged, her strength dried up, and from her lips came constant groaning. To bear every transgression in silence was to strain day and night against the heavy hand of God. When the psalmist *spoke,* however, and confessed her wrongdoing to God ("I acknowledged to you;" "I did not hide;" "I said, 'I will confess'"; 32:5), there was immediate forgiveness. Confessing speech leads to divine pardon. To confess aloud to God says much about the sinner but also about what the sinner believes about God. Penitent speech is a matter of trust (32:10). The psalmist urges the faithful not to be stubbornly silent but, trusting in God's deliverance and protection, to acknowledge their faults, to pray, and *to shout* with joy (32:6-7, 9-11).

PSALM 51 or 51:1-13 (BCP); 51:3-4 5-6 12-13, 17 (RC)

See the comments on the Responsive Reading for Ash Wednesday.

SECOND READING
ROMANS 5:12-19

Interpreting the Text

Drawing on Genesis 2–3 and echoing contemporaneous Jewish understandings about Adam's influence (e.g., 4 Ezra 3:7, 21-22; 7:118; *2 Apoc. Bar.* 54:15), Paul makes a comparison between Adam, the first human, and Christ, the head of the new humanity. The whole of human history, Paul contends, is comprised of two epochs, each established by one man, Adam or Christ. Whereas Adam's sin initiated an age dominated by sin and, through it, death, Christ's death and resurrection ushered in an epoch defined by grace, justification, and life. Paul uses the rhetorical contrast of "the one man" and "the many" throughout to highlight the universal consequences of each man's action. What Adam's disobedience did to distort human life, Christ's obedience undid to restore it. Adam and Christ are thus type and antitype (5:13). For Paul, the parallel is appropriate but not exact. As he argues in 5:15-17, the effect of Christ's act ("the free gift") surpasses that of Adam's trespass. Grace is greater ("much more surely," 5:15, 17) because it overcomes the power and wages of sin.

It is important to note that although Paul identifies the *origin* of human sin in 5:12-19, he does not speak of *original sin* as later Christian theologians would formulate it. Paul ascribes the realities of sin and death to Adam and his "transgression" (5:14; cf. "trespass," 5:15, 17; "disobedience," 5:19) and, secondarily, to individual humans—all of whom have followed Adam into sin (5:12d; cf. 3:9, 23). Paul does not address the question of *how* the effect of Adam's disobedience occurred. The pervasiveness of sin and death is for him here a means to proclaim the radical, life-giving gospel.

Responding to the Text

Paul's words lift up two important themes for the Lenten season. First, he reminds us of the magnitude and pervasiveness of sin that holds us captive. Because of Adam, he contends, the human drama is now played out on a stage dominated by the power of sin and death. Our innate tendency, our deepest instinct, is to sin, to rebel against God. Sin relentlessly crouches at our door. It has from the very beginning. Self-examination during these days, therefore, is about more than acknowledging personal faults or failures and resolving to work harder. It is about recognizing that we are caught up in a distorted existence that we ourselves cannot overcome. We cannot redeem ourselves. The power of sin is too great.

> CHRIST USHERED IN A NEW AGE, A LIBERATING, LIFE-GIVING, GRACE-ABOUNDING REALITY THAT TRANSFORMS AND TRIUMPHS OVER WHAT WAS BEFORE.

The power of Christ's deliverance is even greater, however. Paul proclaims that because of Christ, the human story is told anew. Christ ushered in a new age, a liberating, life-giving, grace-abounding reality that transforms and triumphs over what was before. As a result, our Lenten self-examination takes place in the larger context of God's redemptive work in Christ. Our journey does not end in the wilderness; it ends at Easter.

The Gospel

MATTHEW 4:1-11

Interpreting the Text

Wet with the waters of baptism, his identity as the beloved Son of God just announced (Matt. 3:13-17), Jesus is led by the Spirit into the wilderness to be tempted, or tested, by the devil (cf. Mark 1:12-13; Luke 4:1-13). As the tempter's refrain (*"if* you are the Son of God;" 4:3, 6) indicates, what is at stake is how Jesus understands the nature of his sonship.

Although Jesus' identity is unique, his temptations in the wilderness are not. Matthew underscores that Jesus' experience parallels that of Israel, also called "son" by God (Hos. 11:1). First, Jesus is tested after he returns from Egypt and passes through waters (2:13-17; cf. Exod. 14–15). Second, the Spirit ushers Jesus into the wilderness to be tested just as Yahweh led Israel (2:1; cf. Deut. 8:2-3). Third, Jesus' temptations are identical to and in the same chronological order as those of Israel: hunger (4:3-4; cf. Exod. 16:1-4), testing God (4:5-7; cf. Exod. 17:1-17), and false worship (4:8-11; cf. Exodus 19–32). Finally, Jesus responds to each temptation with quotations from Deuteronomy 6–8, the portion of that book in which Moses teaches Israel how to live faithfully in the land by recalling the exodus and wilderness experience. Matthew thus weaves Jesus' story with that of the people of God. Their temptations are his. Unlike Israel, however, Jesus does not yield to temptation but remains obedient, faithful.

As Moses did on Mt. Sinai before him (Exod. 34:28; Deut. 9:9, 18), Jesus fasts in the wilderness for forty days. Afterwards, when Jesus is famished and weak, the tempter approaches him (4:2-3; cf. Luke 4:2). The first temptation, to make stones into loaves of bread, arises from the immediacy of Jesus' hunger. Use the power that God has given you, the devil entices, and satisfy your needs. Provide first for your own comfort. Jesus' response, a quote from Deut. 8:3, shows that he understands this test to be like that of the Israelites whom God led into the wilderness to discover whether or not it was in their hearts to keep the commandments. There, in the midst of scarcity, a daily diet of manna taught them that God provides sufficiently, even abundantly. Remembering this, Jesus refuses the tempter's invitation to doubt that God's will sustain him. He chooses to wait for bread from heaven rather than to exploit his gifts for narrow, self-serving ends. His response affirms his dependence on God, not bread, for life.

Cleverly, the tempter adopts Jesus' own words ("it is written," 4:4, 6) and strategy of appealing to Scripture for the next temptation. "Throw yourself down," he challenges Jesus, for if God is really so trustworthy, God will command angels to bear you up (4:6; quote from Ps. 91:11-12). The tempter entices Jesus to act in a way that will test publicly the reliability of God's word. To do so, however, requires that Jesus understand God to be at his bidding, that Jesus summon God to fulfill the divine promises for Jesus' ends. Again, Jesus refuses, quoting from Deut. 6:16. At Massah (Heb. "test"), the Israelites demanded water, interpreting its absence as indicative of God's absence (Exod. 17:1-7). For Jesus to jump from the Temple would be, similarly, to call upon God to prove God's fidelity. Such a request would not demonstrate trust in God but a lack thereof.

With the final test, the devil offers Jesus the chance to realize immediately his rightful place as Lord of the earth (cf. Moses being shown all the land on Mt. Nebo in Deut. 34:1-8) without undertaking his ministry. If Jesus will just bow down, he can avoid altogether the work before him.[1] He will not have to gather and teach disciples, heal the sick and the blind, feed the hungry, face opponents, or suffer rejection and betrayal. He will not have to die a criminal's death on the cross. Instead, he can savor now the fruits of victory. With a bold command and words from Deut. 6:13, Jesus dismisses both the tempter and this last temptation. False worship, Jesus claims, renders false triumph. He will arrive at his rightful destination, like the Israelites in the Promised Land, only by trusting God and walking the road that lies before him (cf. Deut. 6:10-15).

Responding to the Text

Matthew skillfully paints a portrait of Jesus as the one appointed by God like Moses (Deut. 18:18), but who never wavers in his obedience to God. Matthew's brushstrokes evoke the familiar stories of human temptation—of Adam, Eve, and a serpent in the garden, of Israel's murmuring in the wilderness—and weave them seamlessly so that Jesus' face is not so unlike our own. Jesus' experience reminds us that temptation is part of the life of faith. The Spirit led Jesus into the wilderness and his encounter with the tempter would not be his last (e.g., Matt. 16:23; 27:40). Testing is inevitable for people charged to serve God in the world.

> TEMPTATION IS NEVER A SIMPLE MATTER. JESUS'
> TEMPTATIONS ARE NOT, ON THEIR FACE, INHERENTLY
> POOR CHOICES.

Matthew also makes clear that temptation is never a simple matter. Jesus' temptations are not, on their face, inherently poor choices. Create bread in the midst of hunger. Call on God to act so that people might believe. Wield power over the kingdoms of the world. Under different circumstances, such actions might well be appropriate. Jesus' temptations appeal to his strengths, not his weaknesses. It is because *he can* that the decisions are difficult.

Even as Matthew paints Jesus' portrait in colors from our own story, we find ourselves, in the end, gazing at the Son of God from afar. Jesus never wavered in the desert. He proved himself unwilling to abuse his power for self-serving ends, to manipulate God into action, to serve another for the sake of quick glory. Rather, this one in whom we meet God chose at every turn not to be like God, but to trust, to remain obedient and humble, to love God with his whole heart, soul, and might (Deut. 6:5). His is the paradigm of discipleship we so often stumble over in our haste be the church in the world.

SECOND SUNDAY IN LENT

FEBRUARY 24, 2002

REVISED COMMON	EPISCOPAL (BCP)	ROMAN CATHOLIC
Gen. 12:1-4a	Gen. 12:1-8	Gen. 12:1-4a
Ps. 121	Ps. 33:12-22	Ps. 33:4-5, 18-19, 20, 22
Rom. 4:1-5, 13-17	Rom. 4:1-5 (6-12), 13-17	2 Tim. 1:8b-10
John 3:1-17	John 3:1-17	Matt. 17:1-9

THE TEXTS FOR THIS SUNDAY PROCLAIM God's sovereignty and grace, God's power to "give life to the dead and call into existence the things that do not exist" (Rom. 4:17). In the Genesis story, God promises life and a future in the face of barrenness and old age. In Romans 4:1-12, Paul stresses that God made promises to Abraham not because Abraham did anything to deserve them, but because God graciously chose to do so. God gives salvation freely. The Gospel account of Nicodemus's night meeting with Jesus reiterates this good news: entrance into the kingdom of God is an outrageously extravagant gift "from above." Such words about divine promises and undeserved gifts invite us to reflect on the nature of faith.

FIRST READING
GENESIS 12:1-4a (RCL/RC); 12:1-8 (BCP)

Interpreting the Text

The human story had nearly run its course. Following creation, the narratives of Genesis 3–11 speak about human disobedience, mistrust, and violence, and about God's judgment by flood and dispersion. Despite God's providential care, the human story was one of brokenness and curse, one that culminated, just before today's text, with the announcement of Sarai's barrenness (11:30). With that, all came to a halt. No way existed, within human capacity, to move the story forward.

It is into this bleak ending that God breathes word of a new beginning. When God speaks to Abram in Gen.12:1-3, it is, as it was in the beginning, speech that creates. God begins with the imperative that Abram leave all that is familiar, all the securities of nation, community, and family, and journey to a strange and unnamed land (12:1). God then makes five promises about the future: "I will make," "I will bless," "I will make," "I will bless," "I will curse" (12:2-3). Repetition of the first person and the word "bless" emphasizes that God is in control and that this new story has a redemptive purpose. Anticipated blessing ("*those who bless you*") outweighs anticipated curse ("*the one who curses you*"). God here initiates, through the life of this person, a history of salvation for Israel and for "all the families of the earth," a history defined by and impelled forward by divine promise.

> GOD HERE INITIATES, THROUGH THE LIFE OF THIS PERSON, A HISTORY OF SALVATION FOR ISRAEL AND FOR "ALL THE FAMILIES OF THE EARTH."

Abram obeys immediately, without objection (12:4a). Graciously chosen by God, he and his family leave behind what is known and set out on a journey not of his initiative to a destination not of his choosing. They journey with hope for a new reality that God alone can create.

Responding to the Text

This text is overwhelmingly about God. God initiates. God commands. God promises. God speaks of possibilities and new life where there seems to be only impossibility and barrenness. What God promises could not be more desirable: land, prosperity, prominence. What God commands could not be more life-altering or world-shattering. In the space between God's promises and God's command, however, the narrative is very much about Abraham. He has a choice to make. Stay with the familiar, the loved, the secure, the ending, or set out toward the unfamiliar, the unknown, the insecure, the beginning. The choice is costly and the journey will be difficult—the wilderness can be a place of struggle and doubt. But it is the way initiated by and paved with divine promise.

RESPONSIVE READING

PSALM 121 (RCL)

It is likely that this psalm, one of the Songs of Ascents (Psalms 120–134), was sung by pilgrims on the way to Jerusalem to worship. It confesses and teaches trust in God to sustain and protect the pilgrim on the journeys in life and the journey of life. The psalmist begins with the confession that God is "my help" (121:1-2). To lift up one's eyes is a gesture of petition (cf. Ps. 123:1-2); "the hills" probably refer to the mountains around Jerusalem, where God's holy mountain, Zion, is found (Pss. 125:1; 133:3). "My help," the psalmist declares, is God, the "maker of heaven and earth," the one whose power to help is boundless.

The psalmist then develops this confession with assurances that God is *your* keeper (121:3-8). There is mention neither of specific dangers (only "all evil," 121:7) nor how God will guard. Rather, the psalmist speaks of God's tireless protection using images of journeying: the foot that does not stumble (121:3), being out in the sun by day and moon by night (121:5-6), going and returning (121:8). The psalmist concludes that God keeps "your life" now and evermore (127:7-8).

The psalmist poses the question for all of us: From where does my help come? If our answer is "from ourselves," the psalmist tells us to think again.

PSALM 33:12-22 (BCP);
33:4-5, 18-19, 20, 22 (RC)

This psalm calls on the righteous to trust in God and offers, in twenty-two verses (the number of letters in the Hebrew alphabet), a comprehensive description of why. After an opening call to worship (33:1-5), the psalmist proclaims that God rules over every realm: the heavens and the earth (33:6-9), nations and peoples (33:10-12), all humankind (33:13-17), and those who "fear the Lord," namely, those who are reverent of and obedient to God (33:18-19). There is no dimension of the cosmos or the human community over which God is not sovereign. God even fashions the human heart and, from heaven, comprehends—looks down, sees, watches, observes (33:13-15)—every person. Furthermore, the salvation of God is more powerful, more reliable, than the greatest human resource (the king's army, a warrior's strength, a horse's might; 33:16-17). God alone can deliver from death, famine, affliction. Finally, the psalmist offers a corporate confession of trust and hope in God (33:20-21) and a prayer for God's steadfast love (33:22).

Second Reading
ROMANS 4:1-5, 13-17 (RCL);
4:1-5 (6-12), 13-17 (BCP);
2 TIMOTHY 1:8b-10 (RC)

Interpreting the Text

This text invites us into a conversation already in progress. Paul is talking about his theology of salvation, that sinners are saved by grace through faith (3:21-26). God freely gives salvation as a gift (3:24), not as wages for doing what the law requires. Believers cannot boast about their salvation, therefore, because it is not of their own doing. It is not their achievement (3:27-28). Does it follow, then, that the law no longer matters? If faith, not law, is the way of salvation, do we "overthrow the law?" (3:31). "By no means," Paul admonishes. Instead, the law may be more rightly understood. He turns to the figure of Abraham to explain.

In contrast to a view held by some of Paul's Jewish contemporaries, that God considered Abraham upright because he was obedient to the law, Paul argues that God did so by grace. Paul reminds his listeners that, according to Scripture, Abraham believed in God and God reckoned it to him as righteousness (4:3; Gen. 15:6). Abraham did nothing to deserve divine favor; his status before God came neither through the law nor through circumcision (4:9-12; cf. Gen. 17:24). Abraham had no reason to boast before God (4:2b). And if *he* didn't, no one else did.

Paul goes on to say that if God's promise to Abraham had been a matter of obedience, a matter of law, the promise never would have been fulfilled. Abraham and his descendants, as sinners, could not have met its demands (4:13-15). Instead, the promise is guaranteed by God's grace, by divine power and generosity that brought life where Abraham and Sarah knew only barrenness and old age (4:17-19). The promise extends to all persons, Jews and Gentiles, who share in Abraham's faith (4:16).

Paul thus underscores that even Abraham, the paradigm of faith, was dependent on God, who alone "justifies the ungodly" (4:5). Moreover, his argument establishes that God's grace (and Abraham's faith) precedes and is the foundation for the law. Believers obey the law, therefore, not as some misguided means to effect their own salvation, but as a lived expression of their faith.

Responding to the Text

Paul's claim that salvation is a gift freely given by God may sound both liberating and unsettling in a culture and time characterized by individualism and self-sufficiency. He rejects the idea that we can make it on our own, establish our worth by our work, earn our salvation as though it were wages. Such thinking, he contends, demonstrates trust in ourselves, not God. Dependency on "following the letter of the law" may cause us to miss, or even refuse, the generosity of God. Paul thus calls us to a grace-filled awareness that our acceptance by God is not—and never will be—our own doing, but because God wants it to be so.

The Gospel
JOHN 3:1-17 (rcl, bcp)

Interpreting the Text

Many people believed in Jesus because they saw the signs that he was performing, John writes, but Jesus did not entrust himself to them; he had no need for their tenuous testimonies (2:23-25). With that, John introduces Nicode-

mus, a leader of the Jewish community, who comes to Jesus at night, a time typically associated with mystery, misunderstanding. Nicodemus's first words indicate that he speaks as one of those many people ("for no one can do these signs
that you do apart from the presence of God," 3:2). His faith is tentative, based on
signs, and his encounter with Jesus will leave him perplexed.

As is characteristic of John, this conversation is full of double meanings, ambiguity, even parody. Nicodemus's repeated misunderstanding prompts Jesus to
explain in more detail. In short, they talk past each other. Jesus responds to
Nicodemus's greeting with a warning: "no one can see the kingdom of God without being born *anōthen*" (3:3). The Greek word *anōthen* can mean either "from
above" (spatial) or "again" (temporal). Jesus uses it in the former sense (3:3; cf.
3:31); Nicodemus clearly understands it in the latter (3:4). Similarly, Jesus plays on
Greek *pneuma,* "spirit" or "wind," to talk about being born from above, born of
the Spirit. Jesus also makes a parallel between "seeing" the kingdom of God (3:3)
and "entering" it (3:5), perhaps suggesting the connection between the revelation
in Jesus and the divine kingdom. Finally, when it seems that all of Jesus' doubletalk
has utterly confounded Nicodemus, Jesus recalls Nicodemus's own words ("are you
a teacher," "we know," 3:10-11; cf. 3:2) to end their conversation.

In the monologue that follows, Jesus responds to Nicodemus's last question
("How can these things be?"). Jesus emphasizes, first, that being born of the Spirit
is a "heavenly thing," something that only he, as the one who comes from heaven,
can speak about (3:12-13). Second, he addresses the *how.* For people to be born
in the Spirit, Jesus must be "lifted up," a reference to the crucifixion, resurrection, and ascension. Just like the bronze serpent Moses raised up on a pole gave
life to the Israelites who looked on it (Num. 21:9), so Jesus "lifted up" becomes
the source of eternal life for everyone who believes in him. In short, entrance
into the kingdom of God is a gift given out of divine love for the world, a gift
from above, an outpouring of the Spirit as mysterious as the wind.

Responding to the Text

The conversation was over so quickly. One can imagine Nicodemus
standing there, an educated pillar of the community, shaking his head in bewil-
derment. It had begun rather simply, with Nicodemus coming to Jesus and
announcing, perhaps proudly, what *we know* about him (3:2). But, somehow, facing Jesus in the dark of night, his certainty gives way to perplexity. Nicodemus
proves unable to keep up with the intellectual banter, the verbal sparring. He cannot make the shift from the "earthly" to the "heavenly," he cannot grasp the words
blowing by him. His rather flat worldview makes it impossible to see, to comprehend who is standing before him. The old formulas do not work. The sure
theologies come up short. How can these things be?

It is into the whirlwind of Nicodemus's confusion, at that point when he is literally speechless in the story, that Jesus proclaims the good news. His words resonate well with those of the epistle for this Sunday. Entrance into the divine realm, he says, is the outrageous, extravagant gift of a loving God. It isn't something we figure out, control, plan, or manipulate. It cannot be achieved or earned. Nicodemus will *see* Jesus, will enter the kingdom of God, by the power of an inbreaking light, a Spirit from above—not by his own volition. The kingdom is not ours to effect. It is ours to receive.

IT IS INTO THE WHIRLWIND OF NICODEMUS'S CONFUSION, AT THAT POINT WHEN HE IS LITERALLY SPEECHLESS IN THE STORY, THAT JESUS PROCLAIMS THE GOOD NEWS.

MATTHEW 17:1-9 (RC)

See the comments on the Gospel for Transfiguration Sunday.

THIRD SUNDAY IN LENT

MARCH 3, 2002

REVISED COMMON	EPISCOPAL (BCP)	ROMAN CATHOLIC
Exod. 17:1-7	Exod. 17:1-7	Exod. 17:3-7
Ps. 95	Ps. 95 or 95:6-11	Ps. 95:1-2, 6-7, 8-9
Rom. 5:1-11	Rom. 5:1-11	Rom. 5:1-2, 5-8
John 4:5-42	John 4:5-26	John 4:5-42 (4:5-15,
	(27-38), 39-42	19b-26, 39a, 40-42)

WATER CASCADING ONTO DESERT SANDS. Living water offered in a hostile land. The motif of water in the texts for this Sunday invites reflection about human dependency on God and God's abundant provision. The texts further affirm the mystery, power, and holy otherness of God. God gives water, but it surges forth from a rock. Jesus offers living water to the Samaritan woman but remains a mystifying figure.

FIRST READING

EXODUS 17:1-7 (RCL, BCP); 17:3-7 (RC)

Interpreting the Text

This story (see the parallel account in Num. 20:2-13) begins with obedience. The Israelites, newly liberated from slavery, are on the move "as the Lord commanded" (17:1). When they make camp at Rephidim and discover no water, however, they worry about their well-being. They anticipate scarcity despite God's prior provision of sweet water to quench their thirst (Exod. 15:22-25a) and feasts of quail and manna to fill their bellies (Exod. 16:1-36). They immediately quarrel and demand that Moses do something (17:1b-3). Their protests grow more strident even though Moses warns them that to contend with him is to test God.

Fearful for his safety, Moses cries to God for help (17:3-4). God responds with instructions that, when carried out, will more than satisfy the people's needs. With God in front of him, Moses takes the rod that once made the Nile undrinkable (17:5; cf. Exod. 7:14-25) and strikes a rock. In an instant, that which was dry and unyielding becomes a source of life-giving springs. As Ps. 78:20 tells it, "water gushed out and torrents overflowed" (see Ps. 78:15-20; 114:8). Moses names the site not for these miraculous waters, however, but for the people's test (Massah) of and quarrel (Meribah) with God. He designates the place a perpetual reminder of the precariousness of faith, of how doubt and fear can give rise to questions about God's presence (17:7), engender a thirst for God to show Godself, and prompt demands that God perform a particular sign or wonder.

Responding to the Text

Standing at Massah and Meribah this season, we are reminded that the journey through the wilderness is not without danger. Redeemed but not yet in the Promised Land, it is possible to get lost in shifting sands. It is possible to believe that there is insufficiency when we have tasted sweet water. To cry hunger when manna falls as the morning dew. To long for security at any price, even that of slavery. At such moments, we may call on God to act, to do something new, to work some wonder in our presence that we might continue to believe. We may require God to be at our beck and call, to demonstrate divine power on our terms. In short, we may try to make God a means to get what we want. This story sternly warns us against such testing of God.

> IN THE MIDST OF CONTENTION AND CASTING BLAME, WE ARE TOLD THAT GOD YET AGAIN PROVIDED FOR THE PEOPLE'S NEEDS.

At the same time, in the midst of contention and casting blame, we are told that God yet again provided for the people's needs. They were dependent on God to do so. God's method was surprising. At God's command, dust and rock unleashed cascades of flowing, fresh water. Standing on the rock in front of Moses, God stirred forth creation so that the people might drink.

RESPONSIVE READING

PSALM 95

Psalm 95 summons its hearers to come into the presence of God with noisy, joyful, song-filled praise, to fall on their knees, and to heed God's warning *today* never to repeat what happened at Meribah and Massah (see Exod. 17:1-7, above). The psalmist opens with a hymn of praise that urges the people to process, shouting and singing their thanksgivings, and to bow before God (95:1-7a). The psalmist invites the people to do so, first, because God is a "great God and a great King above all gods" (95:3). God's power is testified to by God's handiwork: the depths of the earth, the heights of the mountains, the seas, the dry land (95:4-5). The whole of creation rests in the hand of God. The psalmist invites the people to do so, secondly, because this God is "*our* Maker," "*our* God" (96:6-7). This God whose majesty is writ large on the cosmos brought the people into existence and continues to lead, provide for, and protect them (95:7a).

The people's voices now lifted in praise, the psalmist next exhorts them to listen for God's voice (95:7b). Divine speech pours forth a warning to the present from the past (95:8-11). The people are charged not to harden their hearts *today* as the Israelites did on *the day* at Massah and Meribah, not to test or put God to the proof. The consequences were dire for the generation of the Israelites who doubted time and again in the wilderness. God resolved that such a generation would never enter "my rest" (95:11), that is, never set foot in the land of promise (cf. Num. 14:20-25). In the same way, the psalmist contends, not to heed God's voice today is to risk remaining a wanderer in the wilderness, adrift somewhere between redemption and fulfillment.

SECOND LESSON
ROMANS 5:1-11

Interpreting the Text

Paul here interweaves reminder and assurance in a manner appropriate for the season of Lent. The warp of his words, on the one hand, is comprised of blunt reminders about the human condition. People are weak and ungodly (5:6), sinners (5:8), enemies (5:10), and sufferers (5:3). They are self-protecting, rarely willing to risk boldly for another (5:7). In short, they deserve divine judgment (5:9). The woof of his words, on the other hand, is assurance of God's love, Christ's mediation of that love ("through our Lord Jesus Christ," 5:1, 11; cf. 2, 9), and the new realities and possibilities effected by Christ's death and resurrection. Paul emphasizes the unmerited nature of God's grace in Christ. That Christ would die for such sinners, Paul claims confidently, *proves* God's love (5:8).

Paul underscores that because of God's saving work in Christ, Christians now live in the world differently (5:1; cf. 4:13-25) . They rejoice in their new condition (5:2, 3, 11). First, they have been reconciled with God. This assertion frames 5:1-11. Paul opens with "we have peace with God" (5:1) and closes with "we have now received reconciliation" (5:11b; cf. 5:10). Restored in their relationship to God, Christians enjoy access to divine grace (5:2) and need not fear the wrath of God (5:9). Second, Christians have hope that rises out of the divine love poured into human hearts by the Holy Spirit (5:5). Hope that looks expectantly for a sharing in the "glory of God." Hope that is not illusory, does not disappoint, never deceives. Hope that so believes in the divine love shown in Christ and the promise of eschatological salvation that present circumstances—including the realities of suffering—may be transformed and transforming (5:3-4). Hope that affirms that it is God's redemptive power alone that stirs forth life out of death.

Responding to the Text

During the Lenten season, Paul's textual weaving drapes us like a familiar garment, one that enfolds us in our humanness, exposes us to what we know about ourselves, and confronts us with the everyday realities of pain and suffering in the world. It clings to us like an old, well-worn coat. At the same time, it envelops us in the mystery and joy of what God has done on our behalf through Christ: reconciled us, granted us access to divine grace, given us hope, poured love into our hearts, sent to us the Holy Spirit, saved us. The garment wraps us in a way of being that is not warranted by our past and offers assurances of healing, wholeness, and peace we ourselves cannot effect. Its patterns dance with bold colors. Its texture is a delight to the touch. Its threads hold long after optimism is torn and false hopes are tattered. To wear this garment is to witness joyfully to God's saving work in Christ and to hope confidently in a despairing and skeptical world.

THE GOSPEL
JOHN 4:5-42 (RCL/RC);
4:5-26 (27-38), 39-42 (BCP);
4:5-15, 19b-26, 39A, 40-42 (RC, alt.)

Interpreting the Text

John tells two stories early in his Gospel about people struggling to comprehend the mystery of Jesus. The first is that of Nicodemus, a leader in Jerusalem who, try as he might, cannot grasp what Jesus is saying to him about rebirth and breath (John 3:1-21). John soon abandons their conversation in favor of a soliloquy by Jesus. The second is this story about an unnamed Samaritan woman who meets Jesus at a well. Unlike Nicodemus, the woman is a marginalized figure—a woman, a person without apparent office or status, and a Samaritan. Unlike Nicodemus, she talks with Jesus in the light of day, publicly, in what is for him enemy territory. Despite all the gender conventions and ancient antagonisms that would preclude such an encounter, the two strangers engage in the longest conversation recorded by John. The woman works with determination to figure out who this Jesus is, and the two of them shatter ancient barriers for the sake of new truth.

THE WOMAN WORKS WITH DETERMINA-
TION TO FIGURE OUT WHO THIS JESUS IS,
AND THE TWO OF THEM SHATTER ANCIENT
BARRIERS FOR THE SAKE OF NEW TRUTH.

The woman's daily work is interrupted by Jesus' demand for a drink. Brusquely, she names the inappropriateness of his request by highlighting their differences: "How is it that *you, a Jew,* ask a drink of *me, a woman of Samaria?*" Her correction is underscored by the parenthetical comment, "Jews do not use things in common with Samaritans" (4:9). Undeterred, Jesus challenges her to reconsider with whom she is speaking and to ask him for living water. The woman takes up this twofold challenge with tenacity. She asks question after question ("Where do you get that living water?" "Are you greater than our ancestor Jacob?"). She wrestles with ambiguities in Jesus' speech (e.g., water of the well and living water) and engages in ambiguity in her own (4:17). She raises concerns with what he says and considers all of it in light of her own understanding (e.g., 4:19, 25). Eventually, the woman asks for the living water of which Jesus speaks (4:15), but her efforts to understand fully and to recognize him are interrupted by the disciples' return.

While the disciples remain captive to gender conventions (why would Jesus bother with a woman?), the woman sets down her jar for carrying water—she no longer needs it—and returns to the city to tell everyone about Jesus (4:28-30). Unlike Nicodemus who apparently kept his mouth shut, she testifies about Jesus, recounting her experience ("a man who told me everything I have ever done") and asking the question, "He cannot be the Messiah, *can he?*" Her story inspires others to believe (4:39). Her question invites many to ponder the mystery, the incomprehensibility of this stranger. Her call to "come and see" prompts them to seek Jesus for themselves. And, after two days with him, they profess real recognition: "*We* have heard for ourselves and *we know* that this is truly the Savior of the world" (4:42).

Responding to the Text

The woman's encounter with Jesus summons us to diligence in the struggle to know him. What began as a chance meeting, an interruption of the everyday, unfolds into a revelatory moment. After Jesus initiates the conversation, the words fly back and forth as the woman wrestles to determine just who this stranger is in front of her. We find ourselves swept into their dialogue, caught up in her wonderment, participants in her discovery. Then, when their conversation ends abruptly, we are reminded that who Jesus is ultimately remains elusive. There are no simple answers to the many questions. Ambiguity and mystery lingers. Even so, the woman goes forth with what she has experienced, with what she knows, and testifies about it to others. "He cannot be the Messiah, can he?" Suddenly we find ourselves back at the well, asking to know more.

The story also shows Jesus going about the work of reconciliation, engaging someone who, by all definitions, is "other" to

THE STORY SHOWS JESUS GOING ABOUT THE WORK OF RECONCILIATION, ENGAGING SOMEONE WHO, BY ALL DEFINITIONS, IS "OTHER" TO HIM.

him. There, talking face to face, the two bridge the chasm of long-standing disagreements and oppressive assumptions, and engage with one another so that she might know this Jesus. They are on risky ground. Possibilities for misunderstanding abound and, as the disciples demonstrate (4:27), old conventions are near at hand. Yet, as a result of their encounter, the woman cannot help but speak, and Jesus agrees to stay longer so that others might also be with him. There, ancient schisms and old wounds give way to new faith.

FOURTH SUNDAY IN LENT

MARCH 10, 2002

REVISED COMMON	EPISCOPAL (BCP)	ROMAN CATHOLIC
1 Sam. 16:1-13	1 Sam. 16:1-13	1 Sam. 16:1b, 6-7, 10-13a
Ps. 23	Ps. 23	Ps. 23:1-3a, 3b-4, 5, 6
Eph. 5:8-14	Eph. 5:(1-7), 8-14	Eph. 5:8-14
John 9:1-41	John 9:1-13 (14-27), 28-38	John 9:1-41 (9:1, 6-9, 13-17, 34-38)

T HE TEXTS FOR THIS SUNDAY paint in brushstrokes of darkness and light, blindness and sight, death and life, old and new. The 1 Samuel narrative speaks of God at work in the human drama to raise up a new king, David, even as the old, Saul, still reigns. The New Testament texts use vivid contrasts to talk about the significance of Jesus, to emphasize how radically different life in Christ is than life before Christ.

FIRST LESSON
1 SAMUEL 16:1-13 (RCL, BCP); 16:1b, 6-7, 10-13a (RC)

Interpreting the Text

Profound rejection, grief, and regret precede this story, the first in the extended literary unit known as "The Rise of David" (1 Sam. 16:1—2 Sam. 5:10). It is the end of an era. Samuel has announced to Saul, Israel's first king, that because Saul rejected the word of God, God now rejects him as king. God "has torn the kingdom of Israel" from him and given it to someone better (15:22-29). The verdict rendered, the old order in effect finished, Samuel and Saul part company (15:34). Samuel grieves as God regrets (15:35).

Amid these endings, God does something new in Israel. God, the central character of this narrative, initiates a coup d'état. God begins by calling an end to Samuel's mourning and charging him to set out to Bethlehem to anoint the king "I have provided for myself" (16:1). It is a life-threatening command. To anoint a king when another is on the throne is very risky business. When Samuel expresses his reluctance and his fear of reprisal, God provides a ruse, described in detail, and reassures Samuel that the situation will be under divine control: "I will show you what you shall do," and "you shall anoint for me the one whom I name to you" (16:4). Samuel follows the plan, saying exactly what God commands. The stage is set.

The narrator lingers over the next scene, highlighting how freely and unexpectedly God chooses the new king. Samuel is certain when he sees Jesse's oldest son that he must be the one. He is not. God cautions that, unlike humans who trust in appearances (perhaps a barb against Saul who was handsome and "head and shoulders above everyone else," 9:2; cf. 10:23), God sees differently. What matters is the human heart (cf. 1 Kings 3:5-14). The suspense then builds as son after son passes before Samuel and he repeats, "Neither has the LORD chosen this one" (16:8, 9, 10). After Samuel has passed over all seven sons, a number signifying completion, the climactic moment arrives. God chooses the eighth son, the youngest, a shepherd boy (cf. David as a musician, 16:14-23; as a warrior, 17:1-58), the son with the least claim and lowest social standing, to be the new king. David is not even present at first. Everyone has to wait. When God says "this is the one," God thwarts expectations and inverts political structures. The lowliest will be the most powerful. Ironically, the narrator mentions that David happens also to be quite stunning (16:12).

Responding to the Text

With a private anointing and the descent of God's Spirit on David (God's Spirit leaves Saul immediately after; 16:14), God sets in motion a new chapter in Israel's life. Its beginning is in secret; no one—neither Samuel nor David nor anyone else—speaks a word as the oil pours forth. Its unfolding will become most public, a new empire, an eternal dynasty (cf. 2 Sam. 7). Throughout, today's text portrays God at work in the human drama to bring something remarkably and wholly new out of the grief, regret, rejection, and fears of the old. David will become king not because of some historical accident or political campaign but because God intends it.

TODAY'S TEXT PORTRAYS GOD AT WORK IN THE HUMAN DRAMA TO BRING SOMETHING REMARKABLY AND WHOLLY NEW OUT OF THE GRIEF, REGRET, REJECTION, AND FEARS OF THE OLD.

This story, like the Gospel for today, is also about seeing clearly. Where Samuel, Jesse, and the elders see merely a young, inexperienced, practically forgotten boy, God sees a king. Where they see weakness and no claim, God grants power and an eternal dynasty. Out of the least of these comes the one who, with a heart judged as right and a striking appearance, will captivate and reign over Israel.

PSALM 23

This beloved psalm confesses intimately what life is like with God as protector. The psalm unfolds as commentary on its opening verse: "God is my shepherd, I shall not want." The metaphor of God as shepherd evokes pastoral as well as political and theological imagery. In the ancient world, kings and gods, including Yahweh (cf. Gen. 49:24; Ps. 28:9; Jer. 31:10; Mic. 7:14), were described as shepherds of peoples and portrayed with the mace and shepherd's crook (rod and staff; 23:4). To call God "my shepherd" is to entrust God alone, not any human ruler or other power, with the care and protection of one's life.

With God as shepherd, the psalmist knows no lack, no want (23:1b). The psalmist testifies to experiences of grace and abundance, to God's abiding presence even through the darkest valleys of life.

SECOND LESSON

EPHESIANS 5:8-14 (RCL/RC);
5:(1-7), 8-14 (BCP)

Interpreting the Text

This text is part of the larger unit of 5:1-20, which is concerned with Christian conduct. The writer invokes the baptismal experience, the "enlightenment," to remind his readers, individually and corporately, of their Christian vocation. The text is framed by allusions to the believer's dramatic transition from darkness and a deathly sleep before Christ to light and life in Christ (5:8-9, 13-14). The identification of the reader *as* "darkness" and "light" (not "in," 5:8) underscores just how radical the disjunction is between the former things and new life in Christ. Verse 14, possibly the fragment of an early Christian hymn sung at baptism or Easter, might further evoke personal and communal memories of baptism.

The writer implores the readers, as "children of the Light," to live accordingly in a world in which many (e.g., "those who are disobedient," 5:6) live in the darkness of lower ethical standards, a more relaxed morality. The conduct of a Christian ought to be *fruitful,* yielding that which is "good and right and true" (5:9). Specifically, the writer calls on Christians to "try to find out what is pleasing to the Lord" (5:10), to discern what is appropriate behavior in the circumstances of daily living. With minds renewed by faith (cf. 4:23; Rom. 12:2), Christians are charged to live in the world faithfully. Their responsibility is not limited to themselves, however. The writer calls for vigilance in refusing to participate in the *unfruitful* work of darkness. Christians are instead to uncover evil in all of its forms, to expose any wrongdoing (5:11), even as they do not speak of such things among themselves (5:3, 12).

Responding to the Text

Like today's Gospel, the lection from Ephesians employs the vivid language of light and darkness to remind believers of just how radically new life is in Christ compared to life before Christ. Called back to the waters of baptism, we are reminded that "coming into the light" is utterly life-transforming. We cannot live the same way. Conversion has significant moral consequences: to seek to do "what is pleasing to the Lord," to be alert and resourceful, and to be moral agents in the world, standing over against excesses and abuses, exposing, taking no part. This is not the language of compromise, of smoothing-over, of going along to get along. It is a wake-up call, reminding those of us who may have forgotten to get on with the work of living as "children of light."

> "COMING INTO THE LIGHT" IS UTTERLY LIFE-TRANSFORMING. WE CANNOT LIVE THE SAME WAY AS BEFORE.

THE GOSPEL
JOHN 9:1–41 (RCL/RC); 9:1–13 (14–27), 28–38 (BCP); 9:1, 6–9, 13–17, 34–38 (RC, alt.)

Interpreting the Text

John masterfully tells this story about sight and blindness, light and darkness, to teach about the significance of Jesus. The narrative begins with an unnamed blind man and Jesus' claim that he is "the light of the world" (9:5). It ends with the same man seeing the light, physically and spiritually, and instruction by Jesus that those who proclaim they see are, in fact, spiritually blind (9:41). Jesus is, for John, the light that saves, heals, and judges the world (cf. 8:12). For those who believe in Christ and admit their blindness, that light illumines, brings sight. For those who claim to see without Christ, the light is blinding.

The drama opens with a miracle story (9:1–7). For the disciples, their chance meeting of the blind man is an occasion for intellectual exercise. They want to speculate about the causal relationship between sin and suffering, to confirm their assumption that a physical impairment must indicate wrongdoing (cf. Exod. 20:5). Jesus flatly rejects their agenda, their attempts to cast blame. Rather than speaking to the *cause* of the man's blindness, he talks about its *purpose*, to reveal the work of God. Then, without a word from the blind man, Jesus heals him. Note that John emphasizes that the man is healed only after he washes in water, perhaps as an allusion to baptism.

In the scenes that follow (9:8-41), John contrasts the formerly blind man with those who interrogate him. Whereas the man gradually comes to see the truth about Jesus, the Pharisees (9:13, 15, 16; the Jews, 9:18, 22) are increasingly obstinate, blind to what is happening in their midst. The man's responses to their many queries indicate a growing awareness of Jesus. To the neighbors, he identifies his healer as "the man called Jesus" (9:11). To the Pharisees, he calls him "a prophet" (9:17; cf. 4:19) and later a man "from God" (9:33). Throughout the interrogations, the man trusts his experience, does not claim to know more than he does about Jesus (9:12, 25), and refuses to be frightened, as were his parents, by the authorities. By the end, he is weary ("why do you want to hear it again?"), even punchy. He asks with irony whether the Pharisees want to be Jesus' disciples, and declares that, despite their protestations, "he opened my eyes" (9:30-33).

In contrast, John portrays those who interrogate the man as increasingly suspicious of and antagonistic toward Jesus. They are divided (9:16). The neighbors argue about the man's identity while he repeatedly affirms it ("I am the man!"). The Pharisees seem initially to accept the healing, but they disagree about its troublesome aspects. Some point to Jesus' violation of Sabbath laws. Others claim that Jesus, as a sinner, cannot perform such signs. Some eventually charge that the man was never blind and summon his parents to prove it (9:18-23). In the end, the Pharisees refuse altogether to acknowledge the miracle. They call the man a disciple of Jesus and insinuate that Jesus cannot be pious and do the work of God because he is not a disciple of Moses as they are. He cannot be from God. In short, Jesus does not fit their traditional categories, their theological expectations and, as such, the man who testifies to Jesus' power must be dismissed.

Jesus reappears at this point in the narrative to ask questions of the man now rejected by the authorities and a puzzlement to his community. It is the climactic scene. For the man, this is the moment when he finally sees fully and clearly: Jesus is the "Son of Man." The man confesses, believes, and worships him. For the Pharisees, this is the moment of judgment, when those who say, "We see," are convicted of blindness.

Responding to the Text

Preachers do well to be sure that this narrative is read aloud, in full, with all of the dramatic flair that John's storytelling demands. It may be compared to superb street theater in which the characters are bold, their actions and reactions heightened, their movements deliberate, even exaggerated. The story invites listeners into the wonder of the miracle, the suspicion and quarreling over how to interpret it, the heightened tensions, reversals, ironies, and even comedy as the healed man says, again and again, "I was blind, now I see." "*I told you already. Why do you want to hear it again?*" (9:27).

In this season of self-examination, John's story invites us to reflect about the state of our own vision. To what extent are we really blind, despite our protestations that we see? Are there values or traditions to which we so cling that we miss God's revelatory work right in front of us? Are there expectations, loyalties, or prejudices we hold so firmly that we dismiss those who testify before us in truth? It is a messy business of mud and spit in the eyes to see the world differently. But that isn't the hard part. What do we do when we see clearly? Do we tell the story again and again? Do we say with conviction "I was blind but now I see" even when neighbors walk away or powers-that-be make it costly?

ARE THERE VALUES OR TRADITIONS TO WHICH WE SO CLING THAT WE MISS GOD'S REVELATORY WORK RIGHT IN FRONT OF US?

The story, like today's epistolary text, also alludes to baptism. John emphasizes that the man's physical blindness, a condition from birth (9:1, 2, 3, 19, 20), could be healed only by Jesus: "never since the world began has it been heard that anyone opened the eyes of a person born blind" (9:32). Moreover, the blind man is not healed until he washes in water (9:7). Such imagery, and John's contrast of physical blindness with the sin of spiritual blindness, suggests the corollary idea that people are born spiritually blind, in a condition of sin that may be washed away only by the living water of Christ. The church has emphasized this baptismal symbolism. John 9 was and is read as part of the three "scrutinies" or examinations conducted during Lent for catechumens preparing for baptism at Easter. As a story about Jesus as the "light of the world" and a person's "coming into the light," the text is particularly appropriate for this purpose.

FIFTH SUNDAY IN LENT

MARCH 17, 2002

REVISED COMMON	EPISCOPAL (BCP)	ROMAN CATHOLIC
Ezek. 37:1-14	Ezek. 37:1-3	Ezek. 37:12-14
	(4-10), 11-14	
Ps. 130	Ps. 130	Ps. 130:1-2, 3-4, 5-6, 7-8
Rom. 8:6-11	Rom. 6:16-23	Rom. 8:8-11
John 11:1-45	John 11:(1-16), 17-44	John 11:1-45 (11:3-7, 17,
		20-27, 33b-45)

G OD SUMMONS WIND TO BREATHE LIFE into a valley of dry bones. Jesus cries, "Come out!" into a tomb that reeks with four days of death. And then it happens. A vast multitude, the whole house of Israel, rises to its feet. Lazarus, once dead but now alive, steps out from his tomb. In their vivid contrast of life and death, the texts for this Sunday prepare us for Holy Week, proclaiming God's power and Jesus as the life and resurrection.

FIRST READING
EZEKIEL 37:1-14 (RCL); 37:1-3 (4-10), 11-14 (BCP); 37:12-14 (RC)

Interpreting the Text

This prophecy, perhaps the best known of Ezekiel, heralds national revival and restoration for a people in exile. It speaks boldly of new life amid dis-aster and profound crisis. The prophecy is well crafted rhetorically. It opens with a vision narrative (37:1-10) and closes with a divine speech that interprets the vision

> EZEKIEL SPEAKS BOLDLY OF NEW LIFE AMID DISASTER AND PROFOUND CRISIS.

(37:12-14). Linking the two are the exiles' cries of utter hopelessness: "Our bones are dried up" and "We are cut off completely" (37:11). The vision narrative speaks to the former complaint. God's words address the latter.

CHRISTINE
ROY YODER

In the prophetic vision, the Spirit of God transports Ezekiel to the middle of a valley full of bones and leads him around so that he will see their vast quantity and excessive dryness (37:1-2). No longer even loosely held together as skeletons, the desiccated, disjoined bones exemplify the utter despair, the physical and spiritual frailty expressed by the exiles' lament, "our bones are dried up" (see Prov. 17:22; cf. moist bone marrow as indicative of prosperity in Job 21:24). The bones' state of decay heightens the miraculous aspect of what God instructs Ezekiel to prophesy (37:5-6) and then proceeds to do: a recreation of the people from the inside out (37:7-10). There is rattling, bones join together bone to proper bone, sinews attach, flesh appears, and skin covers the bodies. Then, just as God breathed life into the first human (Gen. 2:7), God summons the four winds to breathe life into a vast multitude. "Mortal, can these bones live?" The revived rise up on their feet in answer.

In the divine speech, God explains that the vision represents the restoration of Israel. The resurrection of dry bones (37:1-10) God now describes as the opening of graves and raising up of those in them, a fitting response to the exiles' lament, "We have been cut off completely." The expression "to be cut off" often refers to the dead and buried (e.g., Isa. 53:8-9) and to those who believe they have been forsaken by God, an experience likened to a descent to the underworld (e.g., Pss. 31:22; 88:5). God then announces that the Israelites will return to their land, return to their own soil (37:12, 14). It is a promise of homecoming, one that with the Spirit of God upon them will be lasting (cf. 36:27-28).

Responding to the Text

Ezekiel speaks of life and restoration, good news, to people who consider themselves as good as dead. They are no longer in the land of promise. The temple is looted and destroyed. And they are scattered in a foreign land. The grief is palpable, the despair eats at their bones, and the weight of their sins and those of their ancestors rests heavily upon them. It is the valley of the shadow, a dry, distant place where abandonment and hopelessness hold sway, a place where people are captive to guilt, worry, and loneliness.

But then, says Ezekiel, God breathes. God breathes release from the despair. God breathes hope into the hopeless. God breathes life into the lifeless and calls them home.

RESPONSIVE READING

PSALM 130 (RCL, BCP); 130:1-8 (RC)

This psalm is a concise and fervent call to hope and trust in the steadfast love and redemptive power of God. The psalmist gives voice to the human predicament (130:1-2), petitioning God from "the depths," from the dark, watery abyss of individual (130:3) and communal (130:8) iniquities. If God were to "watch" (so Hebrew; NRSV: "mark") human sin, the waters would surely overwhelm and drown everyone. But God does not, the psalmist proclaims. God's nature is to forgive (130:4). The psalmist then confesses trust in God, a trust that waits for, watches for, and hopes in God, the one who does not watch human sin (130:5-6). Finally, the psalmist exhorts Israel to have hope in God and in God's final and complete redemption of all iniquities (130:7-8). For those in the depths, such hope makes it possible to put one foot in front of the other on our way through the wilderness.

Second Reading
ROMANS 8:6-11 (rcl); 8:8-11 (rc); 6:16-23 (bcp)

Interpreting the Text

Paul opens this chapter in Romans with a declaration of freedom. Those who deserve condemnation under the rule of sin and death have been set free by the work of Christ (8:1-4). The old life has gone. A new life has begun. A new life governed by the dynamic, life-giving Spirit of God.

Paul distinguishes sharply between life in the flesh and life in the Spirit. Paul uses the terms not to describe some sort of duality in human nature but to designate two fundamentally opposed realms, orientations, ways of living. To set one's mind on fleshy things is to remain subject to sin and death. It is to be "hostile to God," to be unwilling, indeed unable, to abide by God's law (8:7-8). To set one's mind on the Spirit, however, is to find life, peace, and the capacity for obedience to the divine will (8:4, 6). Paul portrays life according to the Spirit as a mysterious coming together with God and Christ: believers dwell in the Spirit and the Spirit of God dwells in them (8:9, 11); they have the Spirit of Christ; they belong to Christ; and Christ dwells in them (8:9-10). Thus, Christians exist in the Spirit, and the Spirit exists in them as the concrete expression of God's presence in the world.

> FOR PAUL, THE INDWELLING OF THE SPIRIT MEANS THAT AN INNER TRANSFORMATION IS AT WORK NOW IN BELIEVERS.

For Paul, the indwelling of the Spirit means that an inner transformation is at work now in believers. Although their bodies, their way of living in and knowing about the world, are "dead because of sin," their spirits are alive, resuscitated by the gift of righteousness. God does not stop there, however. Just as God breathed life into a valley of dry bones and raised Jesus from the dead, Paul declares, God will one day enliven their mortal bodies (8:11). Life in the Spirit, the promise of resurrection, is already at hand.

Responding to the Text

During Lent, Paul's antithesis of flesh and Spirit sets us firmly in a familiar moral tension. His stark dichotomy confronts and urges us to think seriously about what it means to "live according to the flesh," how our choices and inclinations reveal a hostility toward God and a captivity to sin and death, even as we seek to set our minds "on the Spirit." Paul names the reality that "fleshy things" all too easily distract our attention and consume our energies.

The good news, Paul proclaims, is that God's Spirit is at work deep within us, transforming and freeing us from the powers that hold us. This liberation is not our doing, not a matter of our will, but an empowerment brought about by God's work in Christ. It is a gift of life when we would know only death, freedom when we would know condemnation. The wind, it seems, already blows in the valley and its stirring invites us onward to Easter and the day of our own resurrection.

THE GOSPEL
JOHN 11:1–45 (RCL/RC); 11:(1–16), 17–44 (BCP); 11:3–7, 17, 20–27, 33b–45 (RC, alt.)

Interpreting the Text

This text is a decisive turning point in John's Gospel. It is the climactic sign of Jesus' public ministry and sets in motion the plot against his life (11:45–53). Set at a narrative crossroad, the story functions on multiple levels. It is an account of the death and raising of Lazarus told "so that you may believe" (11:15) that Jesus is the life and resurrection. Jesus restores physical life as a sign of his power to give eternal life *now* and as a promise that he will raise the dead on the last day (cf. 5:21, 25, 28-29; 10:28). At the same time, the story anticipates Jesus' own death and resurrection. Significant details point the reader beyond Jesus' gift of life to Lazarus whom he loves (11:3, 5, 36) to Jesus' gift of life to the world that God so loves.

John uses wordplay and ambiguity to invite the reader yet again into the characters' struggle to comprehend Jesus. For example, the disciples take literally Jesus' statement that Lazarus has "fallen asleep." Their misunderstanding prompts Jesus to explain more fully what is happening (11:7-16). Martha's first words to Jesus suggest she knows him as a healer and an intermediary heard by God (11:22), but not as himself "the resurrection and the life" (11:25). Next, she interprets Jesus' claim that Lazarus will rise again as a comforting confession of the doctrine of the resurrection (11:23-24; cf. Mark 12:18; Acts 23:8). She does not see that the resurrection and the life stands right in front of her. Finally, although Martha believes that Jesus is God's Son prophesied as the coming Messiah (11:27), the reality of a four-day-old stench of death gives her pause (11:39). Martha knows that Jesus is the "one coming into the world" but knows not that the light and life have already come.

So that all might believe, Jesus raises Lazarus from the dead. Parallels between the miracle and Jesus' promises in John 5 suggest that the present account dramatizes and confirms that earlier discourse.[2] In John 11, Jesus identifies himself as the *resurrection and the life* (11:25). Lazarus is *in the tomb* (11:17), and Jesus cries out with a loud *voice*, "Lazarus, *come out!*" (11:43). In John 5, Jesus claims that "just as the Father raises the dead and gives them life, so also the Son gives life to whomever he wishes" (5:21). Jesus then says, "The hour is coming when all who *are in their tombs* will hear his *voice* and will *come out*—those who have done good, to *the resurrection of the life*" (5:28-29; see 5:19-29). In short, just as Jesus' healing of the blind man in John 9 illuminates Jesus' power as "the light" (John 8:12; 9:1-41), Jesus' resuscitation of Lazarus brings to life Jesus' power as the resurrection and the life.

The story also looks ahead to Jesus' crucifixion and resurrection. Jesus speaks of Lazarus's raising as leading to the glorification of the Son of God (11:4). It does, in fact, precipitate the events that lead to Jesus' death, an integral part of his glorification for John (12:23-24; 17:1). When Jesus decides to go to Judea, Thomas says to the disciples, "Let us go that *we may die with him*" (11:16). When they arrive at Lazarus's tomb, Jesus weeps (11:35; Luke 19:41; Heb. 5:7). The stone is rolled away (11:41; see 21:1). Jesus cries out with a loud voice (11:43; see Mark 15:34; Luke 23:46). And the burial clothes of the one who was dead are removed and left behind (11:44; see 20:6-7). With such details, John tells the story of this miracle while ever pointing his readers toward what is to come—to Jerusalem, Gethsemane, the cross at Golgotha, and the empty tomb of Easter.

Responding to the Text

This story is steeped in human suffering and death. John suggests the critical nature of Lazarus's condition by mentioning his illness five times in the opening six verses. His death occurs inevitably, it seems, as Jesus waits (11:6). Four days in the tomb is long enough to confirm Lazarus's passing, long enough to saturate the air of the tomb with the stench of death. The grief is profound. Martha and Mary mourn Lazarus even as they grieve what might have been if Jesus had arrived a few days earlier (11:21, 32). Neighbors and friends gather around them. There is inconsolable weeping. Mary collapses at Jesus' feet (11:32). Martha becomes the "sister of the dead man" (11:39). And Jesus breaks down in tears (11:35). Everyone is gathered before the tomb. John does not let us avoid the agony. John sets us firmly on this, the Lenten side of the grave.

CHRISTINE
ROY YODER

And then John cries out through the voice of the Jews, "Come and see!" (11:34). There is Jesus in the heart of the suffering with tears on his cheeks crying out to a dead man: "Come out! Come out!" In an instant, life conquers death. In an instant, the one who had been dead is alive. In that instant, some of us may find ourselves standing with Mary, Martha, and the Jews, mesmerized by the sight of Lazarus in the doorway of his tomb, unbound and set free. Our jaws drop in awe and we are speechless in the face of Jesus' power and the reality of the resurrection and the life now in front of us. Others of us, I suspect, find ourselves at the side of Lazarus, hearing Jesus' cry to come out from the darkness of whatever tomb holds us. "Come out! Come out!" So we rise and stumble our way toward the light as quickly as our cloth-wrapped feet can carry us.

SOME OF US FIND OURSELVES AT THE SIDE OF LAZARUS, HEARING JESUS' CRY TO COME OUT FROM THE DARKNESS OF WHATEVER TOMB HOLDS US.

NOTES

1. See T. G. Long, *Matthew.* (Westminster Bible Companion; Louisville: Westminster John Knox, 1997), 39.

2. R. E. Brown, *The Gospel according to John (I–XII)* (Anchor Bible 29; Garden City, N.Y.: Doubleday, 1966), 437.

HOLY WEEK

DONALD JUEL

THAT A LARGE SECTION OF *New Proclamation* is devoted to a single week in the church year is surely an indication that what happens during this period is central to the Christian faith. Each of the Gospels devotes an inordinate amount of space to a narration of this week, moving from Jesus' climactic entry into Jerusalem, through his encounter with merchants in the temple, his "anointing" by an unnamed woman, his last meal with his followers, his prayer in Gethsemane, his encounter with the religious and political authorities that ends with his death and the collapse of his movement, and the first report that he has been raised from the dead.

Perhaps nowhere is the relationship of theology and exegesis so clear as in the interpretation of the relevant passages. And nowhere is interpretation so clearly rhetorical: how we understand the passages determines how we will perform them liturgically and homiletically. How do we understand the movement from Passion Sunday to Easter Sunday? One test case is to see what is done on Good Friday. In some churches there is no service at which Jesus' death is the focus. Easter is celebrated without a genuine sense of death. In other churches, where Anselm's ancient reflections have come to dominate hearing of the biblical texts, the experience of Good Friday may be one of relief, even satisfaction, that some score has been settled or a price paid on our behalf. In such cases the supposed "drama" of an Easter vigil may seem hollow if the important transaction between God and Jesus is already finished. Crucial to an experience of the week is some understanding of what happened and is happening between God and the world that requires such dramatic events. Crucial, in other words, is an understanding of what the church has understood as "atonement."[1] Such reflection involves a sense of the human plight from which we are rescued, why Jesus' death is necessarily involved in that rescue, and where God is in all of it. I have suggested as a regular exercise in Gospel courses that students write a short, three-page reflection on "Why did Jesus have to die?" from the perspective of the narrative they are reading. Such an exercise might prove useful for pastors as well in preparation for Holy Week.

One result of attention to the Gospel narratives may be the discovery that little of the traditional sacrificial imagery is present. The Gospel stories are not told to narrate the story of how Jesus gave himself as a sacrifice for us. That does not mean such interpretations are inappropriate. The Gospels themselves offer hints of these interpretations, and the epistolary literature, particularly the letter to the Hebrews, offers a developed interpretation of Jesus' death in terms of traditional sacrificial categories. The difficulty with such reflection is that it can become abstract and detached—disconnected from the particular story told about Jesus of Nazareth and Pontius Pilate and from the world in which we live. If Jesus' death is somehow essential to God's reconciliation of the world to Godself—one of the central claims of the Christian faith—we should be clear that it is Jesus' death we are speaking about, not a death in general. And our understanding of precisely how Jesus' death accomplishes something positive ought to include attention to the details of the story.

Theology and historical particularity can easily be separated. Students will often, for example, distinguish between the "political" reasons for Jesus' death and the "theological" reasons. According to the Gospels, Jesus' ministry puts him on a collision course with established authorities. It is finally the priests in charge of the temple and the Roman governor who decide that Jesus must die. Yet theories about how God is involved in Jesus' death often ignore these details, focusing more on general theories about how God is obliged to provide a sacrifice if there is to be mercy or how Jesus' resurrection is a triumph over principalities and powers in the abstract. The whole point of the Gospel stories is that the "necessity" of Jesus' death cannot be separated from the social and political features of his career—and that God is invested in precisely this ministry in the midst of the social and political structures within which humans of necessity live.

Helping an audience locate themselves is a critical aspect of interpretation and performance. If the story is about how God removes the obstacles that stand in the way of God's showing mercy, thus achieving some form of satisfaction that is for our benefit, the audience is involved passively, watching from a safe distance as a drama is played out far above their heads. If the story is about how the world in which we live has no way to accommodate God's own presence; if it tells how those responsible for law and order believed they had to decide between Jesus and the common good; if the story argues, in other words, that we are enmeshed in structures that cannot accommodate God's radical graciousness, then the "necessity" of Jesus' death is about us and our bondage, not about God's inability to show mercy without blood. In this case, an experience of the story must involve an experience of our bondage. Sacrificial language may be appropriate as a way of understanding the depths to which God has been willing to go to set us free, but it ought not obscure whose problem is being attended to in Jesus' death. Feminist interpreters and others who have protested the notion that God requires the death of a son in order to be gracious are surely on the right track.

It will become obvious that the textual studies are carried out from a particular perspective that has exegetical, theological, and pastoral components. My bias is that certain forms of Christian piety have misunderstood the cross of Jesus, in particular the way God is involved, and that this misunderstanding determines absolutely how the story is heard. One feature of this misunderstanding is that the "problem" to which Jesus' death is directed is alleged to be God's problem, whether God's obligation is to play within the rules of the game (the Law) or to satisfy the legitimate demands of the devil. The Bible does not argue that God needs to be satisfied before showing mercy or that God is in debt to anyone or anything. It argues that the problem is ours. It seeks to show why it is that God's coming into our midst in Jesus was so threatening to our race that it was necessary to put Jesus to death. And the story indicates what God did—and will do—in the face of that rejection. A second aspect of this misunderstanding is that hearers are

> THE BIBLE DOES NOT ARGUE THAT GOD NEEDS TO BE SATISFIED BEFORE SHOWING MERCY OR THAT GOD IS IN DEBT TO ANYONE OR ANYTHING. IT ARGUES THAT THE PROBLEM IS OURS.

kept from an experience of death—both Jesus' death, which the Bible takes seriously, and the death of human possibilities bound up in that cross, which was a last, desperate act of self-protection. Prevented from an experience of death, we are likewise never allowed to experience resurrection.

Planning Holy Week should involve the most intense theological wrestling in light of a set of biblical passages close to the heart of the whole Christian enterprise. And while liturgical choices will necessarily be limited by local custom and circumstance, planning how we imagine people should experience the week liturgically is part of wrestling with the assigned biblical texts.

Anti-Semitism and the Commemoration of Holy Week

An aspect of the passion tradition that cannot be ignored is the degree to which this material in particular has figured in a frightening history of anti-Judaism in the church. It is a dreadful irony that Holy Week has been a time of particular danger to Jews throughout the history of the church. A major reason is the notion that Jews were responsible for Jesus' death—that they were "Christ killers." There is obviously more behind this notion than history, since all the Gospels make clear that Pilate must finally pronounce the verdict on Jesus, and it is on a Roman cross that he dies. The Gospels, however, encourage focus on the Jewish participants. In Matthew, the whole "people" say, "Be his blood on us and on our children." In John, "the Jews" secure Jesus' death by declaring Caesar as their only king.

Historical study has gone a long way to making sense of the texts. They were written for believers who had a far closer relationship to Judaism and an investment in the Law of Moses greater than most contemporary Christians can even imagine. We do not read the stories through their eyes but through the eyes of a people shaped by distance from Jewish communities and centuries of false and shameful propaganda directed against Jews. The Gospels themselves are far less one-sided in their condemnation of Pharisees, for example, than later tradition has been. A major difficulty is that many Christians know virtually nothing about Judaism and operate with caricatures furnished by the tradition. Conversation with Jews and Jewish scholarship has changed the situation, at least for some. The results need to be shared with others.

While almost two millennia of tradition will not be recast during one Holy Week, pastors can at least take some steps to educate congregations about our religious neighbors. And pastors must realize that without attention to such matters, simply reading the story in which "all the people" say, "'Be his blood on us and on our children'" will only confirm notions that have proved deadly to our neighbors.

THE SUNDAY OF THE PASSION (PALM SUNDAY)

MARCH 24, 2002

REVISED COMMON	EPISCOPAL (BCP)	ROMAN CATHOLIC
Processional Gospel:		
Matt. 21:1–11	Matt. 21:1–11	Matt. 21:1–11
Isa. 50:4–9a	Isa. 45:21–25	Isa. 50:4–7
	or Isa. 52:13—53:12	
Ps. 31:9–16	Ps. 22:1–21 or 22:1–11	Ps. 22:7–8, 16–17,
or 118:1–2, 19–29		18–19, 22–23
		(Heb. Bible 22:8–9,
		17–18, 19–20, 23–24)
Phil. 2:5–11	Phil. 2:5–11	Phil. 2:6–11
Matt. 21:1–11	Matt. (26:36–75),	Matt. 26:14—27:66
or 26:14—27:66	27:1–54 (55–66)	(27:11–54)
or 27:11–54		

THE SUNDAY MANY HAVE KNOWN AS Palm Sunday is now celebrated as Passion Sunday. Two Gospel readings are listed: the first, Jesus' triumphal procession into Jerusalem; the second, the account of the passion. Which reading to use depends a great deal on plans for Holy Week. If there is to be a Good Friday service at which the passion story will be read, it is perhaps unnecessary on Sunday. It is important that at some point in the week the whole story be heard so that congregations can appreciate the sweep of the story as well as individual details. It should be noted that, if Matthew's passion story is read on Sunday, the assigned reading on Good Friday is the passion narrative from the Gospel of John. Pastors should be prepared to attend to the differences if both lections are read.

There are a variety of ways the passion story may be performed. It may be read by a single individual or it may be read with several readers playing the various roles in the story. A chorus is particularly effective.

Decisions about performance should take into account the rhetorical features of the story. By choosing a particular way to

DECISIONS ABOUT PERFORMANCE SHOULD TAKE INTO ACCOUNT THE RHETORICAL FEATURES OF THE STORY. BY CHOOSING A PARTICULAR WAY TO TELL THE STORY, THE NARRATOR LOCATES THE AUDIENCE.

tell the story, the narrator locates the audience. Matthew has chosen to locate readers "outside" the story. Events are not narrated by one of the characters but by a narrator who views events from an omniscient perspective. We are able, for example, to appreciate what is happening both inside and outside the high priest's house where Jesus' trial and Peter's denial are occurring simultaneously. Characters in the story surely cannot know all this. We can hear the explicit and less explicit scriptural (OT) overtones in the wording of the narrative to which the participants have no access: the casting of lots for the garments, the shaking of heads, and Jesus' last words, all allusions to Psalm 22. While telling the story from the perspective of one of the characters may seem more "realistic," it represents a very different narrative strategy that can obscure one of the main features of Matthew's story: the ability to depict events in a way that allows readers to experience them differently from the participants in the story. We can appreciate the irony, for example, that it is Jesus' enemies who announce to the world that he is "King of the Jews." We can appreciate how they fulfill the Scriptures (especially Psalms 22 and 69) without having the slightest idea they are doing so. Irony is the only way to depict a world in which a chasm separates appearance and reality—a chasm of which characters are unaware and are thus powerless to cross. They play their roles believing they understand; readers know that the meaning of events is quite different from what Pilate and the chief priests can imagine. Whether the story is to be performed or read, care should be exercised in not obscuring some of the most powerful rhetorical features of the passion narrative.

First Reading
ISAIAH 50:4-9a (RCL); 45:21-25
or ISAIAH 52:13—53:12 (BCP); 50:4-7 (RC)

The choice of Old Testament readings is obviously dictated by the New Testament passages. Their significance in the history of Christian interpretation has little to do with their original setting. They are important for the way their language has shaped the New Testament. Isaiah 45 in the BCP is chosen for its relationship to Philippians 2. The verses from this portion of Isaiah emphasize Israel's radically monotheistic faith. God alone—Israel's God, with a special name that can no longer be spoken—is the only Savior, beside whom there is none (45:21). It is before this God that every knee shall bow (45:23). The use of this language in Philippians to speak of Jesus (see below), on whom God bestows the "Name that is above every name," is a dramatic move that strained the boundaries of monotheism and to this day is a statement Jews find offensive, verging on blasphemy.

Isaiah 50 and 53 are chosen with an eye to the passion narrative. Several things should be said about the selection of these passages. One is that they have since the earliest days been understood as referring to Jesus. The famous song from Isaiah 53 has furnished numerous details for portraits of Jesus; it has been set to powerful music that has left an indelible stamp on Christian imagination (see below on the first reading for Good Friday). Since the nineteenth century, these passages have been isolated and read as separate "Servant Songs," supposedly depicting the career of a single individual with whom Jesus is then identified. Current scholarship has raised serious questions about the isolation of these passages, and there has always been some question as to whether Isaiah 50 belongs with these "songs." The history of interpreting these passages in postbiblical Judaism is difficult to reconstruct, but there seems little precedent for applying them to Jesus. Since they have now been applied to Jesus, however, there is little question that that is how they will be read.

It should also be noted that there is no evidence in Matthew's passion narrative that either of these passages is in view. While the details of both Isaiah 50 and Isaiah 53 now seem both familiar and appropriate to the story Matthew tells, there are no persuasive verbal hints that the evangelist has these verses in mind as he clearly does Psalm 22 and 69. However appropriate they may thus seem to our hearing of the passion story, it is best not to read too much "servant theology" either into the passages from Isaiah or into Matthew's Gospel.

RESPONSIVE READING
PSALM 31:9-16 or 118:1-2, 19-29 (RCL); 22:1-21 or 22:1-11 (BCP); 22:7-8, 16-17, 18-19, 22-23 (HEBREW BIBLE 22:8-9, 17-18, 19-20, 23-24) (RC)

The choice of the psalm should depend on the Gospel selection. Though not marked by a formula, words from Psalm 118 are chanted by the crowd as Jesus enters Jerusalem (118:26 in Matt. 21:9). Hearing the psalm before the Gospel will allow hearers to make the connection. The same is true of Psalm 22 and the account of Jesus' death. There would be reason to read Psalm 31 if Luke's Gospel were being read. Since it is not, Psalm 22 is appropriate.

SECOND READING

PHILIPPIANS 2:5-11 (RCL, BCP);
2:6-11 (RC)

The famous passage from Philippians has been well studied. The list of significant—and interesting—interpretive debates is long. One question has to do with the general setting of the "hymn": Should it be read in light of later Trinitarian creeds, with a "second person" existing before creation, so that Jesus' "coming" is a "descent" from God? Or should the story be read in light of the biblical account of Adam and Eve, so that the "equality with God not to be snatched at" is understood as the temptation to "be like God," to which humanity has always surrendered? There are strong arguments for both views. The story that results from each view is somewhat different.

Important is that the hymn does not portray Jesus simply as an example to be emulated. While Paul encourages the congregation to "have this mind among you that you have in Christ Jesus," Jesus is a singular figure. He is "Christ Jesus" first of all, and according to the hymn, as a result of his obedience to death God "highly exalts him" and "gives him a name which is above every name"—that is, the divine name itself. The confession in which all will participate is that "Jesus is Lord." While his relationship to God offers a model by which the Philippians may relate to one another in mutual service, Jesus is also the Lord to whom obedience is due and the one who through his death has destroyed death and by his resurrection has brought life to the world.

> THE HYMN DOES NOT PORTRAY JESUS SIMPLY AS AN EXAMPLE TO BE EMULATED. WHILE PAUL ENCOURAGES THE CONGREGATION TO "HAVE THIS MIND AMONG YOU THAT YOU HAVE IN CHRIST JESUS," JESUS IS A SINGULAR FIGURE.

The passage opens a host of fascinating questions. If Paul is quoting a hymn that he did not compose, we must assume that this particular formulation predates Paul and is thus among the earliest worship traditions to which we have access. The Christology in the hymn would be classified as "high": language used of God in the Bible is applied to Jesus. The very presence of the hymn in a Pauline letter, the earliest New Testament writings, suggests that the difference between "high" and "low" Christology is not chronological.

The use of Scripture in the hymn is surely of interest. The words, "To me every knee shall bow, even tongue shall swear," come from Isaiah 45, where the "name that is above every name" is the ineffable name of God. How that name comes to be used of Jesus and with what implications have a fascinating prehistory in scriptural reflection among people who believed in one God and yet could say such things about Jesus, and they have an important subsequent history in the development of the church's trinitarian reflection.

MATTHEW 21:1-11 (For RCL, ALSO THE GOSPEL LECTION)

Several things are clear from the story. One is that Jesus' entry to Jerusalem for Passover is greeted with enthusiasm by festival pilgrims in a way that is sure to cause officials consternation. The incendiary political situation needed only a spark to kindle a revolt. Pilate and his troops came to Jerusalem and stayed in the Fortress Antonia adjoining the temple to head off such a possibility. Another is that, in Matthew's view, the entry is a royal procession, occurring in fulfillment of the passage from Zechariah that he quotes. The concern for detailed fulfillment apparently motivates the somewhat improbable comment that Jesus rode on "them," i.e., on a donkey and on the foal. The crowd apparently senses the imminent possibility of deliverance through this potential savior, since they greet him with lines from Psalm 118, supplemented with a greeting of Jesus as "Son of David," that is, the expected Messiah-King. While throughout his ministry people regarded Jesus as a prophet, here they come to believe he is the King-to-come. What the crowds say is true, though they have no idea in what sense. By the end of the week, they will be utterly disappointed in Jesus and will join in the calls for his death.

Historical questions are tantalizing. Jesus' willingness to ride into Jerusalem in a manner befitting royalty—and the hints in the story that preparations have already been made for the event—seem to suggest Jesus understood himself as the Messiah and was perhaps staking his claim. More than one scholar has suggested Jesus actually sought to liberate the city but was unable to sustain a revolt.[2] Given the presence of Pilate's troops in the city, however, and the fact that Jesus is not immediately arrested make this unlikely. Looking back at the story, Jesus' followers understood his entrance to the city as a royal procession, understood in light of Psalm 118 and Zechariah 9. What this reveals about the actual event or Jesus' understanding of himself, however, is impossible to say.

LOOKING BACK AT THE STORY, JESUS' FOLLOWERS UNDERSTOOD HIS ENTRANCE TO THE CITY AS A ROYAL PROCESSION, UNDERSTOOD IN LIGHT OF PSALM 118 AND ZECHARIAH 9.

THE GOSPEL

MATTHEW 21:1-11 or 26:14—27:66 or 27:11-54 (RCL); (26:36-75), 27:1-54 (55-66) (BCP); 26:14—27:66 (27:11-54) (RC)

Matthew 26–27 follows Mark's account of the passion closely. In both Gospels, there is both a trial before the Jewish court, where Jesus is accused of religious crimes, and a trial before Pilate on political charges ("King of the Jews"). The two sets of titles ("Christ, Son of God" and "King of the Jews") view Jesus' kingship from the Jewish and Roman perspective, respectively. For Jews, the claim is a religious one; for the Romans, it is simply political. Jesus' response to both the chief priests and Pilate ("You have said so") should be read as an ironic acceptance of the titles. The point is that they have spoken the words by which Jesus will be confessed; they have "said so." The observation has implications for performing the story, since irony will be conveyed largely by tone of voice.

One of the differences between Matthew's version of the story and Mark's is Pilate's role. While the story cannot obscure the historical fact that Jesus was executed on a Roman cross, Matthew plays down Pilate's responsibility somewhat particularly by introducing his wife and her dream. Pilate's washing his hands supposedly absolves him of any responsibility for Jesus' death, which would hardly have been convincing to any readers who knew the operation of the Roman judicial system. The washing allows the Jewish mob to take responsibility for Jesus' death in a passage that has had chilling consequences throughout the history of the church: "His blood be on us and on our children."

Interpreting the statement about blood is complex. From the vantage point of Jewish readers in the first century, for example, it would be important to know that Jesus really was out of favor with the people and guilty of crimes against Jewish law; otherwise, he would be regarded as a martyr for the cause of freedom from Rome. From the perspective of Jesus' followers, opposition to Jesus from leaders of the temple in particular helped to explain the later destruction of the temple and of Jerusalem by Titus and the Roman legions at the conclusion of the great revolt of 66–70. The rejection of Jesus by the Jewish leaders—and opposition to the Jesus movement later in the century—remained a significant theological problem for Jesus' followers. That Jesus was executed by a Roman official was hardly surprising. Little more could be expected of Romans. On the other hand, how could it be that the leaders of God's people refused to accept Jesus, the Christ and Son of God sent to save the people from their sins? It is thus not surprising that the role of the Jewish leaders receives more attention as the story is told, particularly toward the end of the first century when the Jewish believers in Jesus found it increasingly difficult to remain within the synagogue.

The statement about bloodguilt has been recalled throughout the history of the church not simply to explain the sufferings of Jews but to justify persecution. A bitter irony is that Holy Week was a particularly dangerous time for Jews. Historically it is clear that the decision to execute Jesus was made by the Roman governor; Jesus was executed on a Roman cross as a political criminal. Even within Matthew's Gospel, however, the statement of the mob must be understood in light of what is said elsewhere about Jesus' death—and his blood in particular. While Matthew's Gospel devotes considerable energy to the controversy between Jesus and his adversaries, even speaking of their opposition as participation in resistance to the prophets and the righteous throughout Israel's history (23:30-35: "so that upon you may come all the righteous blood shed on earth, from the blood of righteous Abel to the blood of Zechariah son of Barachiah, whom you murdered between the sanctuary and the altar" [23:35]), it is difficult to read the story about one who is born to "save his people from their sins" (1:21) and to "give his life as a ransom for many" (20:28) without a sense that having "his blood on us" will include more than condemnation. At the Last Supper, Jesus speaks of his death in terms of his blood that is "poured out for many for the forgiveness of sins" (26:28). There is no justification, historical or exegetical or theological, for reading the passion narrative as justification for anti-Judaism

Echoes of Scripture. Matthew's narrative contains several explicit allusions to Old Testament passages. Unlike some of the references earlier in the Gospel that are marked by introductory formulas ("This was done in order to fulfill . . ."), the allusions (or "echoes") in the passion story are unmarked. Readers do not need to know that the words echo the Scriptures; the passages make sense on their own. If readers recognize the allusion, however, it gives the story depth and texture and shows how intimately Jesus' death is understood as "scriptural."

The most obvious allusions are:

- Jesus' statement to the Jewish court in 26:64: "You will see the Son of man seated at the right hand of Power and coming on the clouds of heaven" = Ps. 110:1 and Dan. 7:14
- the casting of lots (27:35 = Ps. 22:18)
- the passersby deriding Jesus, wagging their heads (27:39 = Ps. 22:7-8)
- Jesus' last words in 27:46, from the opening verse of Psalm 22
- the offering of vinegar in 27:48, probably an allusion to Psalm 69:21

While it is traditional to read the passion in light of Isaiah 52:13—53:12, there is little evidence of allusion to this passage in Matthew. Significant is that the scriptural allusions, largely from the Psalter, do not employ sacrificial language. They are enlisted to interpret the opposition Jesus encounters from his contemporaries. It is important that those unfamiliar with the Old Testament be helped to hear the allusions or echoes. They contribute to the impression that events are unfolding according to the plan of God (i.e., in accordance with the Scriptures) in a way that allows readers to appreciate what characters in the story do not. The priests and the mob and Pilate surely do not recognize that their actions have been scripted. They are serving the will of God but in a way that they cannot understand and that is completely contrary to their intentions.

Irony. The dominant characteristic of the story is irony. It is the chief priests on whose lips the confession of Jesus as Christ and Son of God appears. It is Pilate who calls Jesus "the King of the Jews" and even writes and affixes the title to the cross. It is the soldiers who invest Jesus as king—though in mockery. On the one hand, the characters indicate how the confession of Jesus as Christ and Son of God sounds to people in the know: it is blasphemous and absurd and seditious. On the other hand, they testify to a truth that they cannot understand but that readers know from the opening lines of the story. Crucial is the awareness of the irony—of the distance that separates appearance from reality.

ON THE ONE HAND, THE CHARACTERS INDICATE HOW THE CONFESSION OF JESUS AS CHRIST AND SON OF GOD SOUNDS TO PEOPLE IN THE KNOW: IT IS BLASPHEMOUS AND ABSURD AND SEDITIOUS. ON THE OTHER HAND, THEY TESTIFY TO A TRUTH THAT THEY CANNOT UNDERSTAND BUT THAT READERS KNOW FROM THE OPENING LINES OF THE STORY.

To use Paul's language, it pleased God to reveal God's wisdom through apparent foolishness. And as Paul argues in the opening chapters of his first letter to the Corinthians, the cross discloses a significant difference between the wisdom of God and the wisdom of this age.

Irony is slippery. What if the story is true? What if it is the case that those who supposedly know best are in fact completely in the dark? Every encounter with the Bible should demonstrate that there is always something new to learn, always a surprise. We may well discover that what we have held to be true is a deception intended to shield us from the truth. And if that is the case, we will discover that our privileged position as readers offers no final security. We will find ourselves at the mercy of God who must find a way to free and enlighten us no less than those in the story who decided Jesus had to die. For those in the congregation, the pressing question is whether God will speak in a way that both surprises and reveals.

MONDAY IN HOLY WEEK

MARCH 25, 2002

REVISED COMMON	EPISCOPAL (BCP)	ROMAN CATHOLIC
Isa. 42:1-9	Isa. 42:1-9	Isa. 42:1-7
Ps. 36:5-11	Ps. 36:5-10	Ps. 27:1-3, 13-14
Heb. 9:11-15	Heb. 11:39—12:3	
John 12:1-11	John 12:1-11	John 12:1-11
	or Mark 14:3-9	

FEW CHURCHES WILL HOLD SERVICES ON Monday of Holy Week. The lections might best be used for private devotions or as an agenda for Bible study groups. A useful exercise might be to read from John 12 to the end of the Gospel, since the Gospel lections for the week will be taken from these portions of the Fourth Gospel. This portion of John's Gospel, the so-called Book of Glory, focuses on Jesus' instructions to his followers in an extended Farewell Speech (John 13–17), followed by an account of his arrest, trial, death, and resurrection appearances, characterized in the Fourth Gospel as his "lifting up" and "glorification."

The selection of Old Testament and epistle texts reflects a particular understanding of Jesus' death as a sacrifice. While the imagery emphasizes God's gracious action on behalf of those who cannot help themselves, I have already suggested that there are ways of misunderstanding this imagery that may have unsalutary consequences for an experience of the story of salvation. There is no alternative to a critical reading of the assigned lections with both respect for and suspicion of the traditions in which they come to us. My own suggestion is that the Gospel readings during this week should be central. Why Jesus "must" die has to do first of all not with some eternal rules about sacrifice but with the situation of the world into which Jesus came—and comes. Other biblical material will be helpful in providing richness and depth to our reflection on this story.

FIRST READING
ISAIAH 42:1-9 (RCL, BCP); 42:1-7 (RC)

The passage is the first of the so-called Servant Songs, passages in the later chapters of Isaiah that speak of an unidentified "servant." The isolation of these passages and the suggestion that they be read together was made by a scholar named Bernhard Duhm in a commentary on Isaiah published in 1892. He believed these passages were later than the rest of Isaiah and actually referred to a particular figure, a disciple of the prophet and a teacher of the law, who lived in the postexilic period and died of leprosy. Interpreters, he argued, should therefore read the passages together as "Servant Songs." Few scholars have followed Duhm in his identification of the mysterious figure, but his work has had an enormous impact on later interpreters. Views about the Servant Songs and about a figure known as "the suffering servant," while subject to increasing suspicion among scholars, have found general acceptance especially in nonscholarly circles.[3]

While studying the history of interpretation of the Old Testament is surely not the only appropriate approach, it is significant that there seem to have been no such readings of Isaiah prior to the nineteenth century and certainly no reference to a "suffering servant." In most manuscripts of the Septuagint, the Greek translation of the Hebrew Bible that was read by the New Testament authors and their churches, the translator of Isaiah 42 identifies the "servant" not as an individual but as the nation: "Jacob is my servant . . . Israel my chosen. . . ."

In the New Testament the verses were applied to Jesus. They are quoted in Matt. 12:18-21 to explain why Jesus commands those he heals not to make him known. The form of the passage differs from both the Hebrew and the Septuagint Greek and shows some influence of Christian interpretation. Perhaps first to notice is the echo of the words in the voice from heaven at Jesus' baptism (Matt. 3:17) and at the transfiguration (Matt. 17:5). The words "my beloved [Son] with whom I am well-pleased" are exactly the same as those quoted in Matt. 12:18. Jesus is both the one whom God address as "my Son" in Ps. 2:7 and the mysterious "servant" in Isaiah on whom God puts his Spirit. His task, according to Isaiah, is to bring justice to the nations.

THE PASSAGE IS AN IMPORTANT REMINDER THAT WHAT IS OCCURRING IN JESUS' MINISTRY IS WILLED BY THE GOD "WHO CREATED THE HEAVENS AND STRETCHED THEM OUT." JESUS IS BOTH A "COVENANT TO THE PEOPLE (ISRAEL)" AND A "LIGHT TO THE NATIONS (GENTILES)."

It may not be clear in the English that in vv. 5-9 the "you" whom God has called is singular. While the singular pronoun might be understood as a collective, it is nevertheless possible to understand how it could be read as a reference to a single "servant." There is some evidence that Matthew echoes v. 7 ("to open the eyes that are blind") in Jesus' response to John the Baptist (though the clearest parallel seems to be Isa. 35:5-6):

> Jesus answered them, "Go and tell John what you hear and see: the blind receive their sight, the lame walk, the lepers are cleansed, the deaf hear, the dead are raised, and the poor have good news brought to them. And blessed is anyone who takes no offense at me." (Matt.11:4-6)

In Luke's Gospel, Simeon's *nunc dimittis* speaks of Israel as a "light to the nations," probably an allusion to 42:6.

The passage is an important reminder that what is occurring in Jesus' ministry is willed by the God "who created the heavens and stretched them out." Jesus is both a "covenant to the people (Israel)" and a "light to the nations (Gentiles)."

It may also be of interest that in the Greek Septuagint, the term translated "justice" is not the familiar *dikaiosyne* but *krisis*, "judgment." The vocation of the servant is to declare judgment to the nations. What Jesus' ministry has to do with God's "justice (righteousness)" is another matter.

SECOND READING
HEBREWS 9:11–15 (RCL)

Three of the epistle readings over the next days will be taken from the letter to the Hebrews. In these lections, Jesus' death is interpreted in light of the sacrificial system as reconstructed from the Scriptures. One of the great mysteries about the letter to the Hebrews is its relationship to the historical temple. The argument within the letter works from the Scriptures, giving us little sense of how its reasoning might be related to actual temple practices in the first century.

These verses are part of an extended exposition of Jesus' role as "high priest according to the order of Melchizedek" (Heb. 7:17, quoting Ps. 110:4), the mysterious "King of Salem, priest of the Most High God" whom Abraham encounters in Gen. 14:17-24. Melchizedek, the subject of speculation in the postbiblical period of which only traces remain,[4] provides for the author a way of speaking of Jesus' work that both interprets his activity within sacrificial categories and at the same time provides a way of speaking about the transition to a "new covenant." The tradition of Israel's sacrificial practices—here, the Day of Atonement—provides both an interpretive framework and a foil for speaking about Jesus. Because the letter presumes detailed knowledge of the Scriptures and temple ritual, those wishing to make sense of the letter are obliged to spend some time with the Old Testament.

The most sacred festival in the Jewish year is the Day of Atonement. It was the one time a priest—the high priest—entered the Holy of Holies. The ritual is spelled out in Leviticus 16. It includes both the killing of a goat for a sin offering and the sending off of a scapegoat. Our verses speak of the sacrifice and the sprinkling of blood on the mercy seat to make atonement for the people. According to Hebrews, it is now Jesus who is the high priest; it is his own life that is sacrificed, not that of an animal, his own blood that is shed for the people. It is a sacrifice that need only be offered once. With his death, the sacrificial system comes to an end. Jesus is the mediator of a new covenant.

The passage does not spell out why a sacrifice is necessary. It does not suggest that God requires blood. It argues simply that Jesus' death effectively "cleanses our consciences from dead works" to serve the living God. How and why sacrifice "works" is not discussed. The author accepts that the Scriptures describe how God made provisions for the forgiveness of sins and, within those categories, interprets Jesus' death as a more effective means of forgiveness and the inauguration of a new covenant. The argument presumes an audience that finds sacrifice compelling as a means of purification and forgiveness. This is a point at which those who preach on these verses may have to deal with people who are not so persuaded but who find the whole sacrificial system alien and even offensive. Preachers may have to construct for their congregations some logic of sacrifice in order to make sense of what is said about Jesus. One useful aspect of such an enterprise would be to head off common misunderstandings according to which sacrifice is somehow a response to God's need. The topic, discussed among others by the philosopher Rene Girard,[5] is well worth the investment of time and thought, though this is surely not the kind of reading that should be undertaken at the last moment. That a sacrificial understanding of Jesus' death has been and can still be misleading is perhaps best handled by attending to the particularity of the Gospel stories. Whatever it means to speak of Jesus' death as "sacrificial" cannot be abstracted from the story of his actual trial and death in all its specificity.

> THE PASSAGE DOES NOT SPELL OUT WHY A SACRIFICE IS NECESSARY. IT DOES NOT SUGGEST THAT GOD REQUIRES BLOOD. IT ARGUES SIMPLY THAT JESUS' DEATH EFFECTIVELY "CLEANSES OUR CONSCIENCES FROM DEAD WORKS" TO SERVE THE LIVING GOD.

An aspect of the superiority of this sacrifice is that it is something we cannot provide for ourselves; it is provided for us.

HEBREWS 11:39—12:3

See comments under Wednesday in Holy Week.

THE GOSPEL
JOHN 12:1-11 (RCL, BCP, RC);
MARK 14:3-9 (BCP, alt.)

For the rest of Holy Week the primary Gospel lections are from John's Gospel. The first of these marks Jesus' "anointing" in anticipation of his burial by a woman, a story in Mark that Jesus says will be told "wherever the gospel is preached in memory of her" (Mark 14:9).

There are several differences between the Johannine and the Markan versions of the story. First, while the setting of the meal is in Bethany, in Mark it is at the home of Simon the leper; in John, it is the home of Mary and Martha and Lazarus. The identity of the woman in Mark is unknown; here it is Mary, the sister of Lazarus and good friend of Jesus in whose home he has been dining. It is his feet on which she pours the ointment, while in Mark it is poured on his head. In John, the one who objects to the wasteful use of expensive ointment is Judas who, we are told, objects not because he cares for the poor but because he was a thief (the word used of the false shepherd in John 10:1, 8). And while the story in Luke appears in a different location in the narrative, it includes the unusual detail present in John that the woman wiped Jesus' feet with her hair.

Some interpreters, following the unfortunate English translation in Mark's version of the story ("she has anointed my body beforehand for its burial" [Mark 14:8]), have spoken of the "messianic" significance of this action. The verb in Greek, however, is not *chriō* (from which the word "Christ" comes) but *myrizō*, meaning literally to "pour perfume on" someone. In John, the phrase "anointed his feet" is likewise misleading. The verb is *aleiphiō* and has nothing to do with the "anointing" *(chriō)* for office. In John as in Mark, the action is related to Jesus' impending death and burial.

The story provides an interesting anticipation of Jesus' actions at the Last Supper in John's Gospel, where he washes his disciples' feet.

The comment about Lazarus—that his life is now in danger because Jesus brought him back from the dead—offers a glimpse of the profound irony that moves the story: Jesus' gift of life to Lazarus insures his own death. The "sign" is too dramatic to ignore, and his enemies—the temple authorities—are convinced that if he is not stopped he will bring the Romans down on Jerusalem. Their conclusion is that "one man must die for the people" (11:50). And as long as he is alive, Lazarus is testimony to a power they fear is intended for misuse—to lead the elect astray. Jesus comes to give life, and it is precisely that gift that "his own" cannot receive.

TUESDAY IN HOLY WEEK

REVISED COMMON	EPISCOPAL (BCP)	ROMAN CATHOLIC
Isa. 49:1-7	Isa. 49:1-6	Isa. 49:1-6
Ps. 71:1-14	Ps. 71:1-12	Ps. 71:1-6, 15, 17
1 Cor. 1:18-31	1 Cor. 1:18-31	
John 12:20-36	John 12:37-38, 42-50	John 13:21-33, 36-38
	or Mark 11:15-19	

FIRST READING

ISAIAH 49:1-6 (BCP, RC); 49:1-7 (RCL)

The first reading is from another of the so-called Servant Songs. The passage indicates why the identification of the "servant" has proved to be such an intriguing puzzle. On the one hand, the servant who is speaking seems to be an individual: "The LORD called me from the womb, from the body of my mother he named my name" (49:1). Yet God addresses the servant as "my servant Israel, in whom I will be glorified" (49:3). Further on, however, the vocation of the servant is "to bring Jacob back to him, and that Israel might be gathered to him" (49:5), so the figure cannot be identical with the nation.

There are a few indications in the New Testament that the passage was understood as referring to Jesus. The line of most significance is from v. 6: the servant is to serve as a "light to the nations, that my salvation may reach the end of the earth."

The reading seems an appropriate commentary on the Gospel lection in which "some Greeks" come to Jesus. Their coming is a sign that the hour of his glorification has come. Jesus' death will be not only for "his own"—that is, for Israel—but for "all" whom he will draw to himself.

If we are to see parallels between Jesus and the career of the servant, it is perhaps also appropriate that the servant complains that his career appears to have been for nothing: "I have labored in vain, I have spent my strength for nothing and vanity" (49:4). Jesus' ministry of signs ends with a note of disappointment: though he performed these signs, the people did not believe (John 12:37).

PSALM 71:1–14 (RCL); 71:1–12 (BCP); 71:1–6, 15, 17 (RC)

This psalm, more familiar from Christian liturgy than from the New Testament, contributes to the sense of impending threat. The speaker in the psalm has enemies from whom only God can deliver. The phrase "took me from my mother's womb" in v. 6 is reminiscent of the "servant's" confession in the first reading.

SECOND READING

1 CORINTHIANS 1:18–31

The verses from Paul's letter are both an apt hermeneutical clue to a reading of Jesus' story during Holy Week and a superb example of pastoral theologizing. Paul's eloquent praise of the foolishness of God is a response to challenges to his ministry he has learned about from "those of Chloe" (1:11), perhaps slaves from the household of a prominent member of the Corinthian church who accompanied the official delegation that brought Paul a letter from the congregation. Paul has learned from these "gossips" that the congregation is divided about many issues, most particularly over Paul's leadership. Some criticize him for not returning to them (4:18-21). For others, it is significant that Paul did little baptizing (1:14-17). And in a congregation that has "been enriched in all speech and all knowledge" (1:5), some believe they have outgrown their pastor who is clearly not an eloquent preacher (1:17). Paul takes the criticisms and demonstrates how completely they reveal the Corinthians' lack of real wisdom and understanding.

Paul insists that his lack of rhetorical polish is a strategy. "For I decided to know nothing among you except Jesus Christ and him crucified" (2:2). Because Paul did not give evidence of the expected rhetorical polish, he insists there can be no possible misunderstanding: the faith of the Corinthians is due not to human wisdom but solely to the power of God (2:4-5).

What is the "power of God" and what does it look like? Paul points to Jesus as the embodiment of that power of God. The feature of Jesus' ministry to which he points, however, is his death on the cross. "For Jews demand signs, and Greeks seek wisdom, but we preach Christ crucified." At the center of Paul's preaching and ministry is the gospel of the crucified Christ. Jesus is the Christ, the promised king from the line of David sent by God to deliver the world. But his most royal act is to die on the cross—as the Gospel writers tell it, as "the King of the Jews."

Paul's gospel holds two things together that do not fit: royal office and a shameful death. As a Jew, Paul regarded the message about Jesus as scandalous, even dangerous. He began his involvement with Jesus as a persecutor of his followers (Phil. 3:3-11). An appearance to Paul by the risen Christ turned his life around. What was impossible turned out to be true: God had vindicated the crucified Christ by raising him from the dead. This reality became for Paul not only the source of his call to preach the gospel but the interpretive center of a complete reconstruction of his Jewish faith and his understanding of the world. The embarrassment of a crucified king becomes a critique of a world that construes wisdom and power in such a way as to make Jesus seem like foolishness. God's utter surprise in fulfilling his promises of a deliverer in such an event is purposeful. The reasonable God vanishes behind the cross. The revelation of God's graciousness in the cross is also an act of concealment. God hides, choosing to be known only in the apparent foolishness of the cross.

> THE EMBARRASSMENT OF A CRUCIFIED KING BECOMES A CRITIQUE OF A WORLD THAT CONSTRUES WISDOM AND POWER IN SUCH A WAY AS TO MAKE JESUS SEEM LIKE FOOLISHNESS. GOD'S UTTER SURPRISE IN FULFILLING HIS PROMISES OF A DELIVERER IN SUCH AN EVENT IS PURPOSEFUL. THE REASONABLE GOD VANISHES BEHIND THE CROSS.

That the Corinthians are put off by Paul's lack of rhetorical sophistication indicates how little they understand the gospel of the crucified and risen Christ. Their preference for those who show obvious signs of wisdom indicates that they still operate by standards that are judged in the cross.

Such a "theology of the cross" is tricky. It may seem that Paul is making a virtue of his weaknesses by some theological slight of hand. Friedrich Nietzsche was offended; he regarded Paul's "gospel" as bad news, as the revolt of everything that crawls on its belly against everything that is lofty. Paul's reflection is more than an apology for shortcomings, however. It is wonderfully ironic that Paul's attack on human wisdom and praise of God's "folly" is done with considerable artistry. The passage is an eloquent attack on eloquence, which makes it a particularly useful piece for preachers to study.

What if Paul is right? Among other things, his letter will provide a useful introduction to the story of Holy Week. He suggests what the story is about and what we should listen for. And if in Jesus' death is revealed a new measure of wisdom and strength, the task of the preacher will be to identify those places where the Christian gospel is an affront to conventional wisdom and to offer some glimpse of what it looks like to embody this saving folly. Paul's two letters to the Corinthians are good places to begin.

JOHN 12:20-36 (RCL)

This chapter marks the transition from Jesus' public ministry ("Book of Signs") to the account of his last meal with his followers, his arrest, trial, death, and resurrection ("Book of Glory"). Those using RCL or BCP would be well advised to read both selections together.

Since his first sign at the wedding at Cana, Jesus has spoken of his "hour" that is coming. That "hour" has now arrived: "The hour has come for the Son of Man to be glorified" (12:23). The occasion for this acknowledgment is the arrival of "some Greeks" who wish to "see Jesus." These are contrasted with the crowd, which includes Pharisees, who, because they are blind, do not believe (12:40). While Jesus' ministry occurs almost exclusively among his own people, there have been clear indications that his work is for "the world." When he is lifted up, he will draw "all" to himself.

Noteworthy is that the arrival of the Greeks is treated in a formal way. We do not learn their names, nor does the evangelist report that they actually saw Jesus and spoke with him. Their coming is important for its symbolism—and for the future of the community for whom the Gospel story is told. Jesus' ministry is still principally for "his own"—"the Jews," even those who will not receive him.

Jesus' "hour of glorification" is, paradoxically, the hour of his death. Experiencing the irony is important. John does not have a different view from Paul's; the contrast in John between the wisdom of the world and God's wisdom is more pronounced, if anything. Jesus' death is not glorified; the scandal of the cross is not defined away. The ironic language about being lifted up and glorified is scriptural. The famous passage from Isaiah 53 begins with a general statement about the career of the "servant": he will be "glorified and lifted up" (Isa. 52:13). This is what happens to Jesus. The Greek words in the Septuagint are precisely those used by John. It is his elevation on the cross, however, that is his "lifting up," and his glorification occurs at the hands of enemies who understand nothing of what is occurring. The images of light and darkness, blindness and sight, are present in these verses as throughout the Gospel. One can see the same events through completely different eyes. Whether one sees the truth or only appearances depends on the God who gives sight to the blind and conceals the truth from the sighted (John 12:40).

> ONE CAN SEE THE SAME EVENTS THROUGH COMPLETELY DIFFERENT EYES. WHETHER ONE SEES THE TRUTH OR ONLY APPEARANCES DEPENDS ON THE GOD WHO GIVES SIGHT TO THE BLIND AND CONCEALS THE TRUTH FROM THE SIGHTED.

The "necessity" of Jesus' death is explained here in terms of the operation of nature: seeds must surrender themselves if they are to bear fruit. It is for this that

Jesus has come. The "necessity" must also be understood in light of the narrative, which recounts what happens when the light shines in the darkness (1:5; 3:19-21) and "the Word" comes to his own.

Discipleship is portrayed here as following and "serving" Jesus. It will require "hating one's life in this world." Far more is implied here than simple imitation of Jesus. His followers will prove incapable of following. Peter will choose to save his own life by lying. Something more will be required from God if Jesus' followers are to continue as disciples. The cross will be for them a death not because they choose it but because that is the way Jesus must go.

Part of the conversation between Jesus and the crowd will seem strange to most readers of the Fourth Gospel. The statement of the crowd about the Christ "remaining for ever," the comment about the Son of man being "lifted up," and the question about his identity are strange enough; Jesus' cryptic response about the light leaves most in the dark. Like the discussion about the Christ as David's Son in the Synoptic Gospels (Mark 12:35-37 and parallels), this is a discussion for insiders that we may never fully understand. The comment about the Christ "remaining" presumes a reading of Ps. 89:36. The English translations obscure the Hebrew and Greek, which use the singular "seed": "his seed will remain forever." The statement of the crowd presumes readers know that "seed," used in Psalm 89 and in 2 Sam. 7:12 to speak of the offspring promised David, means "the Messiah"—the king who is to come. The singular noun is important to Paul's argument in Galatians 3 that the promise made to Abraham regarding his "seed" uses a singular form of the noun and not a plural (Gal. 3:16). Paul reads the promise to Abraham as having been fulfilled in God's having kept his promise about a "seed" of David in Jesus. The passage, in other words, presumes a prior history of Christian interpretation of the Old Testament, some of which can be reconstructed, some of which may remain a mystery.[6]

In fact, Jesus is this "Son of man" who will be "lifted up." In so doing he will "draw all to [him]self." Like the bronze serpent on the pole in Numbers, his lifting up will serve for healing (John 3:14-15). And as "Christ," Jesus will "remain forever."

JOHN 12:37-38, 42-50 (BCP); MARK 11:15-19 (BCP, alt.)

John 12:37-50 is the formal conclusion to Jesus' ministry of "signs" in John and serves as a transition to the account of his last days—the "Book of Glory." The passage provides a summary of Jesus' ministry among "his own." After a last warning to the crowd about being overtaken by the darkness, Jesus hides himself. The narrator offers an evaluation: though Jesus did many signs, yet they did not believe. "He came to his own, and his own people did not believe him." The unbelief is explained as the fulfillment of the words of the servant from Isaiah 53: "Lord, who has believed our report, and to whom has the arm of the Lord been revealed?" The reading continues with a comment about those who did believe but were unable to accept the risk of public confession—probably reflecting the situation in which the Fourth Gospel was written. The reading concludes with a final statement of Jesus about the relationship between faith in him and faith in God, the one who sent him.

The most serious difficulty with this selection is the omission of crucial verses. The omission of verses is always somewhat suspect. The decision here to omit vv. 39–41 seems clearly an effort to emend the theology of the Fourth Gospel. The verses offer an evaluation of the crowd's unbelief, again with words from Isaiah:

> And so they could not believe, because Isaiah also said, "He has blinded their eyes and hardened their heart, so that they might not look with their eyes, and understand with their heart and turn—and I would heal them." Isaiah said this because he saw his glory and spoke about him. (12:39-41)

I agree with Raymond Brown that the initial *dia touto* should be translated with a view to what follows in the sentence and not to what precedes: "The reason they could not believe is because [of what] Isaiah said elsewhere. . . ."[7]

The passage offers the same evaluation found in Jesus' discourse on bread from heaven in chap. 6. Several times he indicates to the crowd that understanding is something that comes from God.

> Jesus answered them, "Do not complain among yourselves. No one can come to me unless drawn by the Father who sent me; and I will raise that person up on the last day. It is written in the prophets, 'And they shall all be taught by God.' Everyone who has heard and learned from the Father comes to me." (6:43-45)

Omitting the verses from Isaiah, which appear at the conclusion of Acts (Acts 28:26-27) and, in slightly varied form, in Jesus' comment about teaching in parables in Mark (4:10-12) and at a crucial point in Paul's argument in Romans (11:8), is a serious challenge to the New Testament. That the verses are difficult is hardly an excuse for omitting them from the reading of the Scriptures.

The argument of the verses is that people do not see because God does not permit it. God conceals the truth. If God does not open eyes and ears, words and signs will not help. They will only make matters worse. The result will be not conversion but hardening. The reaction of the lectionary committee to these verses suggests the words speak the truth. The words have scandalized, as they always do—precisely as the Scriptures promise they will. Jesus' signs do not succeed in enlightening those who are not of the light—who are not opened to the light by God—but in fact serve to harden them. Jesus' raising of Lazarus to life brings about his own death. The reaction of Jesus' contemporaries to his words is to seek to silence him. Omitting these crucial verses from the reading of the Scriptures is a strategy that differs little.

The verses strike close to the heart of the Christian enterprise, touching on the freedom or bondage of the human will. Augustine, Luther, and Calvin—following John and Paul—saw this as a crucial theological point. Unbelief is not simply a matter of the human will. Lack of insight is not due to a simple lack of effort. The crowds in John's story cannot see. They are blind—and it is Jesus' words and deeds that provide the occasion for revealing that blindness. "If you were blind," Jesus says to the Pharisees after they have driven from the synagogue the man born blind whom Jesus healed, "you would not have sin. But now that you say, 'We see,' your sin remains" (9:41). Jesus' trial will force leaders to decide about Jesus, and in so deciding they reveal their inability to comprehend the truth (John 1:5).

The other side of the argument is that faith is a gift. Those who understand Jesus and believe are "taught by God." They are born "not of blood or of the will of the flesh or of the will of man, but of God" (John 1:13). They are born "from above," of water and the Spirit (John 3:3-5).

Pastors may shy away from John's—and Isaiah's—words because they may upset people. That they will make a congregation uncomfortable is assured. But perhaps that is precisely the point as the reality of God's graciousness comes painfully close. Can God be trusted with such power? Will God open the eyes of the blind and awaken faith in those who cannot believe? For that we shall have to wait and see. The immediate prospect, however, is that Jesus' coming to bring the grace of God near will get him killed.

JOHN 13:21-33, 36-38 (RC)

See comments on the Gospel for Wednesday in Holy Week.

WEDNESDAY IN HOLY WEEK

MARCH 27, 2002

REVISED COMMON	EPISCOPAL (BCP)	ROMAN CATHOLIC
Isa. 50:4-9a	Isa. 50:4-9a	Isa. 50:4-9
Ps. 70	Ps. 69:7-15, 22-23	Ps. 69:8-10, 14,
		21-22, 31, 33-34
Heb. 12:1-3	Heb. 9:11-15, 24-28	
John 13:21-32	John 13:21-35 or	Matt. 26:14-25
	Matt. 26:1-5, 14-25	

FIRST READING
ISAIAH 50:4-9a (RCL, BCP); 50:4-9 (RC)

Following the pattern established by the lectionary, the reading is another of the so-called Servant Songs from Isaiah. There has been far less agreement among commentators about including these verses with the other three passages in Isaiah 42, 49, and 53. The choice of the passage for Holy Week has less to do with the original setting of the verses in Isaiah than with the conviction that these passages offer insight into Jesus' passion. There is little clear evidence that New Testament writers had these verses in mind. The Fourth Gospel, whose passion narrative is to be read on Good Friday, makes no clear allusion; in Matthew, the only possible allusion is the reference to the soldiers' spitting on Jesus (Matt. 27:30).

As the righteous sufferer in the Psalms, the speaker is oppressed by enemies. We are given no specifics, except that there is no resistance. The sufferer submits to the persecutors with confidence that he will be vindicated by God.

In one sense at least the passage is a helpful anticipation of Jesus' passion. The passage speaks of "contending" and "justifying" and "declaring guilty." The language is taken from the law courts. Opposition to Jesus, who like the speaker entrusts his case to God, will climax in a trial where charges are brought and a verdict announced. On the surface at least, the promises do not seem trustworthy: Jesus is found guilty and put to shame. He dies despised and rejected. Yet God will vindicate him in a way no one could have anticipated. God presides at the court of highest appeal.

Responsive Reading

PSALM 70 (RCL); 69:7-15, 22-23 (BCP);
69:8-10, 14, 21-22, 33, 33-34 (RC)

Those who follow the RCL would be well advised to read Psalm 69 instead of Psalm 70. While a bit lengthy, reading the whole psalm is preferable to the piecemeal treatment it receives in the lectionary. This psalm is important as one of those to which New Testament authors turned to narrate Jesus' story. Jesus' cleansing of the temple in John 2 includes a citation of v. 9: "It is zeal for your house that has consumed me." All the Gospels allude to v. 21: "They gave me poison for food, and for my thirst they gave me vinegar to drink." The omission of this verse from BCP seems particularly unfortunate.

Second Reading

HEBREWS 12:1-3 (RCL)

The opening "therefore" in 12:1 presumes the preceding recital from Israel's history. The "cloud of witnesses" includes especially those whose lives embody a faith that is "the assurance of things hoped for, the conviction of things not seen" (11:1). The list includes the most famous, like Abraham and Moses, but also presumes stories and legends known only from extra-canonical literature. The prophet Isaiah was, according to legend, "sawn in two" (11:37).

All these heroes of faith, according to the author, "did not receive what was promised" but lived only in anticipation of what was to come. Jesus' ministry is the goal of God's history of promises; it is what faithful people lived for, and "apart from us they should not be made perfect" (11:40). Now, Jesus has come, has completed his assigned task, and is "seated on the right hand of the throne of God" (12:2). While Jesus' appearance "once for all" marks the "end of the age" (9:26), there are still trials to be endured until he returns "to save those who are eagerly waiting for him" (9:28). The sense of anticipation is important in these verses. There is more to come. What lies before the faithful is like a race that will involve persecution and shame. Successfully finishing the course will require discipline and endurance. Jesus, like those who came before, is a pioneer whose example should energize the faithful.

THE SENSE OF ANTICIPATION IS IMPORTANT IN THESE VERSES. THERE IS MORE TO COME. WHAT LIES BEFORE THE FAITHFUL IS LIKE A RACE THAT WILL INVOLVE PERSECUTION AND SHAME. SUCCESSFULLY FINISHING THE COURSE WILL REQUIRE DISCIPLINE AND ENDURANCE.

Jesus is far more than a good example, however. The discussion in these verses presumes the whole preceding account of Jesus' ministry. We are able to "lay aside every weight, and sin which clings so closely" because Jesus has accomplished the forgiveness of sins. We can endure hardships because we have an advocate in God's presence who has "taken his seat at the right hand of the throne of God."

The example of the heroes of faith makes for an interesting comparison with the Gospel story. The "cloud of witnesses" also includes those who, like Peter, were not heroes at all, who faltered and collapsed at the crucial moment, and whose place among the witnesses is due solely to God's faithfulness.

HEBREWS 9:11–15, 24–28 (BCP)

See the discussion of Hebrews 9 for Monday in Holy Week.

THE GOSPEL
JOHN 13:21–32 (RCL); 13:21–35 (BCP)

This Gospel lection, which actually follows the lection for Maundy Thursday, tells the story of Jesus' singling out Judas as the betrayer. The betrayal, which resumes in chapter 18, is described with great economy. The reason for Judas's actions is not explored. We learn simply that after Judas had eaten the morsel Jesus gave to him, "Satan entered into him" (13:27). The disciples' speculation about the moneybox recalls the earlier comment about Judas's being a thief, but exploration of his motivation in betraying Jesus is left to novelists and writers of musicals. Important is simply that Judas is the one of Jesus' inner circle who will betray him. The narrator comments at his departure, "and it was night." The darkness of which Jesus has spoken (9:4; 12:35–36) is about to descend.

Interesting is that only the Roman Catholic lectionary (in its Gospel for Tuesday in Holy Week) follows the scene to Jesus' announcement of Peter's impending betrayal. "Will you lay down your life for me? Truly, truly, I say to you, the cock will not crow, till you have denied me three times" (13:38). Not only Judas will betray Jesus. Peter will deny him, and all but the "beloved disciple" will abandon him. While Judas's betrayal is the most spectacular, he is not qualitatively different from the rest of the group. Peter comes closer to greatness, but his courageous act of remaining with Jesus, even if at a distance, only makes possible his explicit threefold denial. His disintegration is the more notable. This is not a story about heroes, and it is important to make clear that

THIS IS NOT A STORY ABOUT HEROES. JUDAS IS THE RULE RATHER THAN THE EXCEPTION. IF THERE IS A FUTURE FOR ANY OF THE DISCIPLES, IT WILL BE BECAUSE JESUS KEEPS HIS WORD NOT TO LOSE ANY OF THOSE GIVEN TO HIM BY THE FATHER.

Judas is the rule rather than the exception. If there is a future for any of the disciples, it will be because Jesus keeps his word not to lose any of those given to him by the Father (6:39; 17:9-12) and because God continues to keep them from the evil one (17:15). If Peter in particular is to assume a position of leadership, it will only be because Jesus forgives sinners.

Some of the details of the story are important for their place in the biblical "script." The formal designation of Judas as the betrayer through the giving of a morsel of bread is important because of the earlier citation of Ps. 41:9: "He who ate my bread has lifted his heel against me" (John 13:18). It is also significant that Judas is included among those with whom Jesus eats.

MATTHEW 26:1-5, 14-25 (BCP, alt.); 26:14-25 (RC)

The Matthean version of the designation of the betrayer is much like the account in the other Synoptic Gospels. Only Matthew indicates the amount Judas receives for agreeing to betray Jesus: thirty pieces of silver. And only Matthew tells of Judas's repentance, his returning the money, and his hanging himself (27:3-9). (Luke offers a different version of the story in Acts 1:16-20.) Once again there is no motivation offered for Judas's action. From Albert Schweitzer's notion that Judas "betrayed the messianic secret" to the elaborate character and motive furnished Judas in *Jesus Christ, Superstar,* those interested in probing psychological motives must resort to invention. The Gospel writers are uninterested in Judas's motives.

There is a considerable difference between reading only these verses and reading them within the context of the rest of the chapter. Matthew does not suggest, for example, that Judas leaves before Jesus' formal words over the bread and cup. He is presumably present for the meal. So are the rest of the disciples, however, who one by one "betray" Jesus as well. Peter is singled out as one who will deny Jesus, but the rest of the group fails him as well. The inner circle of Peter, James, and John are unable to stay awake as Jesus struggles with God in prayer. And as he is arrested, their resolve gives way. "Then all the disciples forsook him and fled" (26:56).

While Judas's failure is perhaps the most spectacular, none of the disciples proves faithful. If they are to amount to anything, it will not be because of any heroic effort. They are incapable of heroism. God will have to bring them to life as well.

MAUNDY THURSDAY (HOLY THURSDAY)

MARCH 28, 2002

REVISED COMMON	EPISCOPAL (BCP)	ROMAN CATHOLIC
Exod. 12:1-4 (5-10), 11-14	Exod. 12:1-14a	Exod. 12:1-8, 11-14
Ps. 116:1-2, 12-19	Ps. 78:14-20, 23-25	Ps. 116:12-13, 15-16bc, 17-18
1 Cor. 11:23-26	1 Cor. 11:23-26, (27-32)	1 Cor. 11:23-26
John 13:1-17, 31b-35	John 13:1-15 or Luke 22:14-30	John 13:1-15

THE LECTIONS TIE JESUS' LAST EVENING with his followers with the tradition of Passover. This is marked in many churches by a Christian seder (service), with elements from the traditional Jewish Passover liturgy recast in the framework of a celebration of the Lord's Supper. The link between Jesus' death and God's deliverance of Israel from Pharaoh, a feature of New Testament traditions, perhaps goes back to Jesus himself. That Jesus and his followers celebrated Passover is hardly surprising. They were Jews. That the earliest church recalled the Lord's Supper in the context of a Passover meal is likewise not surprising, for the same reason. Paul's letter to the Corinthians (the second reading) suggests, however, that the Lord's Supper was soon separated from Passover and became a regular feature of Christian worship. How contemporary Gentile Christians ought to recall our Jewish roots during Holy Week raises significant theological and practical questions.

Ought Christian congregations commemorate Jesus' last supper with a Passover seder? It can be argued that to do so reminds Christians of our roots in the tradition of Israel. We are, the New Testament claims, children of Abraham and Sarah. The deliverance of Israel from bondage to Pharaoh is part of our story. Yet Passover was—and is—a Jewish festival, part of a coherent religious alternative to Christianity. There are other children of Abraham and Sarah who celebrate Passover without any sense that it has to do with Jesus. The relationship of Gentile believers in Jesus to Judaism was a controversial question from the earliest days of the church. Paul must remind his Gentile congregations in Galatia that the Jewish way of life "under the law," the law God commanded Moses, is not something to be dismantled. It has integrity, wholeness. "If you adopt circumcision," Paul tells the men in his Galatians churches, "you are obliged to keep the whole law" (Gal. 5:3). And if life "under the law" is no longer an alternative for those Gentiles who live by faith in Christ—Paul's argument in Galatians—perhaps it is wisest for Christians to respect the integrity of Jewish festivals by not pretending they are something else. Given the reality of supersessionist ideology within the Christian church, it is at least necessary to make clear that Christians are not the "true Israel" at the expense of an empirical Israel whom God has allegedly rejected.

It is quite another matter for Christians to attend a Passover seder at the home of Jewish friends, where their status as guests is clear.

How best to handle such matters ritually will require sensitivity and wisdom. It is likewise the case that the more congregations understand about Passover and Jewish tradition, the richer will be their hearing of the New Testament story.

First Reading

EXODUS 12:1-4 (5-10), 11-14 (RCL); 12:1-14a (BCP); 12:1-8, 11-14 (RC)

These verses mark the beginning of Passover, one of the three great festivals in the Jewish year. A composite of various spring rites, Passover, known also as the Feast of Unleavened Bread, became important for recalling the decisive act in Israel's history: the deliverance from bondage to Pharaoh. Every feature of the meal is to make present an experience of the past events by which God redeemed Israel as well as to anticipate a future in which God will again deliver Israel.

All the Gospels agree that Jesus' arrest and death occurred during the Passover festival. As one of the pilgrimage festivals, Passover required Jewish males in Palestine to celebrate the festival in Jerusalem. The city swelled to twice its normal size, teeming with pilgrims commemorating God's deliverance of Israel from bondage to a foreign ruler. It is no wonder that the Roman governor was particularly concerned with the possibility of political violence and came to Jerusalem with Roman troops. It is not simply the historical setting, however, that makes the relationship between Jesus' death and the Jewish festival crucial. It seems that Jesus himself made a link between his death and Passover. And however we are able to sort out the historical questions, the New Testament writers found the link important in a variety of ways.

Crucial for reading the New Testament is how the celebration of Passover developed over the centuries. The regulations for Passover, as discussed in the Mishnah (compiled about 160 years after Jesus' death), indicate that the celebration had developed considerably since biblical times.[8] One critical matter, for example, has to do with how celebrants understood the lamb that was eaten at the meal. The Mishnah and early liturgies do not view the death of the lamb as a sacrifice. The lamb had to be killed to be eaten; that it was to be slaughtered in the temple had to do with its purity. There are some indications even in the New Testament, on the other hand, that the imagery was available for reflection on sacrificial matters. To the Corinthians Paul writes:

> Clean out the old yeast so that you may be a new batch, as you really are
> unleavened. For our paschal lamb, Christ, has been sacrificed. Therefore, let
> us celebrate the festival, not with the old yeast, the yeast of malice and evil,
> but with the unleavened bread of sincerity and truth. (1 Cor. 5:7-8)

While the Greek verb translated "sacrificed" can mean simply "slaughtered" or "killed," its use elsewhere in Corinthians (1 Cor. 10:20) makes it likely that the term at least connects the slaughter with cultic imagery. The parallel between Jesus' death and the slaughter of the Passover lamb suggests at least that the death of the lamb was the subject of some reflection.

Interesting in this light is the ancient "Poem of the Four Nights," part of a Palestinian targum (Aramaic version) on Exodus that links the first night of Passover with the story of Abraham and Isaac.[9] Still a debated topic, there are clear indications that Jesus' death was understood in light of the story of Abraham, Isaac, and the ram. That these reflections might have been focused on Passover traditions is at least a possibility. The paucity of evidence means that such potentially fruitful suggestions will remain a stimulus to our imagination as readers rather than as any foundation for interpretation.

That Jesus' death was understood in the context of Passover suggests that it was linked with God's deliverance and liberation. The "enemy" from which the people of God are liberated may vary. A major difficulty, of course, is that Jesus does not free Israel from bondage to Rome. That the enthusiastic pilgrims could so quickly turn on Jesus is an indication that he does not meet expectations. The argument of the New Testament will be that "deliverance" is from greater and more dangerous foes.

> THAT JESUS' DEATH WAS UNDERSTOOD IN THE CONTEXT OF PASSOVER SUGGESTS THAT IT WAS LINKED WITH GOD'S DELIVERANCE AND LIBERATION.

SECOND READING

1 CORINTHIANS 11:23-26 (RCL/RC); 11:23-26, (27-32) (BCP)

Paul's version of Jesus' words to his followers at the meal he shared with them before his death, "on the night when he was betrayed," are the earliest record we have of the words that now have so prominent a place in Christian liturgies. Their formulation and the way Paul speaks about the words indicate that they came to him as a tradition, which he passed on to the Corinthians—much like the confession he recounts in 1 Cor. 15:3-7. The point of his remarks about receiving this tradition is that he is not responsible for the formulation. In fact, the tradition claims that the words are Jesus' own.

We learn a number of things from Paul's comments about the Lord's Supper. One is that the commemoration is not a Passover meal. It has become a regular feature of the worship life of the community. His letter presumes an extensive development in which the whole tradition has been cast in Greek and formulated for a gathering that included a meal. To what degree Gentile Christian participants were expected to overhear echoes of Passover in the reference to bread and cup is difficult to say. Another observation is that while the wording is formalized and is remembered in a way that is clearly reminiscent of the accounts in the Gospels, there is no precise uniformity. Each of the versions of Jesus' last words includes some variation.

A unique feature of the Pauline formulation is the linking of the Lord's Supper with the betrayal by Judas. Michael Welker in his book *What Happens in Holy Communion*[10] makes the important observation that, while the Passover meal is eaten with an awareness that the community lives in a world of external threats to its life, commemorating the Lord's Supper "on the night Jesus was betrayed" is a regular reminder that threats are from within as well. Betrayal, as the Gospel stories remind us, was an experience within Jesus' most intimate circle. Judas had already set the process of Jesus' arrest in motion as the meal was eaten; Peter and the rest would soon abandon Jesus, with Peter remaining long enough to deny him three times.

Paul recounts Jesus' words not as part of a discussion of liturgy but as a reprimand to the congregation for what is occurring during worship. Apparently the commemoration of the Lord's Supper is an occasion for fracturing the little community. The meal, which should be an occasion for hospitality, is instead an occasion for showing disrespect for members who are not as well off and do not have enough to eat. In disrespecting one another, the Corinthians are dishonoring the body of Christ and are thus guilty of "profaning the body and blood of Christ." The real presence of Jesus where two or three are gathered in his name has consequences the Corinthians have not considered. "Proclaiming the Lord's death until he comes" means offering hospitality to all those for whom Christ has died.

JOHN 13:1-17, 31-35 (RCL); JOHN 13:1-15 or LUKE 22:14-30 (BCP); JOHN 13:1-15 (RC)

The Gospel is the account of Jesus' last meal according to the Fourth Gospel. As all will recognize, this is a singular version of the event and will relate to the worship service and to the other texts differently. In John there are no words of institution. There is no description of the meal. The meal setting affords an occasion for a lengthy discourse, extending to the beginning of chap. 18. The drama at the supper is Jesus' washing of the disciples' feet.

The particulars of the story suit John's chronology, which is different from that of the Synoptics. Jesus' last meal with his followers, while on Thursday evening, occurs not on Nissan 15, the first day of Unleavened Bread, but on the day before. Remembering that the day begins at sunset, Jesus' last twenty-four hours—including his meal, his arrest, trial, and death—occur in the Fourth Gospel before Passover begins. There are several consequences. One is that Jesus dies on the day the Passover lamb is slaughtered. Another is that Jesus' last meal with his disciples is not a commemoration of Passover. That fact, coupled with the absence of any words spoken over the bread and wine, will create some tension between this Gospel lection and the first two readings for today..

A debated question in Johannine scholarship is what the absence of the familiar words of institution means. One possibility is that the omission of the words is intentional, suggesting an anti-sacramental bias in the Fourth Gospel. This is essentially Bultmann's argument. The author cannot have been unfamiliar with traditions known across the church. The absence of the words must thus suggest something about attitudes toward sacramental practices. Those who argue that John clearly embraces "eucharistic theology" point to Jesus' "bread from heaven" discourse in chap. 6, which climaxes with reference to "eating the flesh of the son of man and drinking his blood" (6:53). Bultmann acknowledges that the verses are derived from eucharistic theology but attributes the verses to an "ecclesiastical editor" who revises John to make the Gospel more compatible with the orthodoxy of the church. Bultmann reads a Gospel without these verses. Others, while not adopting Bultmann's redactional arguments, nevertheless attempt to interpret chap. 6 within the larger setting of an anti-sacramental bias. I find it difficult to imagine that the discourse in chap. 6 does not presume agreement with widespread sacramental piety and theology within the Christian movement; attempts to exclude the verses on redactional grounds are not convincing. If such a view is compelling, the absence of the words of institution need not imply a polemic against sacramental practices. The evangelist rather chooses to use the supper as an opportunity for a different sort of instruction.

Jesus' washing of the disciples' feet has some interesting relationship to themes in Luke's account of the Last Supper, where Jesus' instructions about true greatness are included (Luke 22:24-27). Jesus' statements about true greatness are embodied in John as Jesus assumes the role of slave. That the mark of the community of disciples will be that "they love one another" is given further shape by Jesus' example of service. There is no greater sign of love than the willingness to give one's life for another.

> THAT THE MARK OF THE COMMUNITY OF DISCIPLES WILL BE THAT "THEY LOVE ONE ANOTHER" IS GIVEN FURTHER SHAPE BY JESUS' EXAMPLE OF SERVICE. THERE IS NO GREATER SIGN OF LOVE THAN THE WILLINGNESS TO GIVE ONE'S LIFE FOR ANOTHER.

Determining how far to read into the chapter will depend on how the lectionary has been used earlier in the week. If there is no service on Wednesday evening, it will be important to include in the reading the account of Judas' betrayal. As noted in the introductory comments, the church gathers for the Lord's Supper aware that it is not an ideal community but capable of betrayal and a lack of hospitality. Jesus came not for the righteous but for sinners.

GOOD FRIDAY

MARCH 29, 2002

REVISED COMMON	EPISCOPAL (BCP)	ROMAN CATHOLIC
Isa. 52:13—53:12	Isa. 52:13—53:12	Isa. 52:13—53:12
	or Gen. 22:1-18	
	or Wisd. Sol. 2:1,	
	12-24	
Ps. 22	Ps. 22:1-21 or 22:1-11	Ps. 31:1, 5, 11-12, 14-15,
	or 40:1-14 or 69:1-23	16, 24 (Heb. Bible 31:2,
		6, 12-13, 15-16,
		17, 25)
Heb. 10:16-25	Heb. 10:1-25	Heb. 4:14-16; 5:7-9
or 4:14-16; 5:7-9		
John 18:1—19:42	John (18:1-40), 19:1-37	John 18:1—19:42

SIGNIFICANT DECISIONS MUST BE MADE about the day's focus, whether for personal meditation or for a service of worship. Practices vary widely. In some congregations, there is no Good Friday service. In others, the service of worship still features a reading of the passion harmony and sermons on the "seven last words." Crucial is some sense of what constitutes an appropriate experience of Jesus' death. There are some forms of Christian piety in which Jesus' death is separated from his resurrection. The cross becomes significant in itself, as though with Jesus' death something is settled or satisfied. A sure test of what theoretical model is operative in the engagement of the biblical texts is whether or not the result is a sense of satisfaction. One might ask worshipers leaving a Good Friday service if they sense that Easter is really necessary—or if they believe rather that some decisive transaction has occurred that makes things right and they, with the whole creation, can breathe a collective sigh of relief. There is reason to suspect that behind many of the atonement theories that bear the label "satisfaction" is a desire by the humans formulating the theory to achieve some aesthetic satisfaction, to put things together in a way that makes sense. There is some pleasure in such reflection, though it would be a mistake to regard being satisfied as equivalent to an experience of forgiveness or deliverance from evil or reconciliation with God. Such attempts to solve problems intellectually, at the level of theory, seem rather to serve as protection from any real engagement, preferring to deal with the problem of evil and sin theoretically.

Another significant matter is where worshipers or readers locate themselves in the drama being enacted. The readings from Hebrews that interpret Jesus' death in light of Israel's sacrificial tradition can leave readers in the position of innocent bystanders, watching as some transaction takes place between Jesus and the God to whom sacrifices are offered. The letter does not suggest that God needs blood in order to be merciful, but the preponderance of sacrificial imagery might lead readers to ask what it all means, even if the point is that Jesus' death is the end of the sacrificial system. How does Jesus' death achieve forgiveness for us? It makes a difference if we are implicated in the reasons Jesus must die. "'Twas I, Lord Jesus, I it was denied thee; I crucified thee," an old hymn suggests. That is a rather different argument. That somehow we are enmeshed in systems that have no room for a gracious God may be implied even in Hebrews, but it may be easier to understand and experience in the Gospel stories.

The Gospel narratives are, of course, quite different from one another. The story of Jesus' death in John has a very different tone from Matthew's, with which the week began. The last thing Jesus says in John is, "It is finished," rather than, "My God my God, why have you forsaken me?" In all the Gospels, however, there is no sense that Jesus' death is somehow complete without some further act of God. Jesus' ministry ends in failure and disappointment, with a final verdict executed against him by the religious and political authorities, most of his disciples scattered, and Jesus dead. The story is unsatisfying without some continuation. "Good Friday," in the Gospel accounts, is incomplete without Easter.

This is a theological matter with consequences for an experience of the story. While the Gospel writers may well presume a tradition in which Jesus' death has been understood in terms of various sacrificial categories, none tells the story as the story of a sacrificial death, as though some necessary transaction were completed between God and Jesus. The story focuses on human characters—Pontius Pilate, his soldiers, the temple authorities, the crowds, a few disciples, and some women. It brings to a climax opposition and rejection and misunderstanding that have been building from the beginning. Especially in John, the climax of the story is a trial for which testimony has been gathered since the appearance of John the baptizer in the first verses of the prologue, who is introduced as the first in a long list of those who "give testimony" (1:6-8).

WHILE THE GOSPEL WRITERS MAY WELL PRESUME A TRADITION IN WHICH JESUS' DEATH HAS BEEN UNDERSTOOD IN TERMS OF VARIOUS SACRIFICIAL CATEGORIES, NONE TELLS THE STORY AS THE STORY OF A SACRIFICIAL DEATH, AS THOUGH SOME NECESSARY TRANSACTION WERE COMPLETED BETWEEN GOD AND JESUS.

While the whole Christian story is rehearsed in a setting made possible by God's raising of Jesus from the dead, there is something appropriate about taking the darkness seriously in order to appreciate the dawning of the light. And in the Gospel stories, the darkness takes particular shape and is embodied in specific people and institutions. Friday's service should end with a death—a real death that climaxes a story of growing opposition. It should respect the challenge to God's sending of the Son that concludes with a decisive no. If there is something hopeful in Jesus' death, it will only be because God chooses not to allow the verdict of the court to stand. There can be something positive in the death only if God brings life from death. People ought to finish their Good Friday worship and meditation with a sense that there must be an Easter to make of the violence anything positive. Good Friday services ought not attempt to deny the reality of death—either our own that is sure to come or the death of Jesus, which was the final verdict on his ministry by the established authorities. "He came to his own, and his own people did not receive him." What happens next will depend on God's willingness to raise the dead.

FIRST READING

ISAIAH 52:13—53:12 (RCL, BCP, RC); GENESIS 22:1-18 or WISDOM OF SOLOMON 2:1, 12-24 (BCP, alt.)

The famous verses from Isaiah offer a fine example of the importance of context for interpretation. For most Christians, it is not the writings of Isaiah that have provided the setting within which these words are read but the liturgy and music of the church. The unidentified "servant" in the passage is understood to be Jesus. This identification was made already in the New Testament, though allusions become more frequent in later Christian tradition. Citations and allusions are not nearly as frequent in the Gospels and letters of Paul as we might imagine. The Psalms, particularly 22 and 69, were obviously more formative. There is little indication that the verses from Isaiah informed the telling of the passion story in John, with one possible exception. The Greek version of Isaiah (the Septuagint), which was read by the Gospel writers and their audience, speaks in 52:13 about the servant being "glorified and lifted up." It is important in the Fourth Gospel that Jesus must be "lifted up" in death, and his death is understood as his being "glorified" (John 13:23). Here, perhaps, we can detect the influence of the verses.

The impact of the passage on Christian tradition has been heightened by the work of Bernard Duhm, who was the first to isolate passages from Isaiah and term them "Servant Songs" (see the discussion of the First Reading for Monday in Holy Week). Prior to the nineteenth century, no one had so read the passages. To Duhm likewise is credited the use of the term "suffering servant," a title that appears nowhere in the Old or New Testament. That the famous passage from Isaiah 53 speaks of one person—a specific "servant" of God—and that it is to be read in concert with other passages from the later chapters of Isaiah are the results of scholarship less than two centuries old.

In the first century, it appears that the passage from Isaiah was open to a variety of interpretations.[11] The identity of the unnamed "servant" depends upon the context. Within the setting of Isaiah, "my servant" may apply to the prophet or to Israel or to a group within the people of Israel. If the setting is extended to include the rest of the Old Testament, "my servant" could refer to Moses, Elijah, all the prophets, Israel, the patriarchs, King David, or the righteous who suffer for their relationship to God—Job in particular. Intertestamental literature and the corpus of rabbinic writings include interpretations in which portions of the passage are applied to the whole spectrum of biblical "servants."

It is important for Christian readers of the Old Testament to understand that there was in the first century no single interpretation of the passage that dominated people's reading of the passage. There was no "the servant," which perhaps explains why this is not a "title" used of Jesus. That this passage spoke of one individual—and that this individual was Jesus—would not have been obvious to anyone. The use of the passage represents a special reading of the Scriptures that occurred in light of Jesus' career. It is possible that the reason for the use

> THERE WAS IN THE FIRST CENTURY NO SINGLE INTERPRETATION OF THE PASSAGE THAT DOMINATED PEOPLE'S READING OF THE PASSAGE. THERE WAS NO "THE SERVANT," WHICH PERHAPS EXPLAINS WHY THIS IS NOT A "TITLE" USED OF JESUS.

of this passage depended on the identification of Jesus as the Messiah—and the fact that elsewhere in the Scriptures, the coming king is identified as "my servant" (Zech. 6:12; Ps. 89:50-51). That no one would have imagined this passage as having to do with the career of the coming Messiah-King seems an appropriate reading of the passage itself. Jesus was "despised and rejected" by humans, among whom "we" are included: "we esteemed him not." That the King sent by God to save Israel should end up on a Roman cross may be strangely appropriate to this passage—but it is an insight possible only after the fact.

That also means that what may seem to present readers as an obvious notion of "atonement" in this passage was not at all obvious to earlier readers. That Moses "stepped into the breach" between God and Israel suggested to rabbinic interpreters that so risking his life implied that the words of Isaiah referred to him. When he has delivered God's words of judgment to Israel after the building of the golden calf, and they have repented, Moses makes intercession for Israel: "So Moses returned to the LORD and said, 'Alas, this people has sinned a great sin; they have made for themselves gods of gold. But now, if you will only forgive their sin—but if not, blot me out of the book that you have written'" (Exod. 32:32-33).

Since he risks his life in his intercession, his actions suggest that the words, "He poured out his soul to death" refer to him. And by making intercession, Moses also "bore the sins of many." In fact, in the Babylonian Talmud the whole passage is read as applying to Moses.[12] That the passage is about vicarious atonement, secured by a literal death, is an interpretation made possible by the death of Jesus the Christ.

Such knowledge is important. It helps readers recognize why Jesus' contemporaries would not immediately have recognized him as the Christ and why there are still people who read Isaiah as part of the Scriptures who do not view Jesus as its fulfillment. Awareness of the logic and development of early Christian interpretation of the Old Testament also clarifies how Paul can say both that Jesus' death is "in accordance with the scriptures" (1 Cor. 15:3) and that "Christ crucified" is a scandal to Jews and nonsense to Gentiles (1 Cor. 1:23). Being "called" by God includes the gift of new insight (1 Cor. 1:24) that includes insight into the Scriptures.

Important in this regard is that neither the passage nor its use in the New Testament proposes any real "theory" of atonement. Such reflection is a necessary task for interpreters of these texts. It exists "on this side of the text," to use the language of Paul Ricoeur, and cannot be excavated by means of exegesis. The appropriateness of the various notions of atonement will depend on a logic that cannot simply be read out of the text.

RESPONSIVE READING

PSALM 22 (RCL); 22:1–21 or 22:1–11 or 40:1–14 or 69:1–23 (BCP); 31:1, 5, 11–12, 14–15, 16, 24 (HEBREW BIBLE 31:2, 6, 12–13, 15–16, 17, 25) (RC)

It would make most sense to read Psalm 22, since all the Gospel narratives either allude to the psalm or, as in the Fourth Gospel, actually quote it (John 19:24). Since most of the allusions are not identified, readers will recognize them only if they know the psalm.

SECOND READING

HEBREWS 10:16-25 or 4:14-16, 5:7-9 (RCL); 10:1-25 (BCP); 4:14-16, 5:7-9 (RC)

The two readings from Hebrews are quite different from each other, each focusing on an aspect of Jesus' death. The verses from chaps. 4 and 5, somewhat artificially abstracted from their context, focus on a "pedagogical" view of suffering. Jesus "learned obedience through what he suffered" (5:8). This is important, because we can be confident that our high priest is able to "sympathize with our weaknesses" (4:15). The reading would be more appropriately paired with Mark or Matthew. The Fourth Gospel surely does not give the impression that Jesus "offered up prayers and supplications, with loud cries and tears" (5:7).

The abstracting of the verses from their context may contribute to a false impression that Jesus' death by itself somehow makes things better. Crucial for the interpretation offered in Hebrews is the conviction that God has "exalted" Jesus to a position of honor. The citation of Ps. 110:4 (Heb. 5:6) presumes that God has seated Jesus at God's right hand and that Jesus is the second "lord" mentioned in the opening verse of the psalm (Ps. 110:1). The interpretation here in Hebrews 5 is not far from that in the Philippians hymn (see the discussion of the Second Reading for Passion Sunday): because Jesus was obedient, God exalted him and gave him a name that is above every name. Hebrews further develops the theme, based on v. 4 of the psalm, that identifies this exalted figure as "a priest forever after the order of Melchizedek."

The passage is exhortation based on the confidence that we have an advocate seated at God's right hand. Our high priest has "passed through the heavens" (4:14) and is available to those in need. Statements about Jesus' having resisted temptation and having learned obedience through suffering are important only because they identify the one who is seated at God's right hand until God makes his enemies a stool for his feet (Ps. 110:1). The

THE REASON FOR CONFIDENCE IS THUS NOT THAT JESUS HAS SUFFERED, SATISFYING SOME COSMIC NECESSITY, BUT THAT THE RISEN AND EXALTED LORD IS THE ONE WHO WAS OBEDIENT EVEN TO THE POINT OF DEATH ON A CROSS.

reason for confidence is thus not that Jesus has suffered, satisfying some cosmic necessity, but that the risen and exalted Lord is the one who was obedient even to the point of death on a cross. The passage should not encourage glorification of suffering or a morbid fascination with Jesus' suffering or psychological agonizing—something the Gospels avoid. The emphasis is rather on the identity of the risen Lord with the crucified Christ.

The lection in the RCL from Hebrews 10 is part of a larger argument about the superiority of Jesus' sacrifice to the prescribed sacrifices in the Scriptures. "For it is impossible that the blood of bulls and goats should take away sins" (10:4) is paired with, "For by a single offering he has perfected for all time those who are sanctified" (10:14). It is with this in mind that the author cites Jeremiah, arguing for the fulfillment of the promise that God will "remember their sins and their misdeeds no more" (10:17).

With Jesus' death, the old order ends. In view of God's forgiveness, there is no longer any offering for sin. The statement about Jesus' having "opened a way through the curtain," though the statement is interpreted allegorically as "through his flesh," is reminiscent of the Synoptic accounts of Jesus' death, according to which the temple curtain is torn at the moment Jesus dies. There is a literal end of the temple order—or at least an anticipation of the destruction of the temple some decades later. The use of temple imagery to speak of Jesus' body here in Hebrews is similar to that in the Fourth Gospel, where Jesus' statement about destroying and rebuilding the temple is interpreted as a reference to the "temple of his body" (John 2:21).

The goal of the passage is to encourage the faithful to "draw near with a true heart in full assurance of faith" (10:22). Crucial is that God has proved faithful and can be counted on in the trials ahead. The passage offers a sense of anticipation that "the Day is drawing near" (10:25) and that the faithful are "eagerly waiting" (9:28). The whole chapter anticipates the famous discussion of faith and the faithful in the following chapter.

It is hardly accidental that the lection ends just before the discussion of "deliberate sin" after receiving "knowledge of the truth," for which there is no forgiveness (10:26-31), a passage that was to prove enormously controversial in the time of persecutions. The passage motivated the writing of the *Shepherd of Hermas*, a work that recounts a vision in which God promises apostates a second chance. How Hebrews' picture of a wrathful God fits with the elaborate exposition of Jesus' sacrifice is a topic for another occasion.

The Gospel
JOHN 18:1—19:42 (RCL/RC); (18:1-40); 19:1-37 (BCP)

The Fourth Gospel's version of Jesus' arrest, trial, and death differs in important ways from the accounts in the Synoptic Gospels. For one, the events occur one day earlier on the Jewish calendar. The climax of Jesus' trial before Pilate is set at noon on the Day of Preparation (19:14), when the celebration begins with the burning of leavened products and the singing of a hymn. The explicit mention of the time suggests, as elsewhere in John, that there is a deeper significance. For another, there is no formal trial before the Jewish court but only a hearing. The reason, as "the Jews" must remind Pilate, is that the temple officials have no authority to deal with capital offenses (18:31). The scholarly debate about the truth of the statement continues and, given the paucity and ambiguity of the evidence, will not be resolved.[13] The information is important in the Fourth Gospel because it means Jesus must die on a Roman cross—fulfilling "the word which Jesus had spoken to show by what death he was to die" (18:32). Jesus promised that he would be "lifted up" (3:14; 12:32), and so he is. Jesus dies on a Roman cross even though, the Jewish religious leaders argue, he must be executed for religious reasons: "he has made himself equal to God" (19:7). The trial before Pilate is thus based on a religious charge, even though the political implications of the claim that Jesus is a king are noted.

The emotional high point of the passion sequence—and of the whole Gospel—is the trial before Pilate. Even a cursory glimpse at a concordance will indicate the prominence of court language throughout the Gospel. John the Baptist is the first among many to "give testimony." Even Moses is enlisted in the trial—not, as Jewish tradition suggested, as Israel's defense attorney, but as a witness for the prosecution: "Do not think that I shall accuse before the Father; it is Moses who accuses you" (5:45). The metaphor of a trial at which Israel appears before the heavenly court seems to give shape to the whole story—an image that may well have been borrowed from Isaiah. Appropriately, the story climaxes with a trial at which Jesus is being judged, but at which another case—the case against Jesus' would-be judges'—is being decided as well.

For those who will read the Gospel, a sense of the narrative is crucial. As elsewhere in John, the drama involves the exposure of the participants. Pilate is the first to "reveal" himself. In Pilate's rather strange interrogation of Jesus, Jesus actually questions Pilate. "So you're the King of the Jews?" Pilate asks. "Do you say this on your own, or did others say it to you about me?" Jesus replies. "Am I a Jew?" Pilate asks. At that point Jesus gives an answer of sorts to Pilate's question about his kingship. "So you are a king, then," Pilate says. "You say that I am a king," Jesus points out. The statement is ironic: it is Pilate who says it and Pilate who will write it—not because he believes it to be true, but his testimony is true nevertheless. Jesus then makes a statement that seems to have little to do with the situation: "For this I was born, and for this I have come into the world, to bear witness to the truth. Everyone who is of the truth hears my voice." Pilate responds, "What is truth?" He obviously has no idea—and in saying so he indicates that he is not of the truth. He does not "hear Jesus' voice." And in that regard he is not different from "the Jews."

If the story plays on Pilate's antipathy to considering himself a Jew, it offers a similar play on Jewish antipathy to Romans. Pilate is portrayed as uncertain. He must be persuaded to put Jesus to death. Because he is not convinced by religious reasons, the Jewish leaders make political arguments: "If you release this man, you are not Caesar's friend; everyone who makes himself a king sets himself against Caesar" (19:12). Jews must remind the Roman governor of the law! And when Pilate finally presents Jesus to the crowd as "your king," the chief priests answer, "We have no king but Caesar." The nation would go to war against Rome only a few decades later, led by people who insisted that Jews could not acknowledge the kingship of anyone but God. According to John, in their opposition to Jesus, the Jewish leaders demonstrate that they are no different from Romans: they claim Caesar as their only king. Like Pilate, they do not hear Jesus' voice. And in condemning Jesus they condemn themselves. Far more is decided at the trial than they can imagine.

The tone of the actual crucifixion account is more distant. The narrator is concerned that the various scriptural fulfillments be noted (e.g., from Psalm 22). Jesus' statement to the beloved disciple about his mother—probably symbolic—is one of the matters that must be attended to. "In order to fulfill the scripture," Jesus says, "I am thirsty." And as though some last condition is fulfilled, Jesus says, "It is finished [completed, fulfilled]." With that he dies. The account that follows about why Jesus' legs were not broken and how water and wine flowed from his side when he was pierced by the spear likewise speak almost on a mythological level. The story is told not to move an audience by describing Jesus' pain but to make connections with the Scriptures and the sacramental life of the church.

Most pronounced in this story is a sense that the world in which the characters play their roles is one of appearance and shadows. The evangelist accomplishes this largely by the use of irony. Readers understand the story in a way the participants cannot. The religious and political leaders play their roles as they must, eventually making decisions the situation forces them to make. They decide against Jesus—as they must. And in so doing they reveal their blindness and their guilt. For readers, they fulfill a very different role as well.

> MOST PRONOUNCED IN THIS STORY IS A SENSE THAT THE WORLD IN WHICH THE CHARACTERS PLAY THEIR ROLES IS ONE OF APPEARANCE AND SHADOWS. THE EVANGELIST ACCOMPLISHES THIS LARGELY BY THE USE OF IRONY.

They give testimony to the truth. It is the religious and political leaders who invest Jesus as king. Pilate "says so"; he formulates the charge and writes it for all the world to know. He may intend it as an insult to the Jewish leaders—who are appropriately offended—but the result is the placarding of the truth in Hebrew, Latin, and Greek, foreshadowing the future of this story as it will be told in every language under heaven.

The story does not trivialize the bondage of the leaders. It does not suggest they might have done better if they had been less corrupt or more vigilant. They are part of a world that is cut off from the truth. They do not hear Jesus' voice. If there is to be any hope for such people and for such a world, it will not be because people can try harder but only because God will find a way to break through.

The account ends with Jesus dead, buried, and even embalmed by Nicodemus, identified by the narrator as the one who had come to Jesus "at night" (19:39). While not an enemy, Nicodemus is still in the dark. The outrageous amount of spices he brings suggests both an extravagant love and a deep misunderstanding. He believes Jesus is finished. As readers, we know the story is not over.

THE GREAT
VIGIL OF EASTER

MARCH 30, 2002

Revised Common	Episcopal (BCP)	Roman Catholic
Service of Readings		
Gen. 1:1—2:4a	Gen. 1:1—2:2	Gen. 1:1—2:2
		(1:1, 26-31a)
Gen. 7:1-5, 11-18; 8:6-18; 9:8-13	Gen. 7:1-5,11-18; 8:6-18; 9:8-13	
Gen 22:1-18	Gen. 22:1-18	Gen. 22:1-18 (22:1-2, 9a, 10-13, 15-18)
Exod. 14:10-31; 15:20-21	Exod. 14:10—15:1	Exod. 14:15—15:1
		Isa. 54:5-14
Isa. 55:1-11	Isa. 55:1-11	Isa. 55:1-11
Prov. 8:1-8, 19-21; 9:4b-6 or Bar. 3:9-15, 32—4:4	Isa. 4:2-6; Isa. 54:5-14	Bar. 3:9-15, 32—4:4
Ezek. 36:24-28	Ezek. 36:24-28	Ezek. 36:16-17a, 18-28
Ezek. 37:1-14	Ezek. 37:1-14	
Zeph. 3:14-20	Zeph. 3:12-20	
Lutheran lectionary adds:		
Jon. 3:1-10	Deut. 31:19-30	Dan. 3:1-29
New Testament Reading		
Rom. 6:3-11	Rom. 6:3-11	Rom. 6:3-11
Gospel		
Matt. 28:1-10	Matt. 28:1-10	Matt. 28:1-10

CONGREGATIONAL PRACTICES WILL VARY CONSIDERABLY. Some will celebrate an Easter vigil; many will not. The service will sometimes include baptisms, most often a celebration of the Lord's Supper. The passages are chosen to tell a story that moves from primordial darkness to the rising of the Son. What is important in such a service of worship is the story that is told. The logic of that narrative, the problems to which God's acts of reconciliation and deliverance in Jesus are addressed, should be developed throughout the week. This service emphasizes God's response to the resounding no with which Jesus' ministry ends. Crucial at this service is not nostalgic recalling of a story from long ago but that the living Christ actually appears through word and sacrament to give the gift of forgiveness and new life.

In addition to the appointed readings from Romans and Matthew, I have chosen to comment on two of the many passages that seem particularly appropriate in the context of the other readings for Holy Week.

GENESIS 1:1—2:4

The story of the creation of the heavens and the earth is particularly appropriate at a service that emphasizes darkness and light. It is especially appropriate in view of the readings from the Gospel of John throughout the week. The Fourth Gospel opens with a prologue that offers a new reading of Genesis. The story John tells is of the Word by which God created the heavens and the earth, a Word that was embodied in Jesus of Nazareth and that is now embodied in words both spoken and visible. Neither Genesis nor the Fourth Gospel recounts a drama that is complete. They presume a present in which the darkness is not yet banished and anticipate the completion of creation only in the future, when there will be a new heaven and a new earth:

NEITHER GENESIS NOR THE FOURTH GOSPEL RECOUNTS A DRAMA THAT IS COMPLETE. THEY PRESUME A PRESENT IN WHICH THE DARKNESS IS NOT YET BANISHED AND ANTICIPATE THE COMPLETION OF CREATION ONLY IN THE FUTURE, WHEN THERE WILL BE A NEW HEAVEN AND A NEW EARTH.

> I saw no temple in the city, for its temple is the Lord God the Almighty and the Lamb. And the city has no need of sun or moon to shine on it, for the glory of God is its light, and its lamp is the Lamb. The nations will walk by its light, and the kings of the earth will bring their glory into it. Its gates will never be shut by day—and there will be no night there. (Rev. 21:23-25)

Until then, it is enough to know that when the light shines, the darkness does not overcome it. The darkness takes concrete shape in the people who seek to silence the Word, but God will not allow the Word to be silenced.

Beginning with the story of the creation is an important reminder that the story of Jesus is not simply about individuals. It is about God and the whole created order. Deliverance is not to be taken out of the world but to be enabled to live fruitfully within it. God's Word became flesh. God's Word is spoken in ordinary human words. We do not have to seek God outside the realm of our experience because God has chosen to come to us. The whole story is about what is involved in making it possible for us to live as ordinary creatures made in the image of God.

GENESIS 22:1-18

The story of Abraham and his son Isaac has captured the imagination of interpreters as almost no other. It has horrified some and serves as an inspiring example of absolute faith for others. The story has been interpreted as marking the end of human sacrifice and the institution of substitutionary animal sacrifice, while in times of persecution it has served to help the faithful find positive meaning in the death of martyrs. It is read by some as the last trial of Abraham, or as an example of the "teleological suspension of the ethical" (Kierkegaard). The artist George Segal used the scene of father Abraham preparing to slaughter his son as a memorial for the Kent State shootings—a scene the university found too disturbing to accept. The sculpture is now permanently installed near the chapel at Princeton University.

Perhaps most interesting is the history of the passage within Jewish tradition.[14] It is the assigned reading for New Year's Day in Jewish synagogues. Israel's whole history is understood to flow from God's promise to Abraham:

> By myself I have sworn, says the LORD: Because you have done this, and have not withheld your son, your only son, I will indeed bless you, and I will make your offspring as numerous as the stars of heaven and as the sand that is on the seashore. And your offspring shall possess the gate of their enemies, and by your offspring shall all the nations of the earth gain blessing for themselves, because you have obeyed my voice. (Gen. 22:15-18)

Early Christians offered a daring interpretation of the passage, of which there are the clearest indications in Paul's letter to the Romans. The "offspring" promised Abraham through whom the Gentiles would be blessed was a person, not Abraham's whole progeny (Gal. 3:16-17). It was the same "offspring" promised David, whose throne God would establish forever (2 Sam. 7:12), whom God would call "son" (2 Sam. 7:14), the one later generations would know as the promised Messiah-King. And as Abraham did not spare his son, so God did not spare his Son (Rom. 8:32), offering him as a blessing for both Jews and Gentiles. Jesus' death is the means by which God kept his promise to Abraham, with even the Gentiles in view.

It may be that some New Testament writers saw Jesus as a new Isaac. The story was most important, however, as a statement of God's promise, which Jesus' followers understood to be fulfilled in his death and resurrection. To be the children of Abraham is to be the recipients of God's blessings in Abraham's offspring, in

Christ.

ROMANS 6:3-11

This epistle reading has been selected with the clear expectation that the Vigil service will include baptisms, as has been traditional since ancient times. The famous passage from Romans speaks of baptism as dying and rising with Christ. Baptism is not the topic under discussion at this point in Romans. Paul digresses from his argument in chap. 5 about the superabundance of God's grace to deal with possible objections. The first, provided by Paul for an imaginary objector, is that his argument suggests that if sin has succeeded only in providing an occasion for God's grace, we should "sin that grace may abound." To head off the objection, Paul appeals to a baptismal tradition.

We know this is a pre-Pauline baptismal tradition and not simply a Pauline formulation first by the way Paul introduces the matter. "Do you not know that . . ." suggests the material should be familiar to the Roman congregation. Since Paul has not preached there and the congregation has no prior knowledge of Paul, it is likely that Paul is appealing to a tradition he can presume the Roman congregation will know.

The formulation of the sentences likewise suggests a prior history and a relationship to creedal tradition. In his first letter to the church at Corinth, Paul recalls a summary of the gospel which, he argues, believers have in common throughout the church.

> For I handed on to you as of first importance what I in turn had received: that Christ died for our sins in accordance with the scriptures, and that he was buried, and that he was raised on the third day in accordance with the scriptures, and that he appeared to Cephas, then to the twelve. . . . (1 Cor. 15:3-5)

Verbs from the ancient creedal statement ("died . . . buried . . . raised") are supplied with the Greek prefix "with." What happens to believers in baptism is that they are "incorporated into Christ." They share in what Jesus experienced: they have died with, been buried with, and been raised with Christ. Forms of the same tradition in Col. 2:12-13 and Eph. 2:4-6 indicate that baptism was understood not only as dying and rising with Christ (all aorist participles in Colossians and Ephesians) but that the baptized are made to "sit with him in the heavenly places in Christ Jesus" (Eph. 2:6). Paul's formulation in Romans 6 is more careful. The parallelism is broken. We have died with Christ in baptism and were buried with him, so that as Christ was raised from the dead we too—might walk in newness of life. Paul does not say that we have been raised with Christ—but that we surely will be (6:5).

The language demonstrates that baptism was understood at least in the Greek-speaking forms of Christianity known to Paul as considerably more than a ritual washing for the forgiveness of sins. Christians borrowed baptismal traditions from

John the baptizer, but Christian baptism is baptism into Christ. It is a dying and rising—to newness of life. The setting at the Easter vigil makes other imagery from Ephesians particularly appropriate: "once you were darkness, but now you are light in the Lord" (Eph. 5:8). The experience of baptism links the believer to events that mark the end of the age and the beginning of a new one. Paul is careful to argue in Romans that new life does not remove the faithful from a world still in bondage to evil; resurrection is available only as a foretaste. As long as life lasts, we are part of a creation that groans in travail, awaiting the birth of the new for the whole creation (Rom. 8:18-23).

That these verses might be read at a worship service that includes baptisms offers interesting possibilities even apart from the setting at an Easter vigil. The language of death and life presents challenging imagery to piety that is not accustomed to such drama. The story of Holy Week, into which the faithful are incorporated, is as dramatic as one can imagine. It is about death and the end of possibilities. It tells of a world that has no alternative but to choose darkness over light. It also speaks, however, of a God who will not be denied who is determined to accomplish reconciliation and deliverance whatever the cost.

> PAUL IS CAREFUL TO ARGUE IN ROMANS THAT NEW LIFE DOES NOT REMOVE THE FAITHFUL FROM A WORLD STILL IN BONDAGE TO EVIL; RESURRECTION IS AVAILABLE ONLY AS A FORETASTE. AS LONG AS LIFE LASTS, WE ARE PART OF A CREATION THAT GROANS IN TRAVAIL, AWAITING THE BIRTH OF THE NEW FOR THE WHOLE CREATION.

Relating baptism to this imagery is both promising and challenging, especially in congregations where infant baptism is the norm and where the ceremony includes no drama. It is difficult to imagine, for example, how parents and sponsors and congregations are to imagine that the ritual of baptism has anything to do with death and life when pastors sprinkle a few drops of water on a child's head. It is not at all difficult to imagine, on the other hand, the dramatic experience of newness for those in Paul's congregations whose baptism into Christ involved significant social and political changes. It is also easier to appreciate the drama when those baptized are adult converts. This is not to argue that infant baptism is inappropriate but that congregations miss something important when there are no adult baptisms. Acknowledging the appropriateness of infant baptism ought not obscure what can be an experience of an end—and a beginning. Baptism is not only a ritual washing or an entrance rite; it is nothing less than a death and a new birth.

MATTHEW 28:1-10

Nowhere are the differences among the Gospels more obvious than in the reports of what occurred on Sunday morning, the first day of the week. The only story Matthew, Mark, and Luke share is the story of the empty tomb, and even in this account there are some striking differences. And from this point on, Matthew and Luke tell distinctive stories. This makes historical reconstruction more difficult. What seems obvious is that the endings of the various Gospels are appropriate to themes and developments in each. While in Luke all Jesus' appearances occur in Jerusalem or its environs—the story opens in the temple and concludes in the temple, with the disciples blessing God—in Matthew, Jesus appears only to the women in Jerusalem; the disciples he meets in Galilee, on an unspecified mountain. The Gospel that opens Jesus' public ministry with a sermon from a mountain in Galilee concludes on a mountain with a command to make disciples and "teach all that I have commanded you."

There is obviously a great deal about the experience of the resurrection we do not know. In Paul's recital of Jesus' appearances in 1 Corinthians 15, he speaks of a distinct appearance to Peter, the Twelve, more than five hundred, James, and all the apostles (not to mention the special appearance to Paul) (1 Cor. 15:3-7). The Gospels narrate fewer appearances—and, most importantly, they indicate that it was women who were the first to see the empty tomb and to hear the news that Jesus was alive. In Matthew, Luke, and John, they are the first evangelists, telling the Twelve (or Eleven) the good news.

As readers, we have special seats from which to watch the unfolding drama. We know that Jesus has made promises that the cross will not be the end. And, unlike characters in the story, we learn that there is an earthquake and an angel who descends to roll back the stone. While there are guards at the tomb, they "become like dead men." The women who come to see the tomb are utterly unprepared for what they find. The tomb cannot contain Jesus. God refuses to accept the verdict of the court and raises Jesus from the dead.

AS READERS, WE HAVE SPECIAL SEATS FROM WHICH TO WATCH THE UNFOLDING DRAMA. WE KNOW THAT JESUS HAS MADE PROMISES THAT THE CROSS WILL NOT BE THE END. AND, UNLIKE CHARACTERS IN THE STORY, WE LEARN THAT THERE IS AN EARTHQUAKE AND AN ANGEL WHO DESCENDS TO ROLL BACK THE STONE.

That something comes of Jesus' ministry has little to do with human initiative. Jesus' movement is in shambles after Friday. He has been arraigned before the religious and political authorities, condemned to death, mocked, and executed. Jesus is dead and buried, as the creed emphasizes. The disciples are scattered, the crowds are disillusioned, the leaders relieved if still wary. Though Matthew cannot resist some anticipation of the resurrection in recounting the appearance of saints following Jesus' death, the world seems intact. Jesus seems safely dead, shut up in a tomb at which guards have been posted to insure that the corpse remains undisturbed. The efforts turn out to be futile, however, as an earthquake and an angel open the tomb to demonstrate that Jesus is no longer there.

While Matthew's story of the empty tomb follows Mark closely, there are little differences that are significant for the impact of the story. The women run from the tomb—they do not flee—and not only out of fear but "fear and great joy." While unnerved, the women set out to do as they are told. And while Mark ends without an appearance of Jesus, the women—who alone remained faithful and had the courage to come to the tomb—are the first to meet the risen Christ. Commissioned to report the news to the disciples, they do as they are told.

Jesus' resurrection is not the end of the story but a new beginning. The next chapter will involve those whom Jesus has prepared for leadership. The world into which the Christ is raised is different but not completely changed. There is still the ill will of the religious authorities, the fear of the disciples, and even doubting. There will be tasks to perform—disciples to be made, lessons to be delivered. For the moment, however, what is crucial is that God has refused to allow a human no to stand. Jesus' promised vindication has occurred, and new promises will open a new future.

A significant feature of the situation in which Matthew writes is conflict within the Jewish community between those who believe Jesus to be the Messiah and those who do not. While Matthew does not speak of "Christians," a division is being created that will open a chasm within the community and will lead to the creation of a new religious group, distinguished from Jews, who will be known as "Christians." The guards at the tomb, mentioned only by Matthew, are important, we learn, because they are paid by the Jewish authorities to spread rumors about how the disciples stole Jesus' body.

> So they took the money and did as they were directed. And this story is still
> told among the Jews to this day. (Matt. 28:15).

We get a glimpse here of the setting within which Matthew wrote his account of the good news. Continuing tensions between the two religious groups is part of the groaning in travail of which Paul speaks, which will end only when God finishes the story.

NOTES

1. For an insightful review of various atonement theories as well as an important constructive proposal, see Gerhard Forde, "The Work of Christ," in *Christian Dogmatics,* ed. R. Jenson and C. Braaten (Philadelphia: Fortress Press, 1984).

2. S. G. F. Brandon, *Jesus and the Zealots: A Study of the Political Factor in Primitive Christianity* (Cambridge: Manchester University Press, 1967).

3. See the brief article on Bernhard Duhm in *Dictionary of Biblical Interpretation,* ed. John H. Hayes (Nashville: Abingdon, 1999), 1:310–11.

4. The fragment at Qumran formerly known as 11QMelchizedek (11Q13) seems to view Melchizedek as a figure in the heavenly court. See the standard translations of the Dead Sea Scrolls for the text and bibliography: G. Vermes, *The Complete Dead Sea Scrolls in English* (Penguin, 1998); F. Garcia-Martinez, *The Dead Sea Scrolls Translated: The Qumran Texts in English,* 2nd ed. (Leiden: Brill, 1996).

5. See especially René Girard, *The Scapegoat,* trans. Yvonne Freccero (Baltimore: Johns Hopkins University Press, 1986).

6. See my *Messianic Exegesis: Christological Interpretation of the Old Testament in Early Christianity* (Philadelphia: Fortress Press, 1988), esp. chap. 3.

7. Raymond E. Brown, *The Gospel according to John* (Anchor Bible 29; Garden City: Doubleday, 1966), 1:483–84.

8. The standard translation is by Herbert Danby, *The Mishnah, Translated from the Hebrew with Introduction and Brief Explanatory Notes* (Oxford: Clarendon Press, 1933).

9. Bruce Chilton, "Isaac and the Second Night: A Consideration," *Biblica* 61 (1980), 78–88.

10. Michael Welker, *What Happens in Holy Communion?* (Grand Rapids: Eerdmans, 2000), 43–53.

11. See *Messianic Exegesis,* 119–34.

12. For the text, see ibid., 123.

13. A thorough account of the evidence and the scholarly debates about the precise legal situation in first-century Palestine is available in the magisterial two-volume work by the late Raymond E. Brown: *The Death of the Messiah* (New York: Doubleday, 1994).

14. See the fascinating study by Shalom Spiegel, *The Last Trial,* trans. Judah Goldin (New York: Shocken Books, 1969).

DECEMBER 2001

Sunday	Monday	Tuesday	Wednesday	Thursday	Friday	Saturday
						1
2 1 Advent	3	4	5	6	7	8
9 2 Advent	10	11	12	13	14	15
16 3 Advent	17	18	19	20	21	22
23 4 Advent	24 Christmas Eve	25 Christmas Day	26 Boxing Day (Candada)	27	28	29
30 New Year's Eve	31					

JANUARY 2002

Sunday	Monday	Tuesday	Wednesday	Thursday	Friday	Saturday
		1 Name of Jesus New Year's Day	2	3	4	5
6 Epiphany	7	8	9	10	11	12
13 1 Epiphany	14	15	16	17	18	19
20 2 Epiphany	21 Martin Luther King Day (U.S.A.)	22	23	24	25	26
27 3 Epiphany	28	29	30	31		

FEBRUARY 2002

Sunday	Monday	Tuesday	Wednesday	Thursday	Friday	Saturday
					1	2
3 4 Epiphany	4	5	6	7	8	9
10 Last Epiphany/Transfiguration	11	12	13 Ash Wednesday	14	15	16
17 1 Lent	18 Presidents' Day (U.S.A.)	19	20	21	22	23
24 2 Lent	25	26	27	28		

MARCH 2002

Sunday	Monday	Tuesday	Wednesday	Thursday	Friday	Saturday
					1	2
3 3 Lent	4	5	6	7	8	9
10 4 Lent	11	12	13	14	15	16
17 5 Lent	18	19	20	21	22	23
24 Passion/Palm Sunday	25 Monday in Holy Week	26 Tuesday in Holy Week	27 Wednesday in Holy Week	28 Maundy Thursday	29 Good Friday	30 Vigil of Easter
31 Easter						